£17·95

Friends, for Life

D1434441

Friends, for life

The psychology of personal relationships

SECOND EDITION

Steve Duck

University of Iowa

HARVESTER
WHEATSHEAF

New York London Toronto Sydney Tokyo Singapore

First published 1991 by
Harvester Wheatsheaf
Campus 400, Maylands Avenue,
Hemel Hempstead,
Hertfordshire, HP2 7EZ
A division of
Simon & Schuster International Group

Typeset in 11/12pt Baskerville
by Inforum Typesetting, Portsmouth

Printed and bound in Great Britain by
Biddles Ltd, Guildford and King's Lynn

British Library Cataloguing in Publication Data

Duck, Steve, *1946*—
   Friends, for life: the psychology of personal relationships.
   – 2nd ed.
   1. Interpersonal relationships. Psychology aspects
   I. Title
   158.2
   ISBN 0-7450-0881-X
   ISBN 0-7450-0882-8 (pbk)

2 3 4 5   95 94

This book is dedicated to my father,
Kenneth W. Duck, 1917–86,
who helped so much with the first edition

Contents

1

Our friends, ourselves

Nobody needs convincing *that* relationships are important to our lives, and nobody needs to be told that they are intriguing. This book tries to show *why* they are important, and how they work, by depicting some of the important threads that characterize relationships and by exploring their processes. It also draws occasional lessons from communicational, psychological and sociological research (particularly as we consider children's friendships in Chapter 5), or points out common errors or false assumptions that people make about relationships. While research often makes suggestions about how relationships 'ought' to be conducted, or else tries to find ways in which they can be improved, my goal will be not to give advice as such but rather to indicate practical implications of the growing research on a variety of issues, such as loneliness or conversational skills. My primary goal, however, is to illustrate the excitement and intrigue that surround the research on this most basic of human activities: conducting close personal relationships.

Unfortunately, the evidence is that some people are not good at this basic human activity, and we are constantly reading of the rise in divorce rates, the increase in one-parent upbringing for children, the alleged increase in loneliness, the fragmentation of society, and a host of other relational woes. People seem aware that happiness depends on relationships more than on anything else, but may not realize that such problems as depression, suicide, family violence or alcoholism can often also be traced back to relationship difficulties or relationship experiences, as indeed can truancy,

1

poor performance at school and job failure (Ginsberg *et al.*, 1986). Also increasingly well known are the findings that medical problems attend relationship difficulties, with heart attacks and injury in traffic accidents being much more common in those with relationship problems (Lynch, 1977).

Not only has recent research turned up such intriguing findings, but it shows that relationships do not conduct themselves in the ways that common sense often supposes. Rather it shows that relationships are extremely complex entities that need careful management and demand skills from their participants at all times. The tragedies listed above are partly the result of the fact that our society presently acts as if relationships do not need to be paid any attention. On the contrary, recent research shows that the tragedies are, by and large, preventable if relationships are properly attended to.

The more we can find out about our own relationships, the better we can surround ourselves with human medical insurance. The support of friends, neighbours and relatives is a social support that acts as an important safeguard against occupational stress, psychological illness, unhappy life events and the like, as much of the research detailed throughout this book will show.

The more we learn about the origins and causes of relational success and failure, the better we can deal with a range of important personal and social issues. How can we improve our own relationships? What sort of future can we make for the family? How can we predict or increase our marital satisfaction? How can we increase the chances of our children maturing into stable, sociable, healthy adults? What can we do to prevent loneliness? Is there a 'good' way to end a relationship? What sort of life is there after divorce? We can also learn about the amelioration of general social problems, such as the drug abuse that derives from bad social contacts among teenagers, or how to prevent distressful interaction in disturbed families, to reduce disruption in school classrooms or to create effective and cooperative work and sales teams.

In looking at the growing number of scientific studies of friendship and personal relationships, this book tries to sort out truth from commonsense nonsense and the insightful myth from the unfounded. Many such beliefs exist because relationships feel commonsensical and misleadingly appear to be natural and easy when they are going well. In short, we are not used to concentrating on them or experimenting with them.

Yet this misleading feeling disguises from us the harder truth that 'relationshipping' is actually a very complicated and prolonged process with many pitfalls and challenges. Relationships do not just happen; they have to be made – made to start, made to work, made to develop, kept in good working order and preserved from going sour. To do all this we need to be active, thoughtful and skilled. To suggest that one simply starts a friendship, courtship, romantic partnership or marriage and 'off it goes' is simple-minded. It is like believing that one can drive down the street merely by turning the ignition key, sitting back and letting the car take care of itself.

On the contrary, to develop a close personal relationship (with someone who was, after all, at first a stranger to us) careful adjustment and continuous monitoring are required, along with several very sophisticated skills. Some of these are: assessing the other person's needs accurately; adopting appropriate styles of communication; indicating liking and interest by means of minute bodily activities, like eye movements and postural shifts; finding out how to satisfy mutual personality needs; adjusting our behaviour to the relationship 'tango' with the other person; selecting and revealing the right sorts of information or opinion in an inviting, encouraging way in the appropriate style and circumstances; building up trust, making suitable demands; and building up commitment. In short, one must perform many complex behaviours. These necessitate proficiency in presenting ourselves efficiently, attending to the right features of the other person at the right time, and pacing the friendship properly.

Rather as learning to drive a car does, learning to steer a relationship involves a range of different abilities and these must be co-ordinated. Just as when, even after we have learned to drive, we need to concentrate harder each time we get into a new model, drive in an unfamiliar country or travel through unknown streets, so when entering unfamiliar relationships we have to relearn, modify or re-concentrate on the things that we do. All of us have pet stories about the strain, embarrassment and awkwardness that occurred in a first meeting with a new neighbour or a 'friend of a friend': some clumsy silence, an ill-judged phrase, a difficult situation. It is in such situations that the skills of friendship are bared and tested to the limits, and where intuition is so clearly not enough.

Because it is a skill, relationshipping – even in these novel situations – is something that can be improved, refined, polished (even coached and practised) like any other skill, trained like any other, and made more fluent. It can be taken right up to the level of expertise where it all flows so skilfully and automatically that we can metaphorically focus away from the position of the relational brakes or accelerator and devise ways to drive (the relationship) courteously, skilfully, carefully or enjoyably, so that the others in it can have a smoother ride!

Since we are not usually disposed to think of friendship and close relationships in this new kind of way, people sometimes feel irrationally resistant to doing so. 'How can you represent a close personal relationship as a simple mechanical skill?', they ask. 'Isn't it more mystical, more magical, more moral, less manipulative than you make it sound?' Such people seem happy to see relationships merely as pleasant, passive states: relationships just happen to us and we don't have to do anything particular – let alone do anything properly.

My answer is clear: I am not saying that friendship is all mechanical, any more than making a beautiful piece of furniture or playing an enchanting piano rhapsody or winning a sports championship is simply a mechanical exercise. But each of these activities has some mechanical elements that must be mastered before the higher level aspects of skill can be attempted. You can't paint the Mona Lisa until you know something about painting figures, using a canvas, holding a brush, mixing paints, and so on. Furthermore, research backs this up. Scholars now regard 'relationship work' as a process that continues right through the life of the relationship, with a constant and perpetual need for the right actions and activities at the right time to keep it all alive (for example, Baxter and Dindia, 1990).

This book takes a close look at such research and at the system that is relationship development. I shall explore the general styles and detailed behaviours that are essential to constructive and satisfying friendship, dating, courtship and marriage. I will also point out important differences that characterize successful and unsuccessful styles in friendship, dating and marriage, and the errors that are most often made in creating relationships. I will also look at the ways in which relationships end and the ways in which we can make it all a bit less painful when they do.

There are many advantages to this way of looking at relationships. It leads to a direct and useful form of practical advice for people who are unhappy with one or more of their relationships, or who are lonely or frustrated. It focuses on the things that one can do to improve relationships. It also runs counter to the common, but rather simplistic, assumption that relationships are based only on the matching of two individuals' personalities. This pervasive myth says that there is a Mr or a Ms Right for everyone or that friends can be defined in advance. If this were true, then we could all list the characteristics of our perfect partner – looking for a partner or being attractive to one would be like shopping for or making a checklist of things we liked. By contrast, the new approach adopted here will focus on performance, on behaviour, on the simple mistakes that people make at the various stages of friendship development.

Is it such a strange and unacceptable idea that people can be trained to adopt more satisfactory styles in relationships? Not really. Therapists, social workers, doctors and dentists nowadays receive instruction on the ways to establish rapport with patients and how to develop a reassuring and constructive 'bedside manner'. We know also that insurance or car sales staff are trained in how to relate to possible customers, that airline cabin crew and the police alike receive instruction on relating to the public, and that managers are now encouraged to spend time building up good personal relationships with employees. Such emphasis on skills takes us beyond the trite commonsense advice for lonely persons to 'go out and meet more people'. It focuses us on the fact that relationship problems derive in part, if not on the whole, from people 'doing relationships' wrongly rather than simply not getting enough opportunities to be in them.

The evidence suggests that all of us are probably missing out and not maximizing our potential for relationships. American research (Reisman, 1981) shows that people claim to have about fifteen 'friends' on average, although the numbers change with age (17-year olds claim about nineteen, while 28-year olds have only twelve; 45-year olds have acquired sixteen, while people in their sixties enjoy an average of fifteen). When people are asked to focus only on the relationships that are most satisfying, intimate and close, however, the number drops dramatically to around six (5.6 to be precise).

How can relationships be improved and made more satisfying? It is instructive to look at the nature of relationships and the reasons why we have them in the first place, taking friendship as the first example of 'voluntary intimate relationships'. In that way we will learn what it is that we miss when friendships go wrong. Whatever it is, its absence is so disorienting and disturbing that it must obviously be something fundamental to human experience. What do we need friends for? What do we lose when we experience disruption of friendship?

THE NATURE OF FRIENDSHIP

A friend of mine once defined a 'friend' as someone who, seeing you drunk and about to stand up on a table and sing, would quietly take you aside to prevent you doing it. This definition actually embodies quite a few of the important aspects of friendship: caring, support, loyalty and putting high priority on the other person's interests. We shall see later in the book why these are important. However, when researchers have taken a more precise look at the meaning of friendship, they have focused on two specific things: the general *features* that humans expect friends to have and the *rules* of friendship that humans expect to be observed.

There are certain features that we find particularly desirable in friends and certain characteristics that everyone believes that being a friend demands. K.E. Davis and Todd (1985) found that we regularly expect a friend to be someone who is honest and open, shows affection, tells us his or her secrets and problems, gives us help when we need it, trusts us and is also trustworthy, shares time and activities with us, treats us with respect and obviously values us, and is prepared to work through disagreements. These are things that people *expect* a friend to do for them and expect to do for the friend in return. These features constitute a quite complex picture. However, when one looks at the *rules* of friendship that people actually adhere to, then the strongest ones are rather simple (Argyle and Henderson, 1985): hold conversations; do not disclose confidences to other people; refrain from public criticism; repay debts and favours. These researchers also demonstrate that emotional support, trust and confiding are among the rules that distinguish high quality friendships from less close ones.

In ideal circumstances, then, a friend is an open, affectionate, trusting, helpful, reliable companion who respects our privacy, carries out interactions with all due respect to the norms of behaviour and ourselves, does not criticize us in public, and both does us favours and returns those that we do. In the real world, friendship is unlikely to live up to this ideal and we all have some range of tolerance. However, it is a *voluntary* bond between two people and the above ideals can be seen as part of an unwritten contract between them, whose violation can become the grounds for the dissolution of the relationship (Wiseman, 1986).

Another important view of friendship has been offered by Wright (1984). He too stresses the 'voluntary interdependence' of friendship: it is important that people freely choose to be intertwined together in the relationship. He also places emphasis on the 'person qua person' element, or the extent to which we enjoy the person for his or her own sake, rather than for the things that he or she does for us. More recent research on this idea (Lea, 1989) finds indeed that 'self-referent rewards', or the way the other person makes us feel about ourselves, are just as important as these other things. The way in which the relationship helps us to feel about ourselves, and its voluntary nature, are crucial to the nature of friendship. There are good reasons why this is the case.

THE 'PROVISIONS' OF FRIENDSHIP

There are several ways to start answering the large question: 'Why do we need friends?'. We could just decide that everyone needs intimacy, possibly as a result of dependency needs formed in childhood, just as the psychoanalysts tell us. There may be something to this, as we shall see, but there is more to the need for friendships than a need for intimacy – and there is more to the need for intimacy than we may suppose, anyway. For instance, we might want to ask how intimacy develops, how it is expressed, what else changes when it grows, and so on. We might also note the curious finding (Wheeler *et al.*, 1983; R.B. Hays, 1989) that both men and women prefer intimate partners who are women! Indeed, Arkin and Grove (1990) show that shy men prefer to talk to women even when they are not in an intimate encounter. Not only this, but those people who talk to more women during the day have better health than those who talk to fewer women (Reis, 1986). Clearly the nature of needs for intimacy and friendship is rather intriguing and may be mediated by gender and other social contexts.

Another way to deal with the question of why we need friends is to examine what happens to people who deliberately cut themselves off from their friends or who take jobs that effectively do that for them – people such as hermits, Arctic explorers, religious ascetics and lighthouse keepers. After all, if they have made an informed and calculated decision to go into isolation, the effect should be less extreme because they will already have foreseen it, evaluated it and taken it into account. As expected, early research (Schachter, 1959) found that such people are usually prepared to suffer the effects of their decision. Many ascetic religious orders explicitly begin the training of novices by enforcing

8

periods of silence while still allowing them to meet other novices, or by isolating the novices together for short periods before separating them totally. In this way the order gradually prepares the novices for the full rigours of what is to come. In time, at any rate, the novices are less seriously affected by their isolation than are people who have had it thrust upon them without any choice, or who did not realize what they were letting themselves in for. Many people in solitary jobs (such as delivery drivers or long-distance hauliers) long for time in the canteen when they can talk to others, or else make big use of CB radios to achieve the same purpose. People who live on their own often enjoy 'wasting time' talking to the people whom they meet at work.

These are much less serious (though more familiar) than the very extreme reactions that researchers have found when studying the period of adjustment to total voluntary isolation (Schachter, 1959). Hermits and recluses have been found to dream about people, being in a crowd or meeting friends. (The same thing happens to people in jail, who dream about their loved ones who are still 'on the outside'.) They also report spending a lot of the time daydreaming about other people. In extreme cases, it is found that hermits have the hallucination that other people are present, speaking to them. Such hallucinations are not a mild form of psychological abnormality like schizophrenia, but rather an exaggerated *normal* response. Bereaved persons or isolated prisoners regularly report the same sorts of experience. For example, the bereaved very often experience the feeling that their dead partner is present in the room with them or is just there, watching over them. This familiar response to grief is so well known and so general that we can safely say that it tells us something crucial about the human need for companionship. Yet it does not tell us *why* we need friends, it merely shows us one of the ways in which the human mind protects itself when friends and companions are lost – by manufacturing them for us. This in itself is a finding that dramatically illustrates the awesome but perhaps unexpected effects of friendship upon the human mind.

While some people *choose* solitude, others are doing no more than responding to social pressures when they become recluses: their behaviour may be so odd or unacceptable that withdrawal from the social world is one rational way to escape the scorn and mockery of other people. Other individuals become recluses through fear of the hygienic consequences of meeting others – for example, Howard Hughes, the multimillionaire, built an elaborate castle of defences around himself because he became afraid of catching diseases from other people. Such individuals weigh up the consequences before they embark upon isolation and so they have discounted, allowed for and even actively sought the effects that it will bring.

Although people like this are not typical, they do remind us of an important point: isolation and aloneness are different from loneliness. Loneliness is a feeling about isolation, and people can be isolated without feeling lonely just as they can feel lonely in a crowd. Isolation is physical separation from other people, but loneliness is the feeling that you do not have as many friends, or the sorts of friend, that you wish you had, or enough of the opportunities to meet them that you desire (Perlman and Peplau, 1981). Another way of putting it (Rook, 1988) is that people can either seek or avoid solitude but they experience distress only when their social surroundings do not match their wishes (i.e., when they are in a crowd and want to be alone, or when they are alone and want to be with other people).

Researchers refer to this as 'state loneliness' – a state that lasts as long as the provoking circumstances. By contrast, 'trait loneliness' is the persistent, long-term loneliness that some people experience, and these people are of greater interest in this book because they can be helped more directly. Research has built up a fairly good picture not only of the styles of behaviour of such people but also of the ways to start helping them unlock the doors of the cage of their unwanted solitude (Marangoni and Ickes, 1989).

Isolation creates feelings of loneliness most severely in people who have not chosen it personally (such as those who are put in solitary confinement in jail) or have not anticipated it (such as those who are bereaved unexpectedly) or have it happen to them in less extreme forms – for instance, when people go into hospital they often experience loneliness although they are surrounded by helpful people. Patients with a terminal illness die sooner if they have only a small group of friends than if they are popular and have a happy, supportive family (Lynch, 1977). It surprises me very much that insurance companies have not yet seen the implications of this for their actuarial prediction of life-expectancy. Yet it is conclusively and repeatedly shown that lonely people die younger, and more often risk death through serious illness (Bloom *et al.*, 1978).

We must not assume, because the less extreme effects of loneliness are more familiar, that those mild effects are the only ones. We all know that people in hospitals or people who move house to an unfamiliar neighbourhood experience boredom and loneliness, but few of us have realized that the effects can be serious. Loneliness can be fatal. Bereaved spouses die sooner after the death of their partner than would be predicted from statistical evidence about life-expectancy (Lynch, 1977), and 'death of a spouse' yields one of the highest scores for the widow(er)'s 'dangerous life events' score. Interestingly, such deaths tend to occur on or around anniversaries (such as wedding anniversaries, partner's birthday or anniversary of the death of the partner) that were significant for the relationships (Phillips, 1972). It is not surprising, then, that the time of bereavement is precisely one where our culture requires that our friends, neighbours and relatives rally round, make more effort to exercise the obligations of their relationship, call round more often, and offer help and a sense of community or belonging. Unfortunately society also assumes that such obligations have been properly discharged within a couple of weeks of the crisis, yet bereaved persons often experience the worst loneliness and sense of loss in the long term, say several months following the death (Rosenblatt, 1983).

Belonging and a sense of reliable alliance
In writing about loneliness and the 'provisions' of relationships – what it is that they do for us – Weiss (1974) proposed that a major consequence of being in relationships is a sense of belonging and of 'reliable alliance'. He is touching on something very important about human experience. We all

like to belong or to be accepted; even those who choose solitude want it to be the result of their own choice, not someone else's. No one wants to be an outcast, a pariah or a social reject. Indeed, the powerful effects of being made *not* to belong were long recognized as a severe punishment in Ancient Greece, where people could be ostracized and formally exiled or banished. The modern equivalent is found in the British trade union practice of 'sending someone to Coventry' when they break the union rules: the person's workmates, colleagues, neighbours and associates are instructed to refuse to speak to the person about anything. The US Constitution (Article iii, section 3) indicates a similar line of thinking when it defines 'treason' as 'Adhering to the enemies [of the United States] or *giving them aid or comfort*'.

By contrast, relationships give us a sense of inclusion, a sense of being a member of a group – and, as the advertisers keep emphasizing, membership has its privileges. One of these privileges is 'reliable alliance'; that is to say, the existence of a bond that can be trusted to be there for you when you need it. To coin a phrase, 'A friend in need is a friend indeed' – or in our terms, the existence of a friendship creates a reliable alliance: one of the signs that someone is a true friend is when they help you in times of trouble.

Emotional integration and stability
Importantly, communities of friends provide a lot more than just a sense of belonging and reliable alliance (Weiss, 1974). They also provide necessary anchor points for opinions, beliefs and emotional responses. Friends are benchmarks that tell us how we should react appropriately, and they correct or guide our attitudes and beliefs in both obvious and subtle ways. As an example, consider how different cultures express grief differently. In some countries it is acceptable to fall to the ground, cover oneself with dust and wail loudly; in other cultures it is completely unacceptable to show such emotion, and the emphasis falls on dignified public composure. Imagine the reaction in Britain if the Queen were to roll on the ground as a way of demonstrating grief, or in the United States if the President and First Lady attended military funerals with their faces blacked and tearing their clothes.

Humans have available many different ways of demonstrating grief but they typically cope with this strong emotion in a way particularly acceptable to their own culture.

Like cultures, friends and intimates develop their own sets of shared concerns, common interests and collective problems, as well as shared meanings, common responses to life and communal emotions. Friends are often appreciated exactly because they share private understandings, private jokes or private language. Indeed, communication researchers (Hopper *et al.*, 1981; Bell *et al.*, 1987) have shown that friends and lovers develop their own 'personal idioms' or ways of talking about such things as feelings, sex and bodily parts, so that they are obscure to third parties. By using a phrase with secret meaning, couples can communicate in public places about things that are private. Good examples are to be found in newspaper columns on St Valentine's Day. What, for example, are we to make of a message I found in the local student newspaper: 'Dinglet, All my dinkery forever, Love, Scrunnett'? Presumably it meant something both to the person who placed the advertisement and to the person who was the intended object of it. Be alert: the couple who announce that 'We are going home to make some pancakes' may in fact be planning to have a night of passion!

Such language is just a localized version of the fact that different cultures use different dialects or languages. Equally, friends have routines of behaving or beliefs that are not shared by everyone in a particular country or culture, but for that reason they are more important in daily life. Loneliness is, and isolation can be, wretched precisely because it deprives people of such psychological benchmarks and anchor points. Lonely people lose the stability provided by the chance to compare their own reactions to life with the reactions of other people that they know, like and respect.

This is important for a number of reasons. First of all, it is well established that responses to almost anything can be markedly influenced by others' reactions. For instance, a classic finding of social psychology (Sherif, 1936) is that, if they are placed in a group that consistently claims to see a stationary light move, people will believe that they, too, see

13

the light moving. They can even be induced to offer very precise measurements of the distance that it 'moved'.

Friends provide a stable, meaningful background for responses to many less spectacular and more familiar things, such as political events, other people, work, the weather and life. If these stabilities and comparisons are taken away from someone, he or she becomes uncertain and unstable. This fact has been used by experienced 'brainwashers', whose first rule is to separate prisoners from groups of familiar companions and 'deindividuate' them either by covering their heads with a bag, placing them in isolation or, perhaps, by immersing them in a group of alien prisoners with whom they are forced to deal but to whom they cannot easily compare themselves. Such experiences are intentionally disruptive and often demand great efforts of will by the resistant. Isolation, deindividuation and solitary confinement in such conditions can play havoc with people's sanity – and are *intended* to do so in these circumstances. Nowadays the powerful punishing effects of enforced isolation are recognized in both military and civil prisons. Solitary confinements and removal of association rights are each used as formal punishments in civil prisons, and would not be so used unless they were recognized to be disturbing and unpleasant. Who would give someone solitary confinement as a punishment if they knew that the person merely saw it as a welcome opportunity for some peace and quiet?

Not many people realize that it is a very mild version of this form of disorientation that is experienced when they go on holidays to other countries, or when executives cross oceans and feel 'culture shock'. It can be unbalancing to be confronted with a completely unfamiliar range of beliefs, systems, styles and habits: that, after all, is one of the problems that we try to avoid by creating a stable and familiar group of friends at home. I have noticed that the disorientation is reduced when I travel with people I like and know well, or when I meet close friends at the other end. I suspect that business travellers who are met by disliked or unfamiliar colleagues are actually likely to be more uncomfortable, disoriented and ineffective in adjusting to the new environment. Companies that pay enormous sums to transfer executives across the world are surprisingly inattentive to this small point, which could be easily corrected.

So loneliness and isolation are disruptive because they deprive the person of the opportunity for comfortable comparison of opinions and attitudes with other people – of close friends. People who are parted from friends become anxious, disoriented, unhappy and even severely destabilized emotionally; they may become still more anxious just because they feel themselves behaving erratically, or they may experience unusual mood swings. They often report sudden changes of temper and loss of control, sometimes resulting in violent outbursts; but in any case their judgment becomes erratic and unreliable, and they may become unusually vigilant, suspicious or jumpy in the presence of other unfamiliar people.

Another function of friendship, then, a reason why we need friends, is to keep us emotionally stable and to help us see where we stand *vis-à-vis* other people and whether we are 'doing OK'. It is particularly noticeable in times of stress and crisis. I remember an occasion when all the lights fused in a student residence block where I was an assistant warden. The rational thing to do was to find a flashlight and await the restoration of power. What we all actually did was to stumble down to the common-room and chatter amongst ourselves: the need to compare our reactions to the emergency was so powerful and so universal that even the warden, a medical researcher who had doctoral degrees from both Oxford and Cambridge, did the same. Such behaviour often happens after any kind of stress or crisis, from the crowd of people who gather to swap stories after a fire or a car accident, to the nervous chatter that schoolchildren perform when the doctor comes to inject them against measles or TB.

The value of other people in stabilizing our ability to cope with the world is extensive, then, but we must not forget that it extends to everyday activity as well. Loneliness can be a prison that deindividuates, whether through a person's lack of skills or through physical needs. The elderly and housebound need people too, and may be perfectly capable of the necessary social behaviours, but could suffer the psychological effects of isolation and loneliness for different reasons.

Too often we overlook the tragic social and psychological consequences of such physical challenges, and do not appreciate the extent of the psychological effects.

Opportunities for communication about ourselves

There is a third reason why we need friends (Weiss, 1974). A centrally important need is for communication. This particular wheel was strikingly reinvented by the Quaker prison reformers several generations ago, who attempted to cut down communication between criminals in prison in order to stop them educating one another about ways of committing crime. Accordingly, one of their proposals was that prisoners should be isolated from one another. What occurred was very instructive: the prisoners spent much of their time tapping out coded messages on walls and pipes, devising means of passing information to one another, and working out other clever ways of communicating. Evidently, people who are involuntarily isolated feel a need to communicate. One additional function that healthy friendships provide, then, is a place for such communication to occur – communication about anything, not just important events but also trivial stuff as well as personal, intimate details about oneself. In a study at the University of Iowa, I and my students (S.W. Duck, *et al.*, 1991) have found that most conversations with friends last very short periods of time (about three minutes on average) and deal with trivialities. They are nonetheless rated as extremely significant. They revitalize the relationship, reaffirm it and celebrate its existence, through the medium of conversation.

A mild form of this overwhelming need to communicate is to be found on railway trains, planes and long-distance buses. Here many lonely people strike up conversations – but usually monologues – which allow them to communicate to someone or to tell someone about themselves and their opinions. A striking thing about this is the intimacy of the stories that are often told. Perfect strangers can often be regaled with the life history, family details and personal opinions of someone they have not seen before and will probably never see again. Indeed, that is probably a key part of it, for the listener who will not be seen again cannot divulge the 'confession' to friends or colleagues and so damage the confessor's reputation. (In cases where it is known that the listener and confessor will meet again, as in the case of doctors and patients, priests and parishioners, counsellors and clients, or lawyers and consultants, the listeners are bound by strict professional ethical codes not to reveal what they have been told. On the train, the 'ethics' are simply left to statistical chance, and the extreme improbability of the two strangers meeting one another's friends is a comfort in itself.)

Another example of this same tendency occurs in hospitals. New arrivals communicate feverishly about their medical histories and symptoms, sharing their anxieties with other patients, cleaners, and maintenance staff (K.W. Duck, 1982). This is probably due in part to a need for reassurance about their condition, and in part to the general uncertainty that occurs in strange surroundings. It could also be a kind of magical exorcism of one's fear and anxiety about the physical complaint, a desire to communicate one's worth and importance and to stress what will be lost if one dies.

Such examples illustrate the importance of communication, of an audience for self-expression, and the significance of opportunities to reveal 'private' details about oneself or to have someone show an interest in oneself and one's problems. Loss of such opportunities is one of the more significant consequences of social isolation, and doctors often realize that some patients visit surgeries only for the opportunity to talk to someone. This phenomenon has other less obvious forms, for instance in the case of people experiencing alienation through marital problems or through entering the early stages of divorce. They often want to find someone to 'burst' over, someone who will just listen to them as they talk themselves through the crisis. Often a good listener is all that is needed, and such people do not need advice, they just want a sympathetic ear. The breakdown of a marriage deprives the person of communication with a (formerly) trusted listener, and this deprivation causes some of the same stressful effects as it does in other circumstances.

Given all these points, it is not surprising to learn that lonely people are prone to think that they have poor communication skills and are anxious about the fact (Solano and

17

Koester, 1989). More surprising is the finding that they tend to see other people's communication skills as low also (Spitzberg and Canary, 1985). However, lonely people often express a great deal of negativism and cynicism and react strongly to rejection even when it is expected (Check *et al.*, 1985). So it is likely that their communication skills really are poor. However, communication skills can be developed (see Chapters 2 and 6) and clearly should be.

There is mounting evidence, then, that poor skills and poor attitudes towards communication with other people can be seriously detrimental. Indeed, a thirty-five year study by Peterson *et al.* (1988) showed that people who began the study, as students in the late 1940s, with a pessimism about the world (seeing bad events as caused by stable, global and internal factors) were in much worse health at ages 45 to 60 than were people whose style was not so pessimistic. The authors concluded that pessimism in early adulthood is a risk factor for poor health in middle and late adulthood. These points also suggest the need for us to consider the problems of some special populations who have their communications with friends disrupted. Think not only of such people as divorcing couples, but of prisoners separated from their families, or of people who endure long-distance commuter relationships. As another group who may benefit from research on improving communication in relationships, consider service personnel posted overseas away from their spouses and children. In later chapters I will return to all of these groups, each of which has its own special difficulties in meeting the need to communicate with loved ones – a need normally satisfied by close relationships.

Provision of assistance and physical support
Another 'provision' of relationships is simply that they offer us support, whether physical, psychological or emotional (Hobfoll and Stokes, 1988). This section focuses on physical support and assistance, which are often as significant to us as is any other sort of support.

For example, when people lose a friend or a spouse through bereavement, they report a lack of support – they are cut off from someone who has helped them to cope with life and to adjust to its problems, tasks and changing uncertainties. This can take one of two forms: physical support (such as help with day-to-day tasks) and psychological support (such as when someone shows that we are appreciated, or lets us know that our opinions are valued). Human beings need both of these types of support, but the types are significantly different.

This is very simply illustrated. When your friend gives you a birthday present you are supposed to accept it in a way that indicates your own unworthiness to receive it and also the kindness of the friend ('Oh you shouldn't have bothered. It really is very good of you'). In short, you repay your friend by accepting the gift as a token of friendship and by praising the friend. You 'exchange' the gift for love and respect, as it were. Imagine what would happen if you repaid by giving the friend the exact value of the gift in money. The friend would certainly be insulted by the ineptness: you would have altered the nature of the social exchange and also, in so doing, the nature of the relationship, by focusing on money rather than the gift as a symbol for friendship. Indeed, Cheal (1986) has shown that gift-giving as a one-way donation is rare and gift *reciprocity* is the norm, indicating that it serves an important relational function. Gift exchange serves the symbolic function of cementing and celebrating the relationship.

There are other clear examples of this point – that the nature of the exchange or support helps to define the degree and type of relationship. For instance, many elderly people get resentful of the fact that they gradually become more and more physically dependent on other people for help in conducting the daily business of their lives. The elderly cannot reach things so easily, cannot look after themselves and are more dependent physically, while at the same time they are less able to repay their friends by doing services in return. This, then, is one reason why many people dislike or feel uneasy with old age: they resent the feeling of helpless dependency coupled with the feeling of perpetual indebtedness that can never be paid off. For many elderly people, then, the mending of a piece of furniture, the making of a fruit pie or the knitting of a sweater can be traded off against dependency: elderly people *need to be allowed* to do things for

19

other people as a way of demonstrating to themselves and to everyone else that they are valuable to others and can still make useful contributions to the world. At the same time the elderly do not feel valued for themselves. Gone are the days when old age was a respected time of life, and the elderly were held in high esteem because of their wisdom and experience. The elderly persons' experience is now often felt to be outmoded, or treated as irrelevant to the changing fashions and beliefs of our time, so they can never use it as a bargaining point or 'resource' in their relationship exchange. They can't use their wisdom to 'buy' help and support as in bygone days. People often forget that, when elderly people feel useless and unwanted, they are probably responding sensitively to this key of social life: the relationship between two people is most often defined by what the people in it provide for one another, resources that they distribute and exchange (Cheal, 1986; Chown, 1981). If I provide only *services* to you then we are more likely to remain neighbours than become friends; if we exchange intimate secrets, it is more likely that we are close friends than strangers; if we clearly value one another's opinions and advice, share interests and disclose our deep personal feelings, we are more likely to be thought of as friends than as enemies. A key skill that we need to develop, then, is an awareness of these subtle differences in symbolic exchange, and how they are used to define, contain or develop relationships. It is worth noting that even researchers have often got this wrong and have focused on the literal exchanges that take place in relationships without seeing the deeper symbolic importance.

This all matters because the literalness of exchanges tends to be modified as relationships change and grow. Strangers and very casual acquaintances reciprocate quite literally ('It's my round, you bought the last one'), whereas developing relationships move away from such literalism and exact repayment. When we put elderly people into the position where they receive more services than requests for advice, or more gifts than expressions of our high opinion of them, then, without even realizing it, we are subtly changing the relationship from friendship to a more distant one, if not even one of 'master–servant' or 'parent–child'. Exclusively providing physical help – especially if it cannot be returned like for like – is actually a subtle and unintended way of telling people that the relationship is not a friendship. We all do things for our friends, of course, and these physical provisions – along with provision of assistance, information and goods – are major services that friends offer, and are very important reasons why we need friends. However, in the last analysis, all of these things can be 'purchased' by means other than friendship. Most obviously, services, information and goods can all be purchased by money or, in the case of neighbourliness, by the promise of services, information and help on a future occasion.

One reason why many rich people feel friendless is precisely because they get used to buying help with money rather than by bartering their love or services in return. Society very kindly labels our acts of barter as desirable and honourable ('good neighbourliness'; 'A friend in need is a friend indeed') and so we feel good when we do them. It would be difficult to conduct most of our social lives if such exchange and barter did not create the intimate chains that bind us willingly to friends. Therefore it is essential for a satisfying life that we learn and practise the hidden, subtle skills of social exchange uncovered by research. As Berg and McQuinn (1989) have shown, one of the skills essential for us to be effective in obtaining support is the ability to 'self disclose' – that is, to open ourselves up to other people, to divulge our fears and hopes, concerns, desires, prides and shames. This is not a mechanism for directly requesting support, but an indirect means of establishing a good relationship so that others will be willing to offer assistance, feel warm towards us and generally be supportive.

Reassurance of our worth and value, and opportunity to help others
People who are lonely characteristically say that no-one cares about them, that they are useless, uninteresting, of low value and good for nothing. Studies of the conversation of severely depressed people invariably reveal indications that they have lost their self-respect or self-esteem (Gotlib and Hooley, 1988). In other words, they have come to see themselves as

valueless, worthless and insignificant, often because that is how they feel that everyone else sees them. Furthermore, analysis of suicide notes shows that many suicide attempts are carried out as a way of forcing some particular friend to re-evaluate the person, or to shock the friend into realizing just how much he or she really does esteem the person making the attempt. For this reason, Alfred Adler has claimed, with characteristic insight, that every suicide is always a reproach or a revenge.

One reason, then, that we appreciate friends is because of their contribution to our self-evaluation and self-esteem. Friends can do this both directly and indirectly: they may compliment us or tell us about other people's good opinions of us. Dale Carnegie's multimillion-seller book on *How to Win Friends and Influence People* stressed the positive consequences of doing this. Friends can also increase our self-esteem in other ways: by attending to what we do, listening, asking our advice and generally acting in ways that indicate the value that they place on our opinions. However, there are less obvious and more indirect ways in which they can communicate this estimation of our value. For one thing, the fact that they choose to spend time with us rather than with someone else must show that they value our company more than the alternatives.

There is a subtler version of these points too. Just as we look to friends to provide us with all of these things, so we can get from friendship one other key benefit. Because friends trust us and depend on us, they give us the chance to help them. That gives us the opportunity to take responsibility for them, to see ourselves helping them with their lives, to give them our measured advice and consequently to feel good. Friends provide us with these possibilities of taking responsibility and nurturing other people.

Undoubtedly, these things are important in the conduct of relationships and in making them satisfactory for both partners, and it is critical that we learn to evince them effectively. However, one important point to note is that those people who are poor at doing this (e.g., people who are poor at indicating interest, or who seem to have little time for other people, or never let them help or let them give advice) will find that other people are unattracted to relationships with them. All people need indications of their estimability and need chances to nurture just as we do, and if we do not adequately provide such signs then these people will reject us – just as we would do in their position.

One of the consequences of isolation and social rejection is the loss of this sense of esteem, worth and estimability. It is not surprising that many people become severely disturbed when it is lacking. Nor is it surprising that the nature of fantasy and wish-fulfilling daydreaming in such cases is often recollection of cases where self-esteem was high (for example, past social successes or past instances where other people came for help and advice).

Perhaps it is significant in this context to note how much of our western culture is based on the idea that 'number of friends' is a good measure of social and personal success. Someone who can claim a wide network of friends is usually regarded as happy and successful. One consequence of this is that people tend to exaggerate the number of friends that they have. This can lead to such absurdities as the claim by a well-known public performer to have sent out party invitations to '5,000 of his closest and dearest personal friends'!

Such ludicrous claims are mirrored to a lesser degree in all of our lives in a hundred different ways and we often attempt to 'publicize' our friendships in many minor and subtle forms. Notice how often people put the words 'one of my friends . . .' into a sentence; like name-dropping, 'friend-dropping' is intended to create an impression of involvement in a large circle, in this case a circle of friends. As another instance, when we receive birthday cards or Christmas cards they are not simply noted and thrown away, nor put in a drawer, but displayed on window ledges or hung on walls so that they can be seen by other people and used as an unofficial – but very public – barometer of the recipient's popularity and status. The elaborate consistency of such a performance shows us something important about the reasons why we use our friendships in this way, and testifies to the joint importance of friendships in maintaining our self-esteem and of the techniques and skills that help us to bring about this support from other people.

Personality support

Yet there is something even more fundamental to close relationships than this. Recent research indicates that each feature mentioned above – sense of community, emotional stability, communication, provision of help, maintenance of self-esteem – in its own way serves to support and integrate the person's personality (S.W. Duck and Lea, 1982). Each of us is characterized by many thoughts, doubts, beliefs, attitudes, questions, hopes, expectations and opinions about recurrent patterns in life. Our personalities are composed not only of our behavioural style (for example, our introversion or extraversion) but also of our thoughts, doubts and beliefs. It is a place full of symbols, a space where we are ourselves, a system of interlocking thoughts, experiences, interpretations, expectancies and personal meanings. Our personality would be useless to us if all of these opinions and meanings were not, by and large, supported. We would simply stop behaving if we had no trust in our thoughts or beliefs about why we should behave or how we should behave, just as we stop doing other things that we are convinced are wrong. Some schizophrenics and depressives actually do stop behaving when their thought-world falls apart: they just sit and stare.

Each of us needs to be assured regularly that our thought-worlds or symbolic spaces are sound and reliable. A friend can help us to see that we are wrong and how we can change, or that we are right about some part of our thinking. We may have vigorous discussions about different attitudes that we hold – but our friends are likely to be very similar to us in many of our attitudes and interests, so that these discussions are more probably supportive than destructive. However, we all know the anger and pain that follow a really serious disagreement with a close friend – much more unpleasant than a disagreement with an enemy. What we should deduce from all this is that we seek out as friends those people who help to support our thought-world-personality, and we feel chastened, sapped or undermined when they do not provide this support.

What sorts of person best gives us the kind of personality support that I have described here? In the first instance, it is provided by people who share our way of thinking. The more of these 'thought-ways' that we share with someone, the easier it is to communicate with that person: we can assume that our words and presumptions will be understood more easily by someone who is 'our type' than by someone who is not – we shall not have the repetitious discomfort of perpetually explaining ourselves, our meanings and our jokes.

Yet there is much more to it than this, although it has taken researchers a long time to sort out the confusing detail of the picture. For one thing, the type of similarity that we need to share with someone in order to communicate effectively depends on the stage that the relationship has reached. At early stages it is quite enough that acquaintances are broadly similar, but at later stages the similarity must be more intricate, precise, refined and detailed. One of the skills of friend-making is to know what sorts of similarity to look for at which times as the relationship proceeds. General similarity of attitudes is fine at the early to middle stages, but matters much less later if the partners do not work at discovering similarities at the deeper level of the ways in which they view other people and understand their characters. Very close friends must share the same specific sorts of framework for understanding the actions, dispositions and characters of other people in general, and in specific instances of mutual acquaintance. Such similarity is rare and prized. For that reason, if for no other, it is painful and extremely significant to lose the persons who offer it.

Loss or absence of particular intimates or friends deprives us of some measure of support for our personality, and it is essential to our psychological health that we have the skill to avoid this. Losing an intimate partner or friend not only makes us die a little, it leaves floating in the air those bits of our personality that the person used to support, and can make people fall apart psychologically. Of course, this will depend on how much our personality has been supported by that partner, which particular parts are involved, how readily these parts are supported by others, how much time we have had to anticipate and adjust to the loss, and so on. But essentially the loss or absence of friends and of close, satisfying relationships does not merely cause anxiety, grief or depression; it can cause other, more severe, forms of psychological disintegration or deterioration, often with the physical and mental side-effects noted earlier. Many of the well-known psychosomatic illnesses and hysterical states are actually caused by relationship problems, although this has not been realized by as many doctors as one might expect (see Lynch, 1977). For too long the accepted medical folklore has assumed that the person's inner mental state is a given, and that it causes psychosomatic effects when it gets out of balance. It is now quite clear that the surest way to upset people's mental balance is to disturb their close relationships (Gerstein and Tesser, 1987). We need friends to keep us healthy both physically and mentally: therefore it is doubly important that we perfect the ways of gaining and keeping friends. An important first step is to recognize the different needs that each relationship can fulfil for us, and the means by which this can be achieved.

In the rest of this book I will consider the typical marriage, family, close friendship and casual acquaintance as instances of relationships that need to be cherished and maintained. I will focus on the elements of these relationships that are common and I will point out differences. The nature of distressed marriages, disturbed families and so on will also be given some attention but it is not possible to do justice to those special problems fully in this book. Equally, gay and lesbian relationships are specifically addressed only in certain sections, since in most key respects their conduct and maintenance are very little different from that of heterosexual ones (Kurdek, 1991): there are similar problems of meeting partners, developing the relationship and negotiating suitable behaviours, for instance. There are also, of course, different problems, largely based on homophobia, on heterosexism, on role-socialization as it affects couple relationships, and on other issues to do with 'coming out', but I do not deal with these in much detail as I likewise do not deal with clandestine heterosexual relationships.

Note that there are obvious and less obvious differences between the organization of courtship and that of relationships at work, or between nonsexual male–female adult friendships and parent–child relationships. Each kind of relationship is unique, with its own special style and character. But it is also similar to other relationships, and I am focusing on the general cases; that is, the most commonly occurring ones, the ones familiar to the greatest number of people. I shall look at how these change during a person's life-cycle, how they develop and what can go wrong. In particular I shall stress the actions and skills that need to be accomplished to cope with the beginnings and the subsequent growth of these relationships. Relationshipping involves four separate accomplishments:

1. Recognizing, selecting and making the most of appropriate opportunities for friendship. This involves a sliding scale of subtle judgments about people and about situations: accordingly it is the point where most people go wrong most often.
2. Having a range of strategies and techniques for encouraging and enticing likeable persons into a relationship, and making them see the potential in that relationship for the satisfaction of their needs for personality support.
3. Possessing a strategic armoury and an adequate repertoire of knowledge about the ways in which relationships are helped to develop and grow. This involves knowledge of how to pace a relationship so that it progresses at a rate that is satisfactory to both partners.
4. Having a set of skills that help to maintain and repair relationships. They need overhaul, maintenance and servicing just as any other dynamic structure does, and this is often overlooked.

All of these activities are important for proper and successful relationships, not just the first one (i.e. meeting people). Also important is the fact that relationships can be lost because the individual fails to perform any *one* of these four activities adequately. It is not just because a person does not meet people, or because a person is not outwardly attractive, that he or she may have no friends. Some people meet a lot of other people but simply cannot sustain attraction, or are attractive to the 'wrong sorts of people', or – most unpleasant of all – develop relationships initially and cannot maintain them or cope with them, as soon as they get really intimate.

27

So there are many ideas about friendship that need fuller explanation not only from the point of view of correcting ill-informed or misconceived 'commonsense' notions, but also from the wider perspective of changes in social policy. Very many people who are poor at forming relationships, or who are severely and directly affected by other people's relationship deficiencies, are obvious inhabitants of our social casualty departments, such as the divorce courts, remand homes, prisons, mental hospitals, battered women's hostels and community homes. Other groups are also, at root, suffering from relationship difficulties. Such groups include would-be suicides, depressives, some neurotics, some alcoholics – even some violent prisoners, rapists and child-molesters (Howells, 1981). We should also think of including some people with illnesses that were once thought to be purely physical, but on closer inspection are sometimes caused by relationship problems, such as digestive disorders (Gerstein and Tesser, 1987). All of these people are, in their own way, crying out for a kind of help that only a fuller understanding of relationships can provide – understanding of how relationships start, develop and are sustained.

2

Perfect strangers and the action of attraction

The previous chapter has indicated the needs that close personal relationships satisfy, and has noted that many separable skills compose the means of achieving relationships that are capable of satisfying these needs. In the present chapter I shall survey some of the scientific evidence that has been amassed about these skills, especially as they concern the starting of relationships. It will soon become apparent that many misconceptions have been exposed by such work. The 'commonsense' model is that relationships are based on the mixing and matching of two people's personality characteristics or personal qualities. Two people get to like one another, on this model, because of the fit between their attitudes or interests, for example.

I shall challenge the belief that we start relationships only on the basis of personal qualities. On the contrary, it will begin to become clear that, although each person does undoubtedly bring something to relationships as an individual, it is interpersonal *behaviour* that matters most at the very start, and later the attraction is cemented by joint, not individual, action. There are several levels of skill here, and this chapter starts to explore the most basic one, the skill of *starting* relationships. A relationship has to be created and forged jointly by testing the likelihood that it will work, assessing and displaying trust (and the other person's trustworthiness), sharing of secrets, development of intimacy, confidence in one another's advice, organization of daily life together, and emotional support in times of trouble. These must all be allowed to take time to surface in a relationship and cannot be rushed.

Also, other consequences emerge from the joining of two people into the unit of a personal relationship. 'Similarity' is known to researchers as an important 'emergent property' of relationships: something that is a feature of the fact that two people are compared. (You cannot 'be similar' on your own because it takes two to make a comparison.) Similarities are obviously discovered and demonstrated bit by bit. Initially the two attracted partners can only suspect that they may be similar, but later the delightful commonalities are extensively discovered during the process of acquaintance. How is this crucial entry to a relationship properly devised?

It is a mistake to assume that outward appearance is of most importance in starting off a good friendship, and it is naive to think that physical appearance is the only vital force for attraction, or that people who look attractive just 'have it made'. Such beliefs merely invite the unwary onto a social ghost-train with many nasty surprises in store, and also help to misdirect their attention away from the knowledge, judgments and actions that really matter. Relationships are based on the thoughts, judgments, activities and skills of the partners. Skilful partners comprehend the 'ecology of relating': that is, they understand that not all occasions and places are ripe for relating. They know the places where it can be fostered, the persons to whom it can be offered and the range of activities that is appropriate at each stage of a relationship. They also develop and employ effective skills of discernment and person perception – that is, they are attentive to the telltale signs by which other people give off information about their character, hopes, intentions and secret fears. They know what to communicate, when to communicate and how to do it in a way that avoids their being dismissed, disregarded or rendered 'invisible'. By focusing on these three active constituents of the chemistry of friendship, the present chapter will begin to stress the actions of attraction and flesh out the behavioural skills involved at the very start of relationships.

Attraction – the very first point of a relationship – is not just important for people seeking to set up a long-term partnership, nor is it solely of interest to individuals who sense that they may be bad at it. Each satisfying and long-lasting relationship starts, both for people who are quite good at getting relationships going and for those who are not, at the point where two strangers meet. When the attraction stage goes badly, then the rest of the potential relationship never materializes. This stage is also a key point for sales personnel, doctors, therapists, bank workers and anyone dealing with the public in short encounters whose success depends on getting things off on the right foot, even for a very short time. The skills are different from the ones that come into play later when the encounter gets moving and is turned into a relationship, and I shall take a further two chapters to consider the skills involved there. At the present stage, I shall be looking at ways of arousing relationship drives and dealing with the fears that make people wary of entering relationships; techniques to combat the effects of prejudice and stereotyping; methods of avoiding disregard or 'invisibility'; and the ways people capitalize on the initial attraction stage of relationships. Each of these areas yields a different sort of practical help and advice about how to put relationshipping together into a working whole.

I am writing about *all* relationships, for the most part, though there are obvious differences between sexual and nonsexual relationships (for example, few people go to dating agencies to find friends rather than lovers!). When I do not spell out that I think sexual and nonsexual relationships are different, then I am assuming that their processes work in comparable ways.

FOSTERING RELATIONSHIPS: THE ECOLOGY OF PLACE AND TIME

At first sight it looks as if the best advice that can be given to a lonely person is to try to meet as many people as possible – to go forth and multiply the number of acquaintances that are encountered, and generally get immersed in contacts with other persons. We shall find, however, that this is not all

31

there is to it, but let us start out assuming that it is.

Obviously relationships cannot start until you meet people, so the first problem is how this should be done. There are many straightforward, traditional ways to do this, from joining clubs or groups or talking to neighbours to being friendly to almost everyone. There are also now some nontraditional methods using the many new agencies that have sprung up, such as dating agencies and personal advertisements. There are some important general lessons to be learned from these new, nontraditional methods which work without initial face-to-face contact and which are based on a clear and unambiguous expectation about the ensuing social interaction; yet underneath it all, they use techniques very similar to those underlying the traditional means.

Recently it has become much more popular for people to use dating agencies, or even popular television dating shows, to arrange partnerships. Some people are too busy to spend the time hanging around waiting for the right person just to happen along, and they employ the services of professionals to do some of the searching for them. In a way they are being extremely traditional rather than 'radical': in days gone by, many people were introduced to their marriage partner by a matchmaker. Indeed, in many countries they still are (for example, this practice is common in India, Turkey and several countries in the East). It may be surprising to westerners to learn that the same is true in their own culture in a subtle way. Parks and Barnes (1988) showed that an enormous percentage of people (about 80 per cent) report being introduced to their eventual partner by a mutual friend who foresaw that they would like one another. In a study that I did with Carol Cortez (S.W. Duck and Cortez, 1986), we found that 57 per cent of all dates were likewise arranged by third parties.

Recent analysis of dating agency clients in the United Kingdom (Goodwin, 1990) shows that, far from being bizarre or deviant, the members of dating agencies are likely to be above average in intelligence, social class and income levels, occupying the higher status jobs and having obtained higher educational qualifications than those people who did not use dating agency services. However, the study also reports that dating agency users score relatively low on dating and assertion skills tests. This suggests that such clients may be rather poor at communicating with others and so use shortcut methods of meeting likely partners – probably a good strategy in the circumstances, but one that needs to be supplemented by practice of the skills of friendship. Remember this important point when we begin to have our second thoughts about the wisdom of the advice to 'go out and meet people' if you are lonely.

Other scientific analysis of heterosexual personal advertisements (Koestner and Wheeler, 1988) shows that men 'offer' their status and height when describing themselves, while women 'offer' physical attractiveness. Men usually seek younger women and women usually seek older men. Men describe themselves as emotionally open and expressive, while women seek such expressiveness. It is clear that the advertisers are purposely describing themselves in ways that they expect the opposite sex to find attractive, and to this extent they tend to employ descriptions that have stereotype appeal. We should not forget that such advertisements are intended to persuade other people to think of entering a relationship. This is a good lesson: the very creation of a relationship, its maintenance and development, are all based on persuasion. No-one *has* to be in a relationship with anyone else and all voluntary relationships are therefore rooted in our ability to attract (i.e., persuade) the other person to stay in the relationship. If we bear in mind that most of what is necessary in relating is persuasive, much of what follows will make more sense.

What I am saying is that agencies and advertisements can help people get together but it is then up to the individual to meet the partner and to make it all work. Inability to do this may have been the person's real problem in the first place. Recent work by Berg and Piner (1990) shows that dates are rapidly defined as promising or not (in the first 30 seconds!) and so one's behaviour and actions at the earliest points are greatly influential. The many ways of meeting people – like parties, personal advertisements, singles bars and dating agencies – do all offer the chance of meeting a partner who is interested in a relationship, but they do not offer any general help on how to attract (persuade) other people out-side of these very special circumstances. In fact, they simply stack the cards and do not guarantee anything – especially, they guarantee nothing about the activities of relationship-ping that will ultimately be necessary to make the relation-ship work.

One other subtle reason can be given as to why dating agencies need to be supplemented by other means. These agencies are advantageous for people who have difficulty meeting others or knowing when it is appropriate to 'make the moves'. In the case of a personal advertisement or a dating agency, both people who sign up for the adventure know what they are doing and what is expected – in short, they know what the situation is like because the doubts about the partner's willingness to be involved are minimized. The persons have to exercise no skill or judgment to recognize the situation; they simply have to try and act in a way that encourages other people to play up to the role that the situation demands of them. Because of this the situation actually sidesteps a problem: some people founder in rela-tionships because they do not normally know what is called for or do not recognize the demands, and the limits, of the situation. The member of a loyal, cheering crowd who offers the queen a cigarette is such a person; the job interviewee who invites the chief executive officer out for a meal is an-other. These people fail to recognize that not all friendliness should be taken as personal, nor should it be seen to invite initiation of a close relationship. On the other side of the coin, there are people who do not pay careful attention to the problem of recognizing when friendly advances are called for, and need to have it all spelt out so clearly as to be embarrassing for everyone. They are perhaps too shy or wary to open up and relax, or they may simply not realize what is necessary or, recognizing it, may not have the skills to carry it out reliably.

It is perhaps surprising to realize that such a problem exists, but a whole field of research has been devoted to it (the so-called 'social skills' research that explores the minute behaviours of social interaction (Patterson, 1988)). An example from my personal experience of this difficulty happened when I was in a hurry once, and running to an appointment. One of my pupils, an awkward young woman with minor behavioural problems, rushed up to me in the drizzle and thrust into my hand a piece of birthday cake wrapped in a paper bag. Evidently she had just celebrated her 21st birthday, had a secret crush on me and was trying to start something going. Soggy birthday cake in the drizzle when I was in a rush would seem like a pretty poor way to start, but she clearly did not realize this. Not everyone knows how to 'read' the situation and to reserve the attempt at friend-making until a suitable moment. There is even a story of a boss who once tried to introduce one of his members of staff to a distinguished visitor when they all chanced to meet in the men's urinal, a place that actually makes it rather difficult to carry out normal greeting and hand-shaking in a satisfactory way.

The first stage of making friendships is an understanding of the ecology of attraction; that is to say, a grasp of the situations and circumstances where it is legitimate to lay out one's relational wares and begin to persuade or to strike the bargain that makes the relationship. One must recognize places and situations in which attraction is 'permitted' (or even expected), and also the places or occasions when it is not. Most people would have little difficulty recognizing the fact that situations differ in their demands for sociable action. However, some people need either formal intervention from therapists or clinical psychologists or counsellors, or perhaps just some firm guidance by associates who can indicate that they need to focus on such things. People who seem unfriendly at parties may not be hostile, they may just be ignorant of the ecology of friendship and the skills required to capitalize on it. For instance, Burgoon and Koper (1984) showed that people who are actually shy tend to be mistakenly judged as hostile by other people who do not know them. Something about their behaviour cues people in incorrectly. Interestingly, shy people's own friends do not interpret those same behaviours as hostile.

One of the first skills, then, involves merely the ability to recognize when it is desirable to turn on the range of friendship behaviours discussed in the next two chapters. Other

35

mponents involve recognition or reading of the features
social interactions that are seemingly insignificant and yet
have enormous power.

Some situations are good for friendship and some are not;
some are good for some people and not others; some are
good for starting friendship and some are suitable only once
the relationship has its independent life. Surprisingly,
people who are developing close relationships tend to meet
in public places more often than in private for quite a length
of time (about six weeks, according to S.W. Duck and Miell,
1986). An important skill to acquire and develop, then, relies on two features of 'relationshipping'. First, one must
recognize situations that are appropriate to the starting of a
particular sort of relationship; second, one must learn to
choose, emphasize and seek out those activities and situations that are appropriate to the systematic and successful
development of the relationship so started.

We usually try to meet liked people more often in places
where food and drink are served; disliked people are encountered in places where work is done (Argyle *et al.*, 1981).
Liked people are met for longer periods of time and the
meeting is usually less structured or focused than is a meeting with someone we dislike. In short, friendship and non-
friendship are expressed not only through different feelings
but through a totally different range of activities and situations. Those people who have not learned to do this are
those who appear to others to behave inappropriately.

Relationships happen in many different sorts of environment and also involve many sorts of activity. Work relationships are just that rather than friendships, not simply
because of how the people feel about one another, but because of where the relationships happen and what the
people do together (Mangham, 1981). People define and
accept the relationship because of what they do together, as
much as they do things together because of the relationship.
Argyle (1986) reported that husbands and wives watch more
television together than other people and that this activity is
what differentiates marriage from other relationships – not
the occurrence of sexual intercourse, conflict or anything
else, but of television watching!

Studies have shown that it is possible to alter someone's feelings about another person merely by getting them to do different things together or to meet in different places. Thus, factory workmates who are given the job of organizing a factory outing or a Christmas party, or who are asked to meet outside the factory in a bar or café to discuss such informal matters, will respond to the cues in the situation. Here they are doing friendly things in a friendly environment, therefore they must be friends. This involves so-called 'self-perception'; that is, people catch themselves doing something and explain it to themselves afterwards in a way that makes sense. When workmates meet in a friendly situation, are not focused on their usual work routine, undertake the activities that friends normally do, and enjoy themselves, then they explain all that as being due to their friendship or liking for one another, rather than as due to the fact that they were asked to meet there. Such a result seemed to follow from the careful arrangement of the Camp David talks in the later 1970s where, on expert advice, US President Carter placed Egyptian President Sadat and Israeli Prime Minister Begin – two political opponents – in a situation where they were focused on daily human routine, rather than on political routine. By all accounts they slept in rooms near one another, ate together, saw what each other looked like in the morning and generally came to see the human side of each other rather than the distant, political, stereotyped side. They got on better in their talks and came to trust one another more.

The differences between work and play seem to the unskilled eye to matter very little. In fact they are, on the contrary, extremely significant in relationships, not because of what they *are* but because of how they make people see one another. The activities that we do with another person are crucial ways of defining the relationship, and if we seek to become friends with someone it is essential to enter situations, and create opportunities, where activities that 'feel friendly' can be done. However, there is a gender difference in decisions about the behaviours that count as 'friendly'. As several researchers have shown (e.g., Helgeson *et al.*, 1987), most men define intimacy as 'doing things together' whereas women are likely to define it in terms of the subject matter of their conversations or simply the amount of conversation engaged in. This may create problems in developing relationships between men and women. As the man tries to develop intimacy he attempts to set up situations of 'doing', whereas the woman trying to develop intimacy attempts to set up situations where the two people 'talk'.

There are other differences between men and women in respect of friendship just as there are between older and younger people. For instance, men fall in love sooner than women, but women fall out of love sooner than men. In a long-term study of courtship (Hatfield and Traupmann, 1981) it was found that women operate a last-in-first-out (LIFO) principle in this sort of relationship, whereas men are first-in-last-out (FILO). When one also hears of the studies of marital satisfaction showing that men appear to be generally happier and more content with their marriages than their wives are, then it appears that some general difference between the sexes has been discovered. However, it depends very much on the sort of relationship contemplated. Ball and Robbins (1984) found that married black men in the United States were generally less satisfied with life than were unmarried black men and married white men. My colleagues and I have also found that men are generally much worse at starting friendships when they can be overheard or closely observed, whereas women can do it as successfully under these conditions as under any other (Miell and Duck, 1982).

A very important aspect of friend-making is the fact that there are significant changes in activities as the relationship grows. Just as we behave differently towards people whom we like and those we dislike, meeting in different situations and performing different types of activity, so we distinguish close and casual acquaintances in the same way. This can be as obvious as the fact that we are more likely to meet close friends in our homes than to meet casual acquaintances there, or as subtle as the fact that first dates are typically visits to a cinema while second dates are typically meals (S.W. Duck, *et al.*, 1989). When the relationship is just starting, people tend to feel that the other person initiates activities more than they do. This is important because it gives a strong sense of the other person's desire to foster the relationship, and makes people feel needed and wanted. One of the big distinctions between successful and unsuccessful dates is that bad dates feel as if one person controlled the conversation, while good dates are invariably reported as being mutually controlled (S.W. Duck *et al.*, 1989). We need to *work* to allow control to be mutual rather than taken by one person.

Just as features of activity characterize personal relationships, and just as time and place matter in attraction, so also are these features important in other relationships such as those at work. Meetings with colleagues will usually focus on the task or work involved, but can be transformed and personalized by attention to the so-called socio-emotional content of the interaction. Work can be dealt with briskly in a task-oriented way or it can be handled in a more leisurely, person-oriented way. Comments about the way in which the other person is coping with the task, about the atmosphere in the meeting, about one's enjoyment of the encounter and so on are all contributors to a raised socio-emotional level. All of these can personalize the meeting in a way that emphasizes the relationship between the participants rather than the tasks that they have to complete. In the case of dating or courtship, the important activities in the first encounter are the creation of mutual interest in the partners, an indication of concern over the partner's welfare, and the instigation of a wish for future meetings where the partner's values, opinions and attitudes can be explored. I shall say more about this in Chapter 3 since it is one of the most significant skills in developing relationships

SKILLS OF JUDGING RELATIONSHIP NEEDS

Obviously not everyone is always fully open to new relationships: we may, for example, already have all that we think we need (our 5.6 most satisfying relationships (Reisman, 1981)). A variation on the above necessary skills is the ability to recognize when, even in the right circumstances, the

other person is resistant to entering a relationship. Sometimes this is a matter of understanding what their posture,
facial expression or vocal tone actually means. Sometimes it
requires a deeper appreciation of their character or their
self-image and their beliefs about their own worth. In some
cases the two go very closely together: people who think very
little of themselves give it away by their bodily movements,
facial expressions or tone of voice. For instance, their posture may be dejected, their eye movements nervous and
their tone of voice flat. They mumble rather than speaking
out clearly and confidently; they avoid looking at the person
they are talking to; they lick their lips nervously, hold their
hands in front of their mouths when talking and move in an
agitated way. Many of these signs are similar to those looked
for by police officers and customs officers: it is as if persons
with low self-esteem are feeling permanently guilty – guilty
for being themselves. It is important to spend some time
looking at this because much of what I shall say runs counter
to the usual hidden assumption in western culture that
everyone wants friends, wants them to an equal degree at all
times or in all situations, and wants to expand their network
of friends whenever possible. On the contrary, extensive research shows that there are many misconceptions in this
belief.

For one thing, it has been shown reliably that different
people have different levels of drive for friendship, not only
from time to time but also as permanent features of their
personality (McAdams, 1988). It is as normal to enjoy a close,
small, intense set of friendships as it is to prefer to have lots
of friends. (In fact, one of the famous personality dimensions, noted by Jung, is that of introvert–extravert. Both types
are 'normal', but one takes energy from the world by being
with other people (the extravert), while the other loses energy
to the world by being with other people (the introvert) and
gains energy from solitude.) It is even perfectly normal, but
not very common, for someone to desire no friends at all. As
demonstrated in Chapter 1, a fundamental purpose of friendship is the provision of reassurance that other people need
and want us, but a few self-assured individuals are strong
enough to carry on alone. Other people are absorbed in

work that takes them away from sociable activities. Some have such close ties with their family that they do not need to step outside to find further reassurance of their worth. Equally, not every isolated person is unhappy about being isolated, although many are. What is important in friend-making is that we recognize and cope with these differences, particularly when encountering strangers whose drive for new friendships may be at a very different level from our own. One way to help in this is to try to understand where such differences come from so that we can be most efficient in dealing with them when we encounter them.

Friendship drives are affected by two things: first, the person's global and relatively stable beliefs about his or her general worth and value as a person; second, temporary or transient features of people's lives and circumstances. Stable parts of the person are global self-esteem, experiences in prior relationships, beliefs about one's personal, physical or social attractiveness, and general expectations about the nature of relationships and the rewards or costs that are associated with them. The temporary, transient set of influences comprise the happenstance of recent experiences (for example, whether someone has just broken off or just started a deep relationship, whether they have just had fortuitous experiences that make them feel good).

Whilst transient factors are worth considering in more detail later in the chapter, it is obviously the more permanent features that need closest attention. People who have frequently experienced rejection in the past, and who blame themselves for it, are likely to maintain low drives towards friendship through fears of further humiliation (Mehrabian and Ksionzky, 1974). They will be likely to remain socially unadventurous, reserved and cautious, will feel vulnerable in new relationships, will need to be frequently reminded that the partner likes them, and may be vigilant and suspicious. Such people often express the deepest cynicism and doubts about other people's motives in relating to them (Wittenberg and Reis, 1986). This leads to a constant watch for signs that the other person is insincere, or is entering a relationship with them for instrumental or manipulative reasons, like a desire for sex. Although such fears and doubts are most often shaped by experiences as a young adult, adolescent or child (which is one reason why we should attend more closely to relationship development in children: see Chapter 5), they can be sustained by experiences in adulthood that depend on other people's habitual treatment of oneself.

These fears and doubts can also, however, be broken by the same means, as a very famous experiment shows. This particular study took the view that our personalities and our usual ways of behaviour are based on the ways in which other people treat us, rather than on something 'in' ourselves. It was a study done before the Second World War, and of a kind not ethically acceptable today (Guthrie, 1938). A class of male students was invited to pay attention (unbeknownst to her) to a rather unattractive girl and to treat her as if she were very attractive. They began to compliment her on the way she looked and moved, began to ask her for dates and started to respond to her as if she were highly attractive. At first there was little noticeable effect, but gradually she started to take more care over her appearance, to buy more fashionable clothes, and even to act in a more attractive manner. After a while, the young men were not pretending when they complimented her: she really had become a very attractive young woman and was sought after by other young men on the campus, not just ones privy to the experiment. Her view of herself had been fundamentally restructured by the responses that she received from other people and she acted in accord with the new view. In a more recent study (Snyder, *et al.*, 1977) it was shown that women who were described as 'attractive' to male subjects talking to them over a telephone caused the male subjects to behave in a manner that was attractive and flirtatious (as judged by independent raters of their behaviour). This then fed back on itself. Picking up on the men's behaviour, the women themselves started to behave in ways that the men regarded as more attractive. In part, then, we create reality for ourselves and for other people by the way that we relate to them.

Over time such experiences lead people to think in a very rigid way about their social encounters. In another experiment on people with both high and low self-esteem (i.e., some people who felt that they were valuable people and others who felt worthless), the effects of this were strikingly demonstrated (Stroebe, 1977). The members of the group heard someone say something about them which was either complimentary or critical, and their task was to guess whether the person was giving their true opinion, or was acting under instructions from the experimenter. Subjects with high self-esteem usually guessed that a compliment was 'true opinion', while a criticism was 'instructions'. Subjects with low self-esteem habitually believed the reverse: criticisms were true opinion and praise must have been instructed by the experimenter. In real life this effect would have hidden but far-reaching consequences. For instance, if you are talking to someone at a party who makes an excuse and goes off to get another drink, you may treat this in different ways depending on how you feel about yourself. A person with high self-esteem will assume that the partner was thirsty; a person with low-esteem may assume that the partner was bored by the conversation.

Recognizing that these differences exist and can affect not only an individual's behaviour but also the whole way that one approaches and interprets other people's social actions, we need to sensitize ourselves to their significance. A person who has low self-esteem may not practise considering alternative explanations for other people's social actions, particularly alternatives that do not involve self-flagellation. A cognitive therapist might encourage such a person to think of all the possible reasons why someone would move on at a party, such as the rules about 'circulating', being caught by someone else on the way back to talk to you, going to get food and being waylaid to help prepare some more, and so on. The very fact of being able to create a long list of alternative explanations may help such a person acquire a sense of proportion that focuses less on self-perceived unworthiness, and more on the realities of social life as enjoyed by others.

The opposite style has been identified as characteristic of good conversationalists (Daly, 1990). Such people spend much less time talking about themselves and more time inviting the other person to converse, steering away from disagreement or dogmatic statements and towards an attentive and accepting, if gently interpretative, manner. They adopt deliberate summarizing of what the person says ('I see. So you think that . . .'), attentive reference to past points ('You said a moment ago that . . .') and invitations to expand on their views in an unthreatening way ('That's interesting. I'd like you to tell me more about that.'). These all stress interest in the other person and so lay the ghost of the person's vigilance and give reassurances of his or her worth. They also emphasize that one is listening carefully to the talk, not merely standing there uninvolved. They might even help prevent *the listener* from getting depressed! Notarius and Herrick (1988) showed that people who used supportive listening techniques, such as those above, became less depressed when talking to a depressed person than did people who took it upon themselves not so much to listen as to give advice, especially if it was not tuned specifically to the individuals that they were attempting to help.

These listening skills are routinely taught to couples who are in marital therapy. It is noteworthy that women often feel that men do not listen to them because men give fewer cues that they have heard what was said (such as 'Uh huh' and 'How interesting'). It has been found that when women say 'Uh huh' and so on, it is to indicate continued attention and listening, whereas men typically reserve such vocalizations for specific agreements with the speaker. Thus men do less of it in the first place, but when they do it at all it is in much more limited circumstances, and this can lead to women feeling that they have not been heard.

Adopting these skills is a simple style and strategy that emphasizes one's regard for other persons as people. Placing stress on other people's successful action is also important. As a very subtle example, I know a man who never says 'Congratulations' to someone who has had a success; he always says 'Well done', thus stressing not the chance good fortune itself, but rather the individual's own work and contribution to bringing it about.

Low self-esteem is not the only influence that makes people wary of embarking on relationships. There are complex processes that prevent people from carrying out their desires for relationships. For instance, it is commonly believed that traditionally or classically physically attractive people have better relationships and more opportunities, but this has been shown to be false. Many people have negative reactions to classically physically attractive people, whether through envy or resentment or fear that they will be 'too good for the likes of me', and will reject attempts to be friendly. People are also likely to assume that attractive people have more relationships than the rest of us or are probably already in a close relationship, so there is no point in asking them out.

In fact, people have a series of psychological 'governors' that stop them approaching all the partners who are apparently the best from a purely physical point of view (Berscheid and Walster, 1974). We do not invariably seek out the most attractive partners: we seek out those whom we think we can allure without fear of rejection. The 'governor' here is the person's level of self-esteem and confidence.

The global form of self-esteem, mentioned earlier, has been referred to as 'level of aspiration' and, briefly, it describes the level at which the person sets his or her sights – that is, it defines the level of attractiveness of the kind of partner that the person is confident that he or she can draw (Murstein, 1976; Stroebe, 1977). Research indicates that people with similar levels of aspiration tend to marry one another. A person's 'objective' physical attractiveness may be quite different from his or her level of aspiration: some beautiful people do not think they are very attractive, and some unattractive people are confident that their sparkling wit compensates and makes them more valuable socially. They may be right: people who are seen as attractive are usually those with interesting or lively personalities.

In the case of the temporary level of self-esteem there have been many experiments where men have been given false results on an intelligence test (in order to make them feel either good or bad about themselves) and then tested with a female accomplice of the experimenter (see, for example, Walster *et al.*, 1978). The accomplice is made up in a way that makes her look attractive or unattractive, and the idea is to see whether the man tries to arrange a date with her. Sure enough, men who have their esteem vicariously raised by being told that they have scored very highly on the test are much more likely to 'come on' to the confederate when she is attractive.

The effects of self-esteem are often general and affect all of someone's behaviour, not just actions in a beginning relationship. Researchers have also discovered other psychological 'governors' that affect people's willingness to become involved in relationships. Individuals have other general relationship drives that affect their vigilance and their trust of other people. They also have some very specific beliefs about the level of satisfaction that they can expect in different sorts of relationships. For over three decades researchers (e.g., Thibaut and Kelley, 1959) have talked of an individual's *Comparison Level*; that is, the general level of satisfaction or 'profit' that an individual has come to expect from relationships during the course of his or her life. If the individual suspects that a new relationship will bring rewards in excess of the comparison level then he or she will be attracted to it, but otherwise not. However, sometimes people enter and stay in relationships that are below this comparison level simply because they know that they could not, at present, do any better. In short, they also have a *Comparison Level for Alternatives* – a belief about the level of satisfaction or profit that they could realistically obtain in alternative relationships of a similar type (e.g., with alternative dates or friends). Comparison Level and Comparison Level for Alternatives may be different: the former refers to all relationships in general and the latter refers only to specific sorts of relationship at a particular time. People in a relationship that lies above their Comparison Level for Alternatives (that is, people who do not think that they could 'do better' in another relationship at the moment) are obviously dependent on that relationship, even if they are not happy with it. A knowledge of what people feel about their relationships and their views of alternatives can help an outsider to decide the level of their relationship drive and to direct effort accordingly.

Such things as self-esteem, level of aspiration, drives for relationship and comparison levels are relatively permanent or enduring aspects of an individual's style. There are also some temporary features that affect behaviour in relationships. For one thing, friendship needs are known to be influenced by a kind of 'critical mass' phenomenon: once a person's friendships reach a certain number the person seems to lose the desire to seek out any more friends, and usually does not do so except at the expense of existing friends (S.W. Duck, 1988b). Furthermore, there appears to be a critical threshold before a person feels motivated to do anything about isolation or loneliness (Perlman and Peplau, 1981): it takes time to attack the roots of the person's psychology enough for him or her to take action. To feel loneliness, people must perceive a large discrepancy between what they are 'achieving' in relationships and what they desire. Not only this, but commitment to the relationship must have reached a low point. This is especially true of ending some types of relationship, like marriage, and those at work, in which one's *personal commitment* may be lower than the formal, *structural commitment* (that is, one's liking for the relationship may be lower than the social pressures that keep one in it, such as pressures from relatives or friends, legal obligations or contractual partnerships (Johnson, 1982)).

It is also usual to think of the arrival of a competitor as the cause of a relationship's ending: when a rival turns up, the partner runs off with the rival. A moment's thought enables us to share with recent research the view that this is wrong. What matters is not that a rival just turns up, but the fact that the partner accepts the rival (Pfeiffer and Wong, 1989). In other words, the important feature of the situation is the psychological state of the person who desires the rival. Clearly, willingness to become involved with a new partner at the expense of an old-established one is the key psychological change that has taken place. Personal commitment has reached a point at which structural commitment can be ignored: the repulsion from the relationship reaches a negative force that is powerful enough to overcome the social compulsions that bind one to it. At such points of climactic decision, the person decides to ignore the structural commitments through lack of personal commitment. The decision to run off with the neighbour depends not only on the neighbour, but on one's own views of the alternative. Thus a person's internal relationship drives affect actions more strongly than do external forces and constraints.

A final influence on these relationship drives is presented by a combination of age and place in the life-cycle (Dickens and Perlman, 1981). At certain ages a person is more likely to be searching for particular sorts of relationship and is more likely to be active in attempts to expand a social network. Thus mid-adolescence is the time when a demand to enter heterosexual relationships becomes dominant, and a strong pressure to (start practising to) attract an intimate partner is exerted on people of the age group between 16 and 30. We can expect individuals in these age groups to be on the look out for sexual, cohabital or marital partners rather more noticeably than much older or much younger people would be.

As another example, it is found that specific friendship drives decline sharply after the age of 30 or so, except for people who experience serious disruptions in their life, such as divorce, change of career or death of spouse (Reisman, 1981). For such disrupted people there is actually a sudden and marked increase in social involvements – a fact not without its own psychological problems and stresses, since it runs counter to the social pattern that they would normally have expected. The usual lull lasts until just before retirement age, when a vigorous spurt in social activity precedes a gradual but steady decline in the number of friends (usually through their death rather than from an increase in quarrelling).

The significance of all the foregoing influences on relationship drives lies in their importance not only to people who wish to improve their relationships, but also to those who wish to help and counsel those who have that wish. Friendships, courtships and even casual relationships are begun only when the partners wish to enter them. By attending to the life-cycle position, social circumstances and personality style of the individual one can more easily gauge their likely interest in a relationship. Access to a relationship follows only when we correctly exercise a skilled judgment that the circumstances and the person would both be right for us to make the effort. If the need for the relationship is not present, or cannot be skilfully stimulated, then all the correct friendly behaviour in the world will be to no avail.

The next set of skills relies on different types of judgment. These skills depend not so much on the ability to recognize situations that are ripe with relationship promise, nor on that of recognizing when someone's friendship drive is correctly aroused. Rather they depend on the ability to recognize an individual who has a high statistical likelihood of being a suitable companion. The research shows very clearly that people are boringly uninventive in their choice of partners, and that those who attempt to form relationships outside usual boundaries are probably wasting their time (Kerckhoff, 1974; Rodin, 1982). People making friends actually direct their efforts very discriminately – friendships are usually formed with people of the same religion and socioeconomic level, who have a similar job, background, educational history, level of income, recreational interests, sexual orientation and racial origins.

People usually present themselves in a way that gives the practised observer clues about them. The first couple of minutes of conversation is a point at which people attempt to get across to others the central features of their 'person', their essential 'me-ness' as they see it. For instance, many people start sentences with 'I phrases' like 'Well, I was adopted, and I think that . . .', or 'I live in Surbiton and I've noticed that . . .', or 'I was on a business trip to Singapore once and I think that . . .' or 'That's interesting. I work in a rape crisis centre and I think . . . '. These are all ways of presenting to other people some marker that helps to locate the speakers and defines some feature of themselves that they regard as crucial or overwhelmingly important. It is fundamental to starting off relationships that one listens for such things and attends to them. People very often introduce into their conversations phrases or ideas that are strictly redundant and illogical, but which serve a vital social and relational purpose by telling the listener things about themselves that they want to have known. It can be as simple as the phrases 'Those of us with Italian connections . . .' or 'My Jewish mother always used to say . . .'. People who slip in such information clearly want it to be known, and want the listener to pick it up. It is important to them, and it tells something about their way of life, their inner self and their system of values.

The clearest example of this I ever experienced was from a young woman who spoke to me when I was talking about different cultures and said, 'I was very interested in what you just said because my father died when I was eight and my mother and I lived in America.' The sentence appears to be concerned with the topic of cultures but its actual purpose is to tell me that she has had a difficult life with unusual, tragic experiences. The part about the death of her father is logically irrelevant to the rest of the sentence, but socially very significant to the understanding of what she thinks is important about herself.

There are endless examples of such attempts to locate oneself, to leak information that one thinks is significant, and to get across quickly some feature or characteristic of oneself that one is just dying for the other person to know about. Indeed, the Greeks had a whole myth about these almost uncontrollable urges to leak information: Midas's barber was the only person who knew that the king had donkey's ears underneath his turban, and he was so overwhelmed with the knowledge that he dug a hole and whispered the secret into it. But it looks as if there is something of Midas's barber in all of us. We love to tell things that we know – especially things about ourselves. We should recognize this human tendency and learn its value in helping to understand and get to know other people. What matters for relationships is to watch out for, attend to and use the information that people try to give out in this way. If it matters to them, and makes them feel distinctive or 'individuated', then it will help us to relate to them.

What these individuators are doing is trying to undercut the stereotypes that listeners may otherwise be forced to use, because it is hard to find out much about people in a short space of time without help. In cases where we are not given such individual information, we truly have very little to go on when we meet someone for the first time. Given that the aim of relationships is to obtain some support for our personality, we need to make quick judgments about the people that we meet, and to form quick assessments of how far we would expect that a person like that could offer us the support that we need. In most cases we all rely on stereotypes, both general and personal, to do this. Whole libraries of research papers testify to the existence of cultural stereotypes that describe particular nationalities, groups and subgroups. Each person also has his or her own personal stack of such stereotypes, and the true task that each of us faces is in practising their use so that we make them as accurate as possible, and as far from misleading as we can.

Unfortunately, most people are influenced by outward appearance very strongly, and the only way to combat it effectively is to increase our awareness of the pitfalls. We all draw inferences about someone's personality from the way that they look, and too often these judgments are sweeping, general and unhelpful. For example, a large amount of research has shown that ugly and deformed people are assumed to be more criminally inclined than are normal-looking people (Bull, 1977). In short, inward deviance is invariably assumed from an outwardly deviant appearance. (In fact it is such an assumption, in reverse, that makes it easier for rapists, pickpockets, muggers and con-artists to do their work: they *look* 'normal' and safe, so we assume that they *are* normal and safe.) The same research shows that people with scars on their cheeks are assumed to be criminals – particularly, to be violent criminals. When asked to guess whether a scarfaced man is a lifeboatman or a prison inmate, most people assume that he is a criminal rather than someone who puts his own life at risk for others.

Other research shows that attractive-looking children are judged – even by experienced teachers and other children – to be less naughty and mischievous than are plain or ugly ones (K.K. Dion and Berscheid, 1974). When asked to judge a story of a misdeed done by a child whose photograph is attached to the story, people consistently credit the nice-looking child with nicer motivation or better reasons for doing the misdeed. They are also less likely to claim that the act represents the child's true personality: people seem to believe that attractive-looking children are not really naughty. On the other hand, they do think that ugly children are – and they recommend tougher punishments for them. The same error occurs in court cases (Sigall and Ostrove, 1975). In one study, attractive-looking defendants were rated as less likely to be guilty than were unattractive ones, and several studies have shown that, in experiments, mock jurors recommend shorter sentences for attractive people. The exception is in cases where the persons used their good looks in the crime involved (e.g., if they were confidence tricksters who used their looks to distract people or lull them into unwariness).

Most of these studies use first appearance or just show photographs to people, and there is evidence that some of the effects are less powerful in real life or during extended face-to-face encounters. Even though physical appearance sets off stereotypes in all of us, we overcome them during later encounters. The real skill comes in reining in our stereotyped responses at the start and learning to control their worst effects. One way of overcoming them is to think of alternative personalities for strangers that one meets, to work out what different sorts of personal characteristic they may have, and to explore particularly the ways in which the stereotype does *not* fit.

In the case of physically attractive persons, there seems to be a pretty unrestrained 'halo' effect: we see only the good side and we extend it beyond what we see. Physically attractive people are judged from first appearance to have more interesting personalities, more successful careers, greater capabilities and promotion prospects, and a whole host of other perks. Evidently we like physically attractive people not only because they look nice – indeed, this can actually scare people off, as we have seen. The point is that ordinary people draw flattering conclusions about personalities from the way that other persons look.

The important question that then follows is whether physical attractiveness favourably affects the amount of friendship or social participation that people experience. Most of us would guess the answer to be yes, and we would be right up to a point, but probably we would be wrong in detail. Researchers (Reis *et al.*, 1980) have found that physically attractive people do spend their time in different ways from the rest of us. Attractive males have many more interactions with females than they do with males – but the opposite is not true for attractive females. Evidently, attractive women do not spend any more time enjoying relationships with men than they do with other women. (This could be because friendships and conversations with women are actually preferred by members of both sexes, as we saw in Chapter 1.) However, physically attractive persons of each sex reported having more fun in all their activities than the unattractive people did, even though the attractive males seemed to spend more than average amounts of time (for men) having conversations rather than actively participating in sports or going to parties. This could be because they are interacting with females, who, as we saw earlier, seek intimacy through talk rather than sports or activities. Finally, attractive males are less likely to start off an encounter or take the social initiative, contrary to commonly held beliefs. They report that their activities are usually started jointly when they and their partner just feel like doing something together. So although attractiveness does seem to influence our social participation, it does so more for males than for females and not in the ways we often expect.

While physical appearance affects opportunities for meeting people it does not help to make friends; it is just another circumstantial factor that affects opportunity rather than doing the creation of relationships for people, just like the other factors given so far in the chapter. Effort put into changing one's appearance alone is largely wasted, and it would be better directed to the task of making best effective use of the opportunities for relationships that appearance may provide. The knowledge and skills outlined in the chapter so far are a good starting point, but crucial aspects of communication represent the next most important step – and remember that I am still discussing the very beginning of a relationship, not yet the ways in which it develops.

COMMUNICATION AND THE BEGINNING OF RELATIONSHIPS

The research in the following pages is essentially on how people communicate information about themselves and their attitudes – their attitudes about themselves and about other people. They do this in two ways which often overlap. One concerns their so-called 'non-verbal behaviour' and the other 'self-presentation', although the two are not always utterly distinct. The former concerns very, very subtle and slight actions, sometimes ones so swift that they are hard to detect unless you are looking out for them – like eye movements, changes of posture or variations in voice pitch. Yet the information that they transmit or 'leak' is so important that it is quite enough to stop a relationship before it starts.

Nonverbal style is made up of many microscopic activities, so small that they appear superficially to be meaningless or insignificant. We might overlook the importance of such things as eye movements, however, until we focus on it. If you doubt this then try this simple experiment: talk to people while looking steadily past their right ear. Do not at any time look them in the face. Keep a close look out for what happens, how they treat you and what they do. Be warned – they won't like it!

From ancient times humans have seen the eyes as important socially, and even spiritually. The word 'pupil' for the part of the eye comes from the Latin '*pupilla*', meaning 'little doll', because if you look into someone's pupil you can see a reflection of yourself on a much smaller scale. The eyes were also previously seen as the 'mirror of the soul', and the 'evil eye' was something to avoid.

It is not surprising, then, to learn that our eyes convey significant information about our interest in someone else: when we like someone our pupils dilate or enlarge when we see the person, and stay dilated while we converse (Argyle, 1978). We are normally unaware of this change to our own eyes, yet we notice it on some level of unconscious awareness when it happens to other people talking to us. Even photographs of people with dilated pupils are preferred to photographs of people with undilated pupils, although we are usually not conscious of why we prefer them. Up to the middle ages women used an infusion of deadly nightshade to dilate their pupils as a beauty aid – indeed, the Latin name for deadly nightshade (*belladonna*) means beautiful woman. Chinese jade merchants used to watch a buyer's eyes:

when the pupils dilated, a skilled dealer knew that the buyer had seen a piece that was especially liked, and would bargain harder about its price. The same information is used by expert card players as a sign that an opponent has a good hand.

As our interest in someone increases, so our eyes are likely to 'leak' that information to that person – who is likely to notice, even if we do not know that the hint has been given. More importantly for active relationships, it is necessary for individuals to ensure that they pay careful attention to their partner's eyes in order to pick up any information that is given away about the partner's level of interest in starting a relationship.

The eyes give away other information that doubles their importance as an object of attention at the stages of initial attraction and beyond. Intense looks, gazes and stares convey intense feelings: a stare can be hostile or friendly, depending on the facial expression that surrounds it. Humans look at a person more often and for longer periods of time when they like him or her (Argyle, 1978). An intense stare in a 'soft' expression can be an indication of intense liking, and a long, intimate look at a person can be very rewarding and pleasant for him or her. When we want to look interested in someone or in what a person is saying it is essential that we look at the person closely, particularly at the eyes. By reverse logic, when we look hard at someone he or she is likely to deduce that we are interested, and if we avoid looking or look only for short periods, then he or she is likely to assume that we are not interested. Eye movements are a crucial factor in the smooth development of a relationship just as they are critical to the establishment of initial interest in starting a relationship. Talking intimately to someone while we let our eyes wander elsewhere will be less attractive than intimate conversation accompanied by correct eye movements that centre on the person's face and eyes. Talking about intimate topics is not enough: it must be stage-managed correctly. You must attend to the person and the person's face especially.

There are many other minute behaviours that make up the full nonverbal communication system, and all of them can be used to good effect in relationship beginnings once their impact is understood (Argyle, 1978). Some are simple movements like nods that encourage people and some are to do with postures and gestures that convey one's attitudes about oneself or one's possessions. As an example, we all recognize, not necessarily consciously, that someone who puts two feet on the coffee table or desk is claiming 'owner-ship' of it and simultaneously claiming to be of higher status than the person in whose presence it is done. Two people who put their feet on the same table are indicating that they are equals and that they have a relaxed relationship with one another. Such items as coffee tables, desks, furniture and clothes can be used in this way as props to convey messages about one's social status, or to ensure that one is not over-looked: we can claim space in a library or cafeteria by drap-ing it with our 'props' (e.g., leaving a coat over the back of a chair is a socially agreed way of reserving it, and other people understand that they must ask you first before they sit in that particular chair).

However, the most important ways of presenting oneself concern the behaviours and actions that might encourage other people to contemplate entering a relationship. Their importance stems entirely from the outward information that they convey about the inner person. The outward signs concern posture, gesture and facial expression. Many scien-tific studies have been devoted to this area of research (Ar-gyle, 1978; Patterson, 1988). It is clear from these that if someone adopts a relaxed posture then we shall conclude that he or she likes us and does not find us threatening. Again, if someone smiles or nods as we talk, we shall con-clude that this is an encouragement for us to carry on talk-ing. The lesson, then, is that we should be relaxed and encouraging to other people, and they will enjoy that and like us more. The rewarding force of nods and smiles is so great that people can be induced by them to do something so unlikely as, for instance, to increase the percentage of plural nouns or adjectives in their talk, or to make more personal statements or give more opinions, or to make more sweeping gestures! (There is even a famous story about a teacher whose class conspired to nod and smile whenever he walked to the left: eventually he fell off the platform!) You might want to try out an example for yourself to see how powerful the effects can be.

Such powerful rewards are contained in these simple actions that they are the basic currency of friendship and must be attended to thoughtfully and used carefully. Not only do they act to invite people into relationships, they are also of great value, when properly employed, in getting people to open out and respond to overtures. People who use the nonverbal communication system inadequately will rapidly put people off (perhaps without ever knowing why) unless someone focuses their attention gently upon their deficiency (Trower, 1981). In brief, these people's nonverbal communication system is cold, uninviting and awkward – but they may not know it. Clinics and psychological training schools now exist to inculcate the skills in really bad cases, but for many people it is adequate merely to become aware of this, to think about it or to focus themselves for a while on their use of gesture, their eye movements and their facial expression. Airline cabin staff are trained to smile when talking to people; clients in therapy can be trained to look at people when they talk to them; anyone can be encouraged to use such behaviours satisfactorily, as the cited reading for this chapter details. The important point is that such apparently microscopic activities have major effects on attraction.

Such a system can also be built on by a skilful style of questioning. One good place to watch this style in action is in television interviewers, who are often meeting nervous strangers and having to open them out. Good interviewers are able to encourage even the most taciturn interviewee to speak out. They do this partly by adopting an encouraging posture, an inviting expression and a generally relaxed and interested manner. They also pay attention to their own style of speech, and ask questions that cannot be answered with a mere 'yes' or 'no', as so-called 'closed questions' can. On the contrary, such questions as 'How do you feel about . . . ?' or 'Can you tell us what it was like to . . . ?' are good, open-ended questions that will open people out. Lawyers tend to prefer closed questions because they give them more control over the answers, help them to predict and direct the encounter and appear to produce 'facts' rather than opinions. It is a subtle stylistic difference, but researchers have shown, for instance, that jurors react differently to witnesses' answers to questions like 'Did you feel excited?' (where the answer should be just 'Yes' or 'No'), and to questions like 'How did you feel?' (where the answer may be 'Excited'). It would seem on the face of it to be quite unimportant how we phrase our remarks, but actually there are many important cues concealed in our choice of phrase. In relationship formation, people who adopt closed question styles will appear over-inquisitive, nosey, overbearing and badgering, even though they may in fact be genuinely concerned and interested. On the other hand, someone who uses open-ended questions will be seen as concerned and genuinely interested in the respondent's opinions, advice and judgment.

In recent work on skilled and unskilled conversation, Daly (1990) found that eloquent conversationalists were particularly good at phrasing the same basic idea in many different ways. Also, since they tended to rehearse conversations, they were practised at adapting their phrasing to the particular audience or situation and so avoiding awkward language that did not suit the situation. As an example of awkwardness, consider this case that I heard on the radio. The programme was one that offered to help people meet others and, to show their success, the radio producers paraded people who had tried their techniques and succeeded. One such man reported his success this way: 'I had entered the works canteen and was seeking a place to position myself when a young lady beckoned me.' There was more to the story, but that is enough to illustrate the odd use of language that he employed. It sounds like a legal report to a committee. Do you normally 'enter' a works canteen or go to it? Do you 'seek a place to position yourself' or do you look for somewhere to sit? Do people usually 'beckon you' or call you over? I would expect that this man probably normally struck other people as odd and therefore had problems relating to them, partly because of his stiff and pompously inappropriate choice of phrase. I would bet that that is one of the reasons why he had difficulty being accepted by other people and needed to use the radio programme to train him in how to get dates.

Daly (1990) also reports that good conversationalists remember previous conversations with the same person, as a kind of context for what is happening at the time; that they interpret what is said, rather than attending only to the surface meaning (i.e., they respond to undercurrents, tone, and style); and that they are particularly good at appreciating underlying relationships between parties to a conversation. Such people probably pay deep attention to the nonverbal cues that are available in the situation, but more interesting is the fact that, at root, they simply *enjoy* conversations and focus strongly on the other person rather than on themselves. This outward focusing seems to be one of the most important skills on which to concentrate. Of course, it has also been found that others view one as a good conversationalist when one can get them to talk, particularly if one gets them to talk about themselves.

It is therefore important that people attend to their styles in this particular area and ask questions in a manner that encourages others without compelling them. The differences in style are minute but important, and they depend on the nonverbal and communicational skills above for two reasons. Wrong use of the skills conveys the wrong messages about a person's friendliness; inadequacy in using the skills disrupts the flow of conversation and makes it hard for people to interact (see Chapters 3 and 4). What is significant, however, is that people who lack these so-called 'social skills' can be trained or can train themselves to improve them, with consequent good effects on their social relationships (Trower, 1981). I shall say more about this, particularly in Chapter 5 (on the training of children who show social skill problems). The whole theme, however, emphasizes the importance, in the early stages of friendship, of very small components of behaviour. These unacknowledged aspects of starting friendships have an important part to play in the success or failure of the resultant relationship. If we do not behave adequately in the ways described, then people will soon decide they do not want to explore further – and so the infant relationship will die at its first breath.

The minute behaviours that we perform are much more important than having attractive personal characteristics or attributes alone. Attributes are hard to change, but behaviours are malleable: taking this new line and focusing on behaviour is thus a message of hope. Friendships start well when they are well done at a very basic level. What matters then is making them develop, and that requires further sorts of action and a new range of skills.

3

Initial developments

The moments after an initial move in attraction are busy ones, in both romantic and nonromantic relationships. A first need is for partners to establish that each person is as interested in a relationship as the other. There are several ways in which this is done, depending on whether one indicates one's own interest or tests the other person's interest.

We can indicate our own interest in a number of ways, some of which were covered in the previous chapter. Such things as paying close attention, smiling, asking attentive questions and so on all convey one's interest in the other person. Greater interest can be shown in romantic relationships by flirtatious behaviour, a phenomenon remarkably overlooked by researchers, yet a clear case of deliberate attempts to promote relationships. Montgomery (1986) found that there is agreement between the sexes about the behaviour that is flirtatious: eye behaviour, physical contact and conversational behaviour such as compliments top the list, and such activity as teasing, paying close attention and self-fondling (e.g., playing with one's hair) also figure. There the agreement between the sexes ends, however. Men tend to see it as having a sexual objective, while women tend to see it as having a primarily friendly purpose. It is clear that both sexes see flirtation as a means to promote relationships, but they disagree somewhat concerning the type of relationship that is being promoted.

The other side to promoting any relationship is trying out the other person's interest, or 'affinity testing', as Douglas (1987) calls it. He explored the strategies that people use in order to test out whether a new acquaintance really is interested or is just being polite. These strategies involve gentle indirect tests. One good example is 'I stopped talking for a while to see if she was interested in picking up the conversation.' Another is 'I told him that I lived 16 miles away and needed a ride home. I wanted to see if he was interested enough to go to all that trouble', and a third is 'I asked her if she wanted to talk to anyone else – you know, to find out if I was keeping her from something. I wanted her to say "No".' There are several types of such strategy and they serve to show that the tests are quite subtle and natural-sounding, but nonetheless effective for that.

Once the partners are clear that they are both interested in developing a relationship (whether romantic or non-romantic), much intelligence work has to be done, many activities have to be co-ordinated, and much sharing of viewpoints is necessary. Over and above this, a major task of developing a friendship is to translate it from the private, shared feelings of two individuals into a fully accepted, working, active relationship. That is, the association moves from the private to the public domain, and the partners have to let *other* people know that they are now partners, friends, mates or companions. To achieve this public acknowledgement of the relationship, the partners carry out various skilled behaviours that they have not needed before. To continue with the car-driving analogy that I have already used earlier, the partners have to become less concerned with looking at the pedals, their feet, the steering wheel and the gear lever: they must begin to look down the road, steer a sensible course and make their activity fit neatly into the available pathways and patterns familiar to other road-users.

This is a crucial stage in relationships: the point where they turn from mere attraction into a full working relationship is the point where they become most full of promise and rich in personal fulfilment. The developmental period is, however, also fraught with difficulty and risk, and a number of different tasks have to be skilfully performed. The intentions or desires for a relationship still need effective execution, and the developing relationship has to be put together into a working model, stage-managed and encouraged to burgeon. According to Van Lear and Trujillo (1986), the development of relationships has four stages: reducing uncertainty about the partner, exploring one another's feelings, growing together into the relationship and stabilizing the relationship. In the present chapter I shall look at these very early stages where partners move from the attraction stage to a well-established partnership, like friendship; in Chapter 4 I shall examine the research on the growth from well-established partnerships to deep and intense relationships with special forms, like cohabitation, courtship, marriage and sexual relations. In the first case, the research explores the intensification of feelings and the means by which people negotiate the necessary adjustments in their patterns of activity, their knowledge of one another and their search for personality support. In the second case, the largest efforts of the partners are focused on changing the nature of the relationship, altering the public beliefs about the relationship, having it accepted by other people as an exclusive relationship, and negotiating the problems of satisfying physical needs as well as social ones.

In the present chapter we are dealing with matters that people readily overlook, unless they are pointed out strongly. When I ask people how they make relationships, I hear them tell me what they talk about with strangers, but they overlook the really important thing: *how* they talked about it all. Were the topics handled intimately? Did the topics make them embarrassed? If they shared opinions about some contentious issue, did their partner's opinions seem genuine or ingratiating? Were disagreements serious or playful? The manner in which such matters are dealt with is just as important as the topics themselves at this stage. Intimate topics such as sex handled in an off-hand or flippant way do not convey the message that the conversation is caring, friendly, accepting or truly intimate. Casual topics discussed in a relaxed and friendly way do convey such messages. The point is that while the words create the topic of conversation, the manner or style of communication concerns, defines and exhibits the relationship between the speakers.

Another aspect of developing friendships which we easily overlook is the activities that we perform to develop them. If we attend only to what we say to strangers, then we ignore that most crucial aspect: what we did next, and where we did it. Friendships do not start until people do friendly things in friendly places: they are not created merely by friendly talk. In fact, it is easy to forget that relationships start when we *do* something sociable, like invite a new acquaintance or new neighbour for a meal or coffee or a drink, or when we suggest going for a meal, visiting the local shops together or going to a film. People may have liked what their acquaintance said, but until they have cooperated, socialized, joked or accompanied one another somewhere they have only the bricks to build a relationship, and no foundation. In fact, once the point is pressed, people usually come round to recognizing or recalling that they did actually do such things and that these joint activities were what truly set the relationship going. Yet the activities are so easy to overlook and so easy to underestimate in importance that advice to lonely people hardly ever mentions them. Unfortunately, without attention to such matters no friendship can get far off the ground.

The present chapter therefore deals closely with these topics. I shall focus on three main aspects of them. First, I shall examine the ways in which acquaintances progressively attend to the attitudes of their partner through both word and action. Secondly, I shall explore the means by which people increase their intimacy with one another and learn to reveal intimate information about themselves in proper and effective ways. Lastly, I shall deal with the recent research that has shown the overwhelming importance of the signals that partners must send out to the rest of the world about their new relationship. Together, these three areas comprise the early stages of development in acquaintance, the final resting place of many a relationship that might have been.

GETTING RELATIONSHIPS GOING: SEEKING SIMILARITY AND SUPPORT

The main need of persons who are beginning acquaintance is for information about each other. It is a time of great uncertainty: the other person and his or her mind, style and habits are large, uncharted continents. Nonetheless, information has to be imparted systematically, noticed when it is imparted, judged in relation to one's need for personality support, and treated publicly as useful and important. The second need is for behaviour to be altered in a way that matches up with the partners' feelings for one another. Such behavioural signalling of developing feelings is important. It causes major changes in the rules of conduct, in the matters that draw their attention and have significance, and in the expectations that the partners have about the future course of the relationship. The third need is for the creation of a pattern of communication that reflects their new relationship to each other. Formal, superficial styles of communication must be replaced with others that convey and adequately represent the level of intimacy that now obtains in the relationship. Formal, stylized, brisk, uninvolved, unpersonalized ways of communicating about intimate matters, or during activities which are personal and intimate, are characteristic of instrumental relationships like prostitute–client ones. In deeper, lasting, working relationships the style of communication and the style of activities must be made to correspond. Accordingly, the communication style must be monitored and developed as a part of the development of the relationship itself. Each of these three topics will be dealt with separately in the present chapter, although what is, of course, ultimately most important is how they are combined.

Ask an ordinary person in the street what makes relationships work and you receive one of two contradictory answers. Some people assume that similarity is attractive ('Birds of a feather flock together'), while others assume that 'Opposites attract.' In order to tidy up the confusion that these two contradictory 'commonsense' ideas represent, a vast amount of work was carried out by research psychologists and demographers to try to find out which accounted best for friendship, courtship and marriage (see S.W. Duck, 1977, Chapter 6). The research soon divided into three piles: lots of studies showing that similarity worked best, one or two studies showing that dissimilarity did, and one uninterpretable pile showing that neither of them worked at all. It is not hard to see why these different conclusions were reached, and researchers were soon made aware of the fact that they were all looking at different things in the first place. What has to be similar or opposite? Similar heights? Similar shoe sizes? Similar physical appearance? (There was even one study that found a mutual interest in dentistry was important for courtship!) Opposite personalities (whatever that means)? Opposite levels of educational achievement? Opposite political attitudes? For instance, it was found that friends are similar in attitudes, but courting couples are similar in their level of attractiveness (i.e., they do not necessarily look the same, but are about equally attractive). Married couples were found by other less clear, less numerous, and less convincing studies to be opposite in major personality characteristics and showed 'complementarity of needs'. That is to say, married couples complement or fit one another's personality: a common finding would be, for instance, a dominant person married to a submissive one, or a helpful, initiative-taking person married to a dependent one.

If we take the view outlined earlier about the importance of personality support then this all makes perfect sense. People need the reassurance of knowing that their partners share and accept many of their own attitudes and beliefs, but they also need to be interested, intrigued and even taught or challenged by their partner. One reason why people would not want to be totally similar to their partner is that this would 'deindividuate' them, or make them lose their uniqueness. Partners could be expected to prefer to be very similar to one another in major attitudes and outlook, but to enjoy being different in other ways. What better ways to be different than in those that complement one another? Someone who likes to be led, for instance, obviously needs to find the complementary person, a leader. It seems perfectly understandable, then, that as relationships proceed the persons will attempt to discover major similarities first, in order to give one another basic reassurance and security, but later will try to look for differences. So at the very early stages of relationship development, similarity is what counts and what should be demonstrated, revealed and displayed. A different strategy is needed later on, and I shall come to this in the next chapter.

Similarity of what, and when? What sorts of similarity do intending friends, colleagues, workmates and lovers need to be good at showing at this stage? I have already mentioned in Chapter 2 that the very first similarities that usually emerge are those that 'locate' the partner: similarities of race, educational background and interests. At the next stage of developing friendship a different sort of similarity takes over and assumes a greater importance: basic similarity of attitudes and beliefs. One of the largest programmes of research in the last thirty years has shown the deep and extensive ways in which similarity of attitudes influences the early development of relationships, including relatively swift and infrequent meetings between various professional groups and their clients. Bank managers, teachers, jurors and therapists have all been investigated in such research, alongside friends, lovers and married couples.

The basic finding is that the more similar two people's attitudes, the more they like one another (Byrne, 1971). Most effective is similarity in attitudes that the two partners believe to be most important to them and/or which are rarely found in the population at large. A person who fervently believes that the world is flat is particularly likely, therefore, to be attracted to someone else who holds the same belief. It is especially one that they wish to have supported and yet one that, by its very nature, rarely is: therefore another person who shares it is a godsend and will be highly attractive because of it.

The initial stages of friendship development are thus characterized by active search for information about the other person's beliefs and attitudes. A major skill, therefore, consists in the ability to reveal one's attitudes in a way that gives the partner evidence about their importance and extent, and a major demand is for similar information from the partner. There are many techniques for opening up partners about their attitudes, and both of these needs and demands can be handled in skilled conversations. The most obvious way is the direct question that asks for someone's view on a particular topic. This is risky, however, until one knows a little bit about how the person responds to such a question, since one wants to keep open the possibility of agreement, if the topic is important. To announce your most preciously important belief without first testing the possible response is to run the risk of having it rejected outright by the other person, who may not be perceptive enough to recognize its importance. A better strategy is to skirt around it, or to broach it in a tentative way, perhaps by the simple device of saying 'I know that some people believe that . . .', and seeing what the partner's response is like. A considerable amount of shadow-boxing goes on in these early encounters until the partners find a safe topic to agree on and use it as a base for excursions into more doubtful attitudinal territory.

In any case, a careful attention to the nonverbal signs of facial expression and tone of voice permits a person to learn more than is actually said in words. We can deduce people's strength of feeling about a particular issue from careful observation of their posture, their hand movements and their breathing rate or facial colouring as they talk about it. Do they look engrossed or uninvolved, angry, impassioned or couldn't-care-less? By attending very carefully and thoughtfully to such clues it is possible also to work out the extent of someone's interest in a particular topic. Finally, from a person's general manner and demeanour when discussing attitudinal topics or matters of opinion, we can tell a lot about his or her personality style. We can learn about partners' openness to other views, their tolerance, their passions and flat spots, their dogmatisms and their assumptions about life. We can also learn a considerable amount about their attitudes to other people, to relationships and to the expression of feelings, as well as about their views on how other people should be treated. All this information is over and above the information conveyed directly in words, but it helps us to see whether they are like us, and whether they offer the kind of personality style or support that we need and enjoy.

It is not an easy task to be so attentive to other people's manner of discussing attitudes and beliefs. It takes work and effort to concentrate so fully not only on what they say but on how they say it, and on what that manner of delivery means about their inner 'clockwork'. Yet ultimately it is essential for the proper development of relationships. One can unwittingly and unnecessarily extend the length of time that it takes to get to know someone if one is careless, inattentive or unskilled at this stage. By attending very carefully, we gather valuable information about the other person's attitudes as well as about his or her expectations and predictions about the relationship. But one also communicates interest and concern. Of course, the other person will find this encouraging and is likely to reciprocate with a corresponding interest in the discussion.

Most social scientific researchers make fine distinctions between values, opinions, beliefs, attitudes and personality. Attitudes are specific, value-laden statements about contentious issues; they are evaluations of probabilities or dogmatic views about large-scale political, religious or social issues. Personality, on the other hand, is the system in which attitudes are organized and the framework within which attitudes are expressed. Values are organizing structures for attitudes. Attitudes are the books in the personality library, as it were, while values are the shelf marks. Just as books can be packed neatly and tightly in rows or left higgledy-piggledy, classified carefully or just tossed anywhere, taken out and clustered for some special purpose, so it is with attitudes. They may be tightly or loosely organized according to the needs or values of the person who has them. Also, just as the library contains things other than books – such as the facilities that keep the reader warm and comfortable – so the personality 'contains' other things than attitudes. It consists also of needs, fears, hopes, ambitions; it comprises characteristic ways of doing things ('niceness', 'high-handedness') and a whole lot of other traits and modes of action. Accordingly, when we learn about someone's attitudes we learn an awful lot about what the personality contains, and how it is organized in some gross way – but there is still a lot to find out about (see next section).

Nevertheless, attitudes give us knowledge of the basic outline, the peaks and troughs, of the partner's personality, and this knowledge is such a central goal of personal relationships that the effects of discovering attitude similarity are very extensive. For instance, Byrne (1971) has shown that bank managers give bigger loans to customers who are similar in attitudes. Juries recommend lighter sentences for defendants who have attitudes similar to those held by the jurors, prejudiced white people give more favourable treatment to black people who have similar attitudes than they do to whites with dissimilar ones, and so on.

These delightful peripheral findings of the research are sometimes disturbing, sometimes merely amusing and captivating. More significant in many ways are the findings in respect of teacher–pupil relationships and doctor–patient relationships. Several different studies have shown that teachers prefer and give more attention to pupils with attitudes similar to their own (e.g., Menges, 1969). For either this reason or the reason that the similarity improves communication between them, pupils learn more and learn faster from teachers who have similar attitudes, right the way up to very advanced levels. In the case of doctor–patient relationships, particularly psychotherapist–patient relationships, there has been shown to be an astonishing effect of attitudinal similarity upon the patient's recovery. Doctors and patients who get on well work better together and the patients recover sooner than those who do not get on well (R. Hays and DiMatteo, 1984). Not only this, but psychotherapists have a much lower success rate in dealing with patients who have dissimilar attitudes, and report that these patients were harder to get on with, had intractable problems and were not truly committed to the treatment (Takens, 1982). It also seems probable that effectiveness in selling (e.g., selling insurance) is increased by sales personnel who can adopt the customer's attitude framework rapidly, and can stress similarities between themselves and the customer.

Disclosure of attitudes and a search for similarity are not merely luxuries in starting relationships: on the contrary, they serve a major function and help the partners to estimate the advantages of continuing or the benefits of closing down the development. The ability to reveal and assess attitudes is thus essential to the development of relationships, and consists largely of extensions of the skills described in the previous chapter, except that these are now focused on a different topic. The early signals about personality that are provided by the other person's attitudes are useful, quick, structured ways of communicating information about the person's inner life and framework of values. These provide major clues upon which to base the development of relationships.

INCREASING INTIMACY

The development of relationships is not automatic but rather occurs through the skills of partners in revealing or disclosing first their attitudes and later their personalities, inner character and true selves. This is done in a reciprocal manner, turn by turn, and in a way that keeps pace with the revelations and disclosures made by the partner. The main feature that stabilizes, establishes and develops relationships of all types is proper and dexterous control of *self-disclosure*: that is, the revelation of personal layers of one's self, one's personal thoughts or even one's body (Jourard, 1971). In this last case, where self-disclosure can mean body disclosure, it refers to the different amounts of access to our bodies that different people have. The better we know someone, the more we relax the complex rules governing the availability of our bodies, as the very metaphor of 'close' friends suggests. For instance, we are 'permitted' to sit closer to people whom we know than to people whom we do not; we are 'allowed' to touch the arms, shoulders or waists of close friends, but not of strangers; we are 'entitled' to wear informal clothes, to sprawl around and to be less polite when we are with friends rather than with people we do not know.

People sometimes do this inappropriately and cause offence. A friend of mine used to irritate a lot of people, unintentionally, simply by standing too close to them. They could not verbalize what it was he was doing wrong that annoyed them, but when I pointed out that he was offering too much access to his body, they readily recognized this as the problem. Intimate friends expect close contact and physical closeness, to sit next to their friends, and so on. People who are mere acquaintances do not, and may feel hustled or overborne by someone who is too close. In tightly packed lifts or trains we become distressingly aware of this, even though the contacts that we receive there from strangers are ones we would expect and even enjoy from friends and people that we know well. To balance out the fact that we are touching strange people, we usually avoid looking them in the face – something we do not avoid with people we like. Since bodily closeness is such a powerful signal of intimacy, it is something that must be carefully gauged in social relationships and should be tested out warily.

Self-disclosure is a key to relationship development because it applies to so many different features of relationships, each of which must be executed effectively. Although the physical kinds of disclosure are significant, the most important aspects undoubtedly concern disclosure of personality and inner self. Here the circumstances have to be appropriate: frank, open, honest disclosure is not always attractive. People who tell strangers exactly what they think are usually regarded not as open, honest and frank so much as rude, tactless and insensitive – yet exactly the same things can be said to a friend without being thought rude or tactless. The appropriateness or inappropriateness of disclosures is defined by the relationship between the two people and the level of intimacy that they seek to achieve.

Another aspect of self-disclosure that is important is that it should happen at all. Someone who never says anything about personal opinions, inner thoughts, deeper feelings and intimate wishes will be cast aside as a closed, defensive and unrewarding person (Jourard, 1971). People *like* to know what their friend's intimate views are. More than this, they *need* to know, in order to find out about the person's true personality and the support that it can provide to their own. They also assume that someone who is open and disclosing is a mentally healthy person who has nothing to hide psychologically, and is balanced, mature and self-possessed. Some people never get this right, ranging from the person who clams up when personal topics come up in the conversation, through those who coolly disguise, dissemble and overcontrol their true feelings, right down to the person who is a toadying ingratiator, laughing at all the boss's unfunny jokes and going along with other people's opinions while privately believing them to be wrong. Such people make it difficult for others to get to know them properly, and are often excluded from social relationships or kept in only superficial ones for this very reason.

Other people try to get their feelings across, but do it in an embarrassing or inappropriate way. For instance, they may insist on getting serious about a topic that everyone else was enjoying taking lightly, or they may forever find that, whatever anyone says, they can turn the conversation around to something about themselves or some opinion they persist in going on and on about. In extreme cases they may just ignore what everyone else is talking about and keep droning on about themselves and their views of life, their own personal concerns or their present problems and anxieties. This has the same effect, at this early stage of relationships, of making other people draw back, because the task of 'reading' the stranger's personality is made so awkward or because they are self-disclosing in the wrong way. They are easily dismissed as people with complex personality problems that make them unattractive company.

In recent studies of boring communication, Leary *et al.* (1986) found that boring communicators tend to be egocentric and to make banal remarks (obviously), but they also have a tendency to offer less information about the subjects under discussion, to ask relatively large numbers of questions, and to merely acknowledge what the other person has said rather than to add anything to it or take the conversation along. My own studies (S.W. Duck and Condra, 1987; Leatham and Duck, 1990) confirm this pattern and suggest that self-preoccupation is the major problem, since it excludes the listener and, by so doing, implicitly discredits and derogates the importance of the other person. In terms of the argument that I made in Chapter 1, the boring person does not offer support for the personality of the listener. Boring people are also relatively low on self-disclosures, such as information about feelings and inner thoughts, which again gives the listener little to go on in the search for personality support.

There are many other aspects of proper self-disclosure

that will be discussed in the rest of this chapter. It will become clearer and clearer just how much self-disclosure matters to successful relationship growth for many reasons. These range from the fact that it gives people direct information about personality (whereas attitudes give only indirect hints) to the fact that it also supplies indications to the other person on just how far you trust them, and finally indicates how fairly you 'balance up' by telling them as much about yourself as they tell you about themselves. Clearly, the more you tell them about your inner self the more vulnerable you make yourself, and so the more trust and confidence in their loyalty you are expressing. All this amounts to an indirect but very clear signal that you feel that the two of you can get along.

Self-disclosure embodies many components, the first of which is clearly its communication aspect, because it involves openly communicating about our personality and is the fastest means of establishing and developing personality support (Montgomery, 1984). It would be unhelpful and confusing to reveal and communicate a whole personality in one giant disclosure, since the context for understanding its complexity has not been provided. Accordingly, it has to be revealed bit by bit, stage by stage, layer by layer. Naturally this is where the first piece of craft comes in: knowing which part matters at what point in the relationship.

Our personality and our partner's personality are both composed of many different features which can be described in a variety of ways, and revealed in different forms. Practically everyone has their own idea about personality, and although the proper measurement of personality has become something approaching an exact science, popular ideas about it are vague and conflicting. Of course, we recognize that we can classify someone's personality as being 'extravert' or 'introvert', or located somewhere on the dimension 'conforming–nonconforming' or 'generous–mean', and we can also use labels like 'warm', 'friendly', 'twisted', 'devious' and 'arrogant'. There are scores and scores of more precise scientific systems of measurement. Some of them measure people into broad classes like extravert–introvert, while some of them work out scores on a number of dimensions separately, such as emotionality, orientation to justice, intuitiveness, thinking/feeling and judging/perceiving. Finally, some measures try to assess the very precise ways in which the person thinks, anticipates the future or interprets events.

Naturally, someone can be both extravert and conforming as well as generous, a Capricorn, impulsive, diplomatic and resentful. It all depends on how an investigator decides to classify personality – whether one stops short at 'extravert' or at 'Capricorn'. More sophisticated views of personality suggest that there are very many ways to characterize the same person, and this is important because different parts of the personality come into play at different stages in a relationship's development (S.W. Duck, 1977, Chapter 6). At the start of a relationship it matters how sociable someone is (i.e., whether that person is an introvert or an extravert), but later on, people's sociability is less important than the way they co-ordinate with their partner and the ways they think (e.g., whether they are rigid and dogmatic, or flexible and open-minded). Partners must demonstrate or self-disclose the relevant parts at the relevant times and places in the relationship's progress.

Second, it is not so much the 'true' personality of yourself and your partner that matters at the early stages as what you think or believe about each other's personality (Cahn, 1990). In the early stages of relationships, individuals make lots of guesses and inferences about the other person's personality, and those are what start to be very important. As discussed earlier in this chapter, attitudes constitute one major source of such guesses at the early stages. Longitudinal studies of developing relationships have shown the ways in which, as the relationship develops, we start to look deeper (S.W. Duck and Craig, 1978; Van Lear and Trujillo, 1986). We probably do this unconsciously, like breathing, but occasionally we do it deliberately and in a measured way. Individuals try to find out more detail about their partner in order to assess whether their first impressions were accurate or completely off the mark. As things proceed, so they get more information about the other person and can check their impressions for their accuracy or inaccuracy. The more they can get their partner to self-disclose, the easier is this job of checking first impressions, and if they are wrong (as they often will be) the easier it is to create newer, better, more useful and accurate impressions about the other person.

This is all very fine, but it implies that we know what to look for. It so happens that a lot of research shows conclusively that many people do not know what to look for, and so they do not develop relationships satisfactorily. One extreme example is provided by schizophrenics: they often do not understand other people's personalities in normal terms. For instance, they are likely to describe someone's personality – personality, mind you – on dimensions such as 'tall–short' or 'heavy–light', and they seem to have no good grasp of the psychological dimensions that the rest of us use, like 'generous–mean', 'interested in other people–self-centred' or 'likes to control things–more relaxed'. If such persons do not know what a personality is, nor how best to understand it, then we can hardly expect that they will be able to form with other people those deep friendships that are based on personality judgments.

For those of us who do make reasonable sorts of assessment about other people's personality, our relationships will be more successful as our judgments are more accurate – and both accuracy and inaccuracy in judgment are learned for the first time in late childhood and early adolescence (see Chapter 5). They can nevertheless be improved in adulthood by various means, such as psychotherapy, sensitivity group-training and various methods designed to increase awareness of other people's points of view, motivations, biases, moods and psychological structures – in short, their personality and psychological mainsprings. These methods are not particularly complicated, they merely make people attend to something that they normally do not scrutinize especially closely. Some people do not spend long enough getting other people to talk about or share their feelings nor long enough assessing the meaning of any such expression (e.g., whether the expression is true, or caused by self-presentation or by interpersonal strategies). For those people, it is often enough of a corrective for someone to urge them to think about this more carefully. Once a person recognizes that it matters, the problem can be solved by oneself.

There is another point to note – another side to the coin – in relation to assessments of personality. It is that we ourselves not only need to make assessments about the other person's self-disclosure, but must also help the other person to make assessments about us. This requires demonstration of our feelings, our biases, our motivations and our character through our behaviour.

To draw the moral from all this, we simply need to note that personality does not just affect relationship development in any simple, obvious way. Once more we come to the idea that it is what you *do* with personality information in friendship that makes it have significance in making friendships grow. In this case what you do is to communicate about your personality and get your partner to do the same thing. Both partners need to communicate their views, opinions, preferences, needs and attitudes – but they also need to ensure that their partner wants to hear them, and give the partner a fair chance to do the same.

Developing a friendship does not mean monopolizing the conversation, nor is it adequate merely to allow a prospective partner to do so. Personality gets its importance in friendship from the manner in which it is displayed (choosing the right thing to display at the right moment), and from the 'decoding' of the personality of one's partner. We do this decoding partly through direct use of deliberate self-disclosure and partly through indirect, unintentional disclosures (Miell *et al.*, 1979).

If these two points are added together, we end up with a much more sophisticated and practically useful idea about what is going on in relationship growth. The advice about improving relationships and relationship growth is consequently given a more sensible foundation. Instead of suggesting that people have face-lifts, haircuts and new clothes or take up new hobbies or join clubs, we end up pointing to a range of judgments and indirect disclosures that may need to be practised or 'trained up' in people whose relationships are presently unsatisfactory. It is easy to rehearse these skills privately, without formal training.

But what skills and what indirect disclosures? Let us assume that the nonverbal behaviour mentioned in Chapter 2 (eye movements, posture, gesture and so forth) is adequately mastered in the ways described earlier. That is, let us assume that the person knows that smiles and eye movements, for example, are important as indicators of general interest in the other person, and that he or she uses them appropriately. We can now take this a step further and show that these same things fit into the more advanced kinds of disclosing activity required in developing satisfying relationships.

Smiles, nods and eye movements in appropriate places do not serve only to show general interest, nor just to stress important points in conversation, nor even to keep the conversation going. They have a fourth, separate function – they indicate aspects of our personality. We are called 'rude' if we do not look at people when they are talking to us, although we hear with our ears wherever our eyes are looking. Equally it is rude to stare, that is, to look at a person too much or too long. Our use of such nonverbal behaviours, then, also shows that we know the proper rules of polite conversation, and that we are not abnormal or deranged. The system of such nonverbal cues relates closely to the *content* of speech and it is the mark of a competent communicator that he or she works the two systems closely together. So we should look at people when we are nearing the end of what we want to say, but look away when we have not finished and do not want to be interrupted. In this case, the 'eye contact' indicates our willingness to let the other person talk. Also, a competent communicator establishes eye contact when he or she is saying something especially important. In short, eye movements have a role to play in the control, emphasis and regulation of conversation, when they are done appropriately.

My point is simply that the rules are sometimes broken or used inappropriately, and poor communicators reap a bad harvest of other people's negative judgments about their personality. People who interrupt when we talk are thought to have 'rude' personalities; people who do not talk when the conversation pauses for them are called 'socially inept'; people who monopolize the conversation are called 'boring'.

Equally, people are hard to cope with when they do not make the normal use of eye movements to indicate the main points or the boundaries of their conversation. These people tend to become isolated simply because others cannot cope with them: they do not give the right signals, we do not know whether they are interested or not and we cannot tell much about their personality. Accordingly, we do not know whether we are giving them the right information and whether our indications about our own personality have been helpful to them or not. Equally, it will probably be hard to get them to disclose relevant information about themselves because we cannot properly conduct a conversation that makes it possible to 'draw them out'. For instance, if I am prepared only to talk about the weather then no-one will learn much about my personality, except that it is narrow, closed and unintriguing. Yet if I talk about the most crucial decisions I have ever had to make, or behaviours that I am ashamed of in my past life, then my personal feelings are being brought out more obviously. My priorities, my values, my hopes and fears are all being exposed to the other person's view.

Naturally, there are some cultural differences here, and in some countries (e.g., the United States) an open style of disclosure about one's personal feelings is expected and encouraged. In others (e.g., Japan) self-disclosure of feelings is thought to be inappropriate and self-indulgent, but information about family, status and social position is entirely suitable for disclosure. In all cultures, however, normal people open themselves up in the appropriate ways more and more as their relationships grow, and they are increasingly prepared – at the right sorts of moment, and in the right circumstances – to reveal these personal thoughts.

Another key aspect of self-disclosure, then, is the management of the intimacy level of what we reveal (Derlega *et al.*, 1985). Usually, researchers examine the information that people disclose about themselves and whether or not it is intimate. For instance, they may look at the extent to which people talk about private thoughts, feelings about personal matters, and intimate experiences, and at whether they do it at the right times and in the right ways, or are always telling perfect strangers the sorts of private detail that strangers do not really want to know. The research has shown two main aspects to this: the pacing of the deepening of intimacy, and the timing of revealing negative or positive information about yourself (Chelune, 1979). Increasing intimacy of disclosure is a key problem in developing normal friendships because the intimacy and privacy of disclosed information has to be increased steadily so that you reveal more and more about the deeper and more private aspects of your personality. These parts are precisely the ones that are most important for your partner to test out as providers of support for his or her own personality. However, the person who discloses too intimately too soon is likely to be thought peculiar, indiscreet or untrustworthy. On the other hand, the person who tries to get you to disclose too intimately will be thought driving and pushy, unless there are special reasons why they are doing it (e.g., a doctor or a therapist exercising professional techniques is 'allowed' to push).

The other aspect of pacing intimacy that must be right is the timing of negative/positive information about oneself. Researchers have consistently shown that people are disliked if they disclose positive information about themselves early in a relationship, but not if it comes later (E.E. Jones and Gordon, 1972). Negative information should be disclosed early, however, if the people caused it themselves (e.g., if the negative information is some misfortune they brought upon themselves by heedlessness). Evidently people are attracted to someone who seems willing to own up to responsibility early on. Someone whose negative information is to do with bad luck which is not their own fault should keep quiet about it as long as possible! What this research shows is that people are less influenced by the positive or negative aspect of the information itself than by the timing of its disclosure and the manner in which it is done. (The same goes for evidence in court: Frankel and Morris (1976) have shown that if a defendant has positive information about himself or herself to tell the court then he or she should get someone else to tell it. In controlled experiments using exactly the same bit of information, defendants who told it themselves to a mock jury got harsher sentences than defendants who had an independent outsider tell it for them.)

Pacing and timing of self-disclosure help us to find out about each other in a systematic way. They also assist us by controlling the amount of information that is available to us at a given time and so do not overload our minds with things that are too detailed to understand: they give us time to absorb it systematically. Finally, such rules of disclosure again teach us something fundamental: when they are incompetently done, there is a whole range of rather negative judgments that will be heaped on a person who does not do this 'right'. Not only, as has been said, will someone who is too free with personal information probably be labelled boring, bizarre or even mad; more significantly, we are likely to assume that he or she tells *everyone* such things, and not that we are being told about it because he or she specifically likes us. So we shall treat it as indicating, not a wish for a friendship with us personally, but indiscretion.

Just as necessary as the fact that we reveal things about ourselves, pace it correctly, and observe the usual 'rules', is that we should reciprocate what the partner does. If a person reveals something intimate, it helps the relationship if the other partner reveals something equally intimate – not necessarily about the same topic, but something at the same depth of intimacy. If a person asks direct questions about some particular area of personality, then it helps to develop the relationship if the partner offers reciprocal disclosure about that area of personality too. If someone shows reluctance to talk about a particular sort of topic, it is better not to question and probe directly. Indirect reference should be made to one's own feeling on the topic or a similar one so that he or she is encouraged to reciprocate and will feel less vulnerable.

Self-disclosure is still a major topic of research and there is much about it that we do not know. However, many unexpected things have been found out. For one thing, there are very clear differences between the two sexes when we look at the amounts of intimate information that are disclosed to a partner. Females generally disclose more intimate information to their partners than males do, for instance. It does not seem to matter whether the partner is a male or a female: females are simply more open than males.

Various explanations have been offered for this highly consistent finding. At one extreme are those theorists who stress the cultural experiences of women as more 'relationship-oriented'; women, in this view, are encouraged to be more personal, intimate and open in relationships, while men are encouraged to retain a 'masculine' aloofness from personal relationships. Another sort of explanation assumes that women are less competitive than men and do not worry so much about becoming vulnerable in relationships by exposing their more personal thoughts. A third possibility is that women are implicitly taking the initiative in offering the chance to form a better relationship by presenting the building-blocks at an earlier point than men do.

Whichever of these explanations is correct, it is certain that people of both sexes expect women to disclose themselves more than they expect men to do, and that those women who do not do so will risk dislike, rejection and avoidance. This is particularly the case in dating and courtship, where men tend to take involuntary control of disclosure by asking more direct questions than women do – usually also more intimate and probing questions (J.D. Davis, 1978). By contrast, women lead by example – that is, they disclose personal information in the expectation that the men will reciprocate. Men are attracted to a female partner who responds suitably, but they do not like one who attempts to avoid the question, or answers it with information less intimate than was expected. Equally, men do not like to be probed too early themselves – whether by women or by other men – and many a promising relationship has been uprooted by a male's negative reaction to a too-questioning partner. Nevertheless, it has recently been shown (Derlega *et al.*, 1985) that in cases where a man likes a woman whom he has met for the first time, he will disclose much more freely and openly than usual.

However undesirable such sex differences may be, it is clear that they represent some strong cultural norms at work. The effects are so widespread, being reported in the United States, Great Britain and Europe, that they are clearly ingrained in our present western cultural make-up. Yet they represent such a subtle difference that it is unlikely that many people are conscious of them. People do, however, react negatively when the 'rules' are broken, and it is likely that considerable effort would be needed in schools and other places of cultural learning before equality of disclosure expectation can be achieved.

Recent research indicates that people use self-disclosure strategically in getting to know other people (Miell, 1984). Skilful relaters are careful to choose their moment for probing a particular area of personality or behaviour or attitudes. They wait to see how the partner responds, or they throw in a comment of their own that helps the partner to reciprocate. They press into new areas swiftly when they want to force the pace a bit, but quickly withdraw for a while before probing into them again more gently. Rather than producing a steady pressure on a particular area, they seem to use a sort of 'battering-ram' approach – push, withdraw, wait; push harder, draw back, wait; push further, and so on.

But just as such people make skilful use of self-disclosure so, conversely, the people who have most difficulty with normal relationship development seem to be least adept at this part of it. People can be trained to get self-disclosure right, partly by guided exercises that indicate the different depths of information that are appropriate at different stages of relationships, and partly by putting them in a warmly accepting atmosphere that encourages them to open up.

It is important to focus on self-disclosure because the person who self-discloses inadequately or inappropriately will certainly be labelled negatively, be avoided and eventually be cast out – perhaps without anyone ever explaining why. The processes here are subtle, so that people may not be able to tell why. It is difficult to verbalize this, and there are also strong social taboos that prohibit discussion of such things. It is very difficult to break the liking taboo and look someone straight in the eye while telling them that you like them, for example. Except in dates, where 'I love you' is an accepted gambit, we are supposed not to express ourselves so directly. We do it more subtly by nonverbal means – by smiles, friendly looks, evident happiness and enjoyment of the other person's company.

Equally, we are not supposed to talk directly about the way someone behaves. Even though best friends can tell you about most of your shortcomings, they would find it hard to say, 'Do you realize everyone thinks you are shifty because you never look them in the eye?'. It is very hard to indicate that someone is a social clam or a bore because of inappropriate self-disclosure. Even if someone asks you whether he or she is boring you, it is either a brave person or a rude one who will give the straight answer 'Yes', and take the social consequences. For these reasons it is very unusual and often very difficult for people to draw attention to someone's self-disclosing habits and to cope with the social and emotional disruption that follows. If you do not believe me, just try doing it. People do respond very fiercely when this taboo is broken.

So the satisfactory development of a relationship will depend on the 'proper' use of self-disclosure and personality communication. That is to say, in the present western cultural climate, men will tend to take the lead by encouraging females to disclose, but they will not disclose so much themselves; females are expected (even unfairly pressurized) to disclose more information at an earlier point in an acquaintance than males are. People look for reciprocation, for proper pacing and for deepening intimacy of disclosure, and notwithstanding the recent development in the United States of 'outing' (or forcing the revelation of homosexuality, willy nilly), disclosure is normally expected to be voluntary.

The circumstances must also be right: in some situations it is not permissible to disclose what not only would be right but would probably be expected in other circumstances. The classic example of this is in the job interview, where very personal information is often sought in a direct way that would be regarded as highly offensive in other circumstances – for instance, in talking to a stranger in a bar, or in talking to acquaintances at work (unless they were new arrivals, who are generally regarded as fair game for interrogation).

Despite the fact that self-disclosure is uniformly associated in general with relationships progress, there are topics that are taboo even in well-established relationships. Baxter and

Wilmot (1985) showed that such things as former deep relationships and 'the state of our relationship' should, on the whole, be avoided. Obviously if I spend a lot of my time telling my partner about my deep attachment to a former lover, then that will not do my present relationship a whole lot of good. Equally, focusing on 'the state of our relationship' tends to make people wary, anxious, defensive and uncertain, though there is some possibility that such negative reactions are more true for men than for women. Such topics, then, are best left off the conversational agenda until both parties feel comfortable with them.

Although such exceptions exist, they are rare, and self disclosure is generally regarded as a good thing. A recent four year longitudinal study by Sprecher (1987) found that the amount of overall disclosure in a relationship was the best predictor of whether a romantic couple remained together. Indeed, it was found to be such a powerful predictor that amount of disclosure, measured *today*, can predict whether or not the couple will still be together *four years from now*!

SHOWING THAT THE RELATIONSHIP IS GROWING

There is more to developing satisfying relationships than merely extracting the abstract information that ought to help them to grow. Their growth must be indicated in behaviour, and they must be maintained. In this section I shall look at the research which shows how activity changes as relationships grow – indeed, how it must change. Later, I shall consider the effects of 'publishing' a relationship in this way, particularly as it affects the rest of the social group that the partners belong to. The attitudes and responses of the group are often very influential in the development of relationships, particularly as they get very close.

Researchers have been loath to look at what people actually do in friendship for fear that the research will interfere with the relationship, and it is only in the last ten years or so that such studies of human social behaviour have really got off the ground (Huston *et al.*, 1981; Duck *et al.*, 1991).

Indeed, we found out a lot more about what monkeys and ants actually do in relationships than we did about humans – except humans in the sterilized, scientific laboratory, and they do not always behave the way they normally would.

One reason for this omission is that everyone assumed that they *knew* what people did, and so did not need to make records or do observations. It is not surprising, then, that there were several shocks in store when the job of cataloguing social behaviour was begun. For instance, if most people were asked what distinguishes the husband–wife relationship from all others in terms of reported activities done together, then we would probably expect something to do with sex to make the top of the list. In fact occurrence and amount of sexual activity does not distinguish husband–wife pairs from many other sorts of couple (Argyle, 1981). As I have already mentioned, the activity that statistically separates married couples from everyone else is that they spend more time watching television together.

Joint activity is more than just fun: it serves an accepted social signalling purpose. Quite simply it helps to indicate – both to the partners and to the rest of the world – that the partners are friends, and although friendship is based on feeling, the feelings have to be demonstrated or else people will not know that they are there. Equally, people have to change what they do together as the relationship grows, since this is a necessary means of showing that the friendship is developing and changing too. In some countries there used to be a very clear example of this when the partners formally agreed to switch from the distant form of address ('*vous*' in French, '*Sie*' in German) to the intimate form ('*tu*' in French, '*du*' in German). Even in our own language system the same person may be called 'Sir', 'Mr Jones', 'Robert', or 'Bob', depending on the degree to which we are getting to know him personally.

The pattern and diversity of interactions, joint activity and shared pursuits will also gradually alter as a friendship grows. Tolhuizen (1989) shows that dating partners deliberately focus on increasing the amount of contact time spent with the partner as well as the rewards that they give to the partner. Not only will the partners do more together and spend a higher percentage of their time in one another's company, they will also tend to do different things together. (In technical language, this is referred to as making the relationship multiplex rather than uniplex.) For instance, people may originally meet at work, and so pattern their meetings within certain particular hours of the day, talking about a relatively narrow set of topics (e.g., the supervisor, the job, the news in the day's papers) and doing a very restricted set of things together (e.g., eating lunch together, chatting). As the relationship grows so they may meet outside work and at different times of day or evening, do a wider range of things together (e.g., playing sport, going to the cinema), and talk about a wider range of issues. Many other aspects of their activities also change (Hinde, 1981). For instance, the intensity of the actions will increase: where they used to kiss tenderly they will now kiss passionately; where they used to smile politely they will now smile affectionately; where they used to laugh dutifully they will now laugh from genuine joy or happiness. Finally, the breadth of a couple's interaction – the range of activities that they do together – will extend itself considerably if they are to become a lasting couple (R.B. Hays, 1984). Pairs of people who do not diversify their interactions are quietly strangling the relationship in these early stages.

Furthermore, there are important consequences of the fact that a relationship is not merely something abstract or some rarefied feeling. It is a way of acting; it is a way of behaving. It is here that we can usefully revisit the idea brought up earlier in the chapter about complementarity; the idea that, for example, dominant people marry submissive ones – that people work well together when they have complementary skills. This is where it actually matters: when people behave in conjunction with one another. For instance, if two friends can work out complementary ways of behaving with each other then they will create a good working friendship.

Consider two people sharing a house: if both persons actually enjoy doing the dishes and neither likes to clean the carpet then not only will they fight about who does the dishes, but also they will soon be ankle-deep in dust.

However, if they can work out a complementary system where they each take turns at each job, then things will run smoothly. So it is in the sharing of a relationship. If both partners like to run the relationship, it will get out of control, but if they can work out a bit that each of them 'runs' it will go well. Under these sorts of circumstance complementarity is attractive; otherwise it is not. But in any case it involves work, discussion and give-and-take. The partners have to negotiate and create a complementary system for their relationship as it develops; these things do not just happen. Doing the necessary negotiation is one of the very complex skills of relationship development that needs a lot of thought and practice.

Because of these negotiations and these necessary alterations to activity, and because they mean, demonstrate and clarify things about two persons' relationship to one another, people come to expect them as signs of the growth of their intimacy. They become distressed, annoyed or hurt if the patterns of activity in the relationship do not seem to change in a fashion that indicates a growing relationship. So it is important to demonstrate affection and feeling once relationships are begun, both directly by verbal means and indirectly through nonverbal behaviour or changes in type of shared and negotiated activity.

Conversely, people indicate to one another their willingness or their reluctance to become more intimate and allow the relationship to grow. In some cases there are various normative forces that help here: there are quite wide ranges of tolerance for the friendliness or openness with which they may be conducted. For instance, teachers and pupils, or therapists and clients, or doctors and patients, may behave in a very friendly way to one another – be on first-name terms, for example – or be very distant and formal. Whichever is true, there are very strict sanctions that would be employed if the two became lovers, because of the built-in power differences.

Recently there has been considerable interest in the implications of other sorts of workmate romance. Dillard (1987) has shown that not only organizations themselves but also the people who are humble workers in them have become increasingly concerned about the high level of romances at work. A full 31 per cent of people surveyed have been involved in a romantic relationship at work and as many as 71 per cent of those surveyed had witnessed or observed one between workmates. Several different motives for these romances exist, with 36 per cent of them due to passionate love, 23 per cent due to simple desire for affection and companionship, 19 per cent due to 'flings' where people sought ego gratification, and a mere 8 per cent conforming to the stereotype of the exploitative relationship where one person was on an ego trip while the other had fallen in love. Dillard (1987) finds evidence that organizational romances do *not* inevitably cause a decrease in work performance in the involved couple. Nonetheless, the common view persists that they do cause lowered job performance. While these stereotypes continue, performance loss is likely to be caused as much by the gossip as it is by the relationship itself.

When the situation itself is less prominent and forceful, people still have to let one another know the limits that they perceive to the relationship, whether they see it as likely to grow, whether they want it to do so, and so on. This need can be problematic. It is often important to us to know how committed our partner is to growth in the relationship, but to ask directly is to break a taboo. How do skilled people manage this dilemma? Baxter and Wilmot (1984) found that secret tests are used: one partner faces the other with little trials and traps that cause him or her to act in a way that betrays the extent of commitment to the relationship. For instance, talking fondly about someone else who showed an interest in one *ought* to make one's partner respond in a jealous fashion if he or she feels committed to the relationship. So by watching carefully the extent of the reaction, one can assess the extent of the commitment. As another example, the apparently harmless question 'Why don't you come and meet my parents?' contains a secret test. If the invitation is accepted, then the partner is also accepting that he or she is committed enough to the relationship not to mind other people witnessing it and seeing it as a committed relationship.

Some people are uncomfortable when relationships get more intimate, and prefer to keep them distant and superficial, feeling that they will otherwise lose control over them. As their feelings get stronger, so they draw sharply back or indicate nonverbally that they want room, distance, space. How then do these desires and their opposites get indicated and communicated? The answer is 'subtly rather than directly'. Whenever someone shows keenness to enter a relationship, there is a risk of vulnerability. If someone asks directly 'Will you be my friend?', the question risks the straight answer 'No'. Such an undesired answer will obviously be threatening and offensive. Thus, except in very special circumstances (e.g., in making a proposal of marriage), people do not ask directly, but make the indications subtly and, usually, by nonverbal means or through style of behaviour. For instance, the wish to become closer can be shown by indicating greater interest in the person, by showing that you enjoy his or her company, by confiding, by asking for personal advice and seeking opinions, or by generally creating more opportunities for further meetings in a wider variety of circumstances. When the invitation is thus indicated obliquely, indirectly and ambiguously, it may be acknowledged or ignored without offence. For example, if someone asks a partner for advice about a private or personal matter, then the 'target' can treat this either as a move towards friendship and reply in a confiding or intimate way, or as a neutral matter by replying in a detailed but matter-of-fact way, or merely as a business matter for which the advice is given very formally and in a distant tone.

This social fact has several implications. First, we often may not realize what the other person intended until later. Second, some people will be better and some worse at detecting the subtle differences that are possible in such responses. So some will take, and others miss, opportunities simply because of their different abilities to detect – detect fast enough, that is – what their partner is intending. Third, some people will be better, and some worse, at putting their own intentions across in suitably subtle ways. Intentions or desires that are too explicit can be offensive or simply amusing, and there are many more subtle ways in which people avoid direct or explicit expression of them. People cut down both the risks and the offence by making characteristic changes in the 'contents' of what they do in relationships and in the ways in which they communicate about it. Such changes in the patterns and diversity of their activities, the frequency of their meetings and their communication styles, are all ways of indicating, cementing and establishing increases in intimacy and commitment. They convey the same desires and intentions, but do so in a safer and socially more acceptable way.

The most recognized way of doing this is by altering the 'currency' of the relationship (La Gaipa, 1977). In all meetings with other people, various tangible or intangible rewards are exchanged. To take a simple example, if I go into a shop I may buy a tie and give money for it: I receive the 'reward' of the tie and the shop assistant receives the 'reward' of money. Or I may go to an evening class to learn about basket weaving, in which case I receive the reward of information in exchange for a part of my enrolment fee. Or I may win a difficult sales order and be promoted to vice-president on the spot, receiving the reward of status for the service of marketing. Social psychologists have long conceived of social behaviour in terms of rewards and exchange of resources, as indicated briefly in Chapter 1.

Whether or not one accepts that these general principles apply to *established* intimate relationships, it is clear that *developing* relationships can usefully be seen in terms of the economic analogy. As the relationship grows, so there are systematic changes in the economy of the relationship (Hatfield and Traupmann, 1981).

For one thing, the type and value of the rewards change (La Gaipa, 1977). Friends do not spend most of their time exchanging goods for money: they are more likely to swap information for information, services for services, or love for love. In short, they move away from concrete items as the predominant content of their activity, and instead spend more time on the abstract. The quality of the rewards changes in personal terms also: money has the same value whoever gives it to you, but love is valued (or not) as a result of the person who offers it. Finally, as relationships become deeper there is less concern over immediate repayment of rewards: while casual acquaintances are concerned not to do too much for each other without being rewarded in return, close friends are more likely to be prepared to do favours without expecting instant 'payment'. Acquaintances return invitations to dinner, but friends do not keep track to such an extent. Part of the key development of friendship thus concerns the extension of the timespan for the return or reciprocation of rewards. Someone who is always keeping score will be difficult to relate to. Indeed, insistence on acting in a manner consistent with only casual acquaintance will make it hard for the partner to feel any closer. This is quite simply because it is acting in a way that is not consistent with the growth of the relationship and the changing definition of it as expressed in its exchange or reward pattern.

Another major way of indicating change in the relationship is through change in the patterns of communication within it (Morton and Douglas, 1981). A simple change at the developmental stage is that partners begin to communicate more vigorously about attitudes and beliefs. The change from discussion of 'locating information' (as in Chapter 2) to attitudes, values and beliefs is thus one subtle alteration to the communication structure in the relationship and one that, in properly conducted relationships, rapidly gives way to disclosures about personal feelings and the deeper aspects of personality. Partners at this stage of all relationships begin to share more interpretations of life and to communicate at a level that consists of personal judgments and values.

However, the pattern of communication changes not only in terms of its subject matter but also in terms of its style (Morton and Douglas, 1981). Not only does formality decrease as the partners become more familiar with one another, but relaxation of rules of behaviour is accompanied by a greater openness and a greater willingness to share secrets. Private stories about the past are shared, and the partners make their weaknesses and mistakes as much a part of the debate as their strengths and successes. This serves to make each person more vulnerable, of course, since each partner begins to build up a picture of the other person's private life, the things they dislike about themselves, and their errors, omissions or past failures. However, such vulnerability is usually reciprocal because both partners expose themselves in this new communication style. It serves to bind them together and to increase commitment to the relationship, therefore, and is very important to the development of the relationship.

The purpose of many of the communicational changes that occur is indeed to set up a new structure of assumptions in the relationship. As the relationship grows, so partners communicate more about their shared past rather than their separate pasts. This often involves them talking about their feelings on some shared experience, and has the consequence of making them focus on the relationship itself and their feelings about it. It thus promotes an agreed definition of the relationship and its form, which is essential for its growth. Partners need to work towards an agreed definition of the future of the relationship, and to set up shared expectations about its ultimate shape. Indeed, Honeycutt *et al.* (1989) have recently shown that *memories* of the development of relationships are extremely important to people, especially to women, who tend to monitor the track or path of the relationship very closely.

Couples, will, however, often disagree about the way in which their relationship started, particularly when it is in its early stages (S.W. Duck and Miell, 1986). As the relationship matures, the discrepancies between the 'origin stories' get ironed out and the couple evolves a standard and agreed story. One interesting example in my own studies of dating couples was of two people whose initial reports were quite different. When we asked them, only two weeks after it had happened, to describe where they first met, one of them reported that the meeting occurred in a coffee bar and the other that it happened in a lecture class. Intriguingly, when we asked them again six months later, they both agreed that it happened as one was going from a coffee bar to a lecture that both of them had to attend! Clearly the creation of such stories and the making of agreements about them are important to the couple making the relationship. I would go so far as to say that the creation of such stories is a part of the creation of the relationship itself.

Another way of looking at this same point is to observe the ways in which people react to their relationship when they cannot continuously create a story of its development. In the dating studies that I carried out, one of the most frequent reasons for breaking up was that the two partners had different expectations about the relationship. 'It was getting too intense. My partner wanted more from it than I was prepared to give just yet' was a very frequent type of response. By communicating about the relationship, its past, its future and its probable length, the partners contribute to creating an agreed picture of it that helps them to shape and stabilize it.

A further unconscious consequence of such talk is that it increases the partner's feelings of security in the relationship, enhances his or her commitment to the partner and beliefs about the partner's commitment, raises or creates trust and strengthens the stability of the relationship. By stressing the links between the partners in both the past and future, it also raises their feelings of relatedness or interdependence, and hence serves an important function in increasing intimacy in the relationship. It may be characterized by the development of symbols in the relationship – 'our tune', 'our restaurant', photographs that conjure up particularly happy or significant times in the relationship, and so on (Baxter, 1987). Such symbols can also take the form of special language or 'personal idioms' that couples evolve to make their relationship special, as I have already noted in Chapter 1. But the growth in intimacy stems from the structural and stylistic changes in communication just as much as from any changes in the content of the conversation.

These changes in the economy of the relationship, in the activity patterns and in the communication styles matter most to the two partners themselves in defining their relationship, but the changes also have another function. They indicate to outsiders that the relationship has been formed. Outsiders can interpret the nonverbal signals between people, the communication changes and the change of perspective just as well as the insiders can. Outsiders can often tell when two people are in love from the way that they behave in public, even when they do not know the people at all.

This is all obvious enough, but it is important because outsiders exert an influence on relationship development and, in some cases, can influence the form that it eventually takes – the father with a shotgun being the clearest example. For most partners it is important to gain other people's acceptance of their new friend, date, lover, spouse or companion, not only as a person but as 'my friend', 'my date', and so on. In short, the partners need the seal of approval that their other friends and associates can provide.

Studies consistently show, for example, that parental approval is positively related to marital adjustment: when parents fully accept the marriage partner, that marriage is a happier one. In general, such approval helps to prevent break up of the marriage and speeds up the prospects of the relationship during its formative period. In other cases, particularly in teenage gangs, a new date often seeks the approval of the whole group (La Gaipa and Wood, 1981), and a person risks losing membership of the gang if the chosen partner is not so approved. It can come down to a simple choice between the new partner and the gang – give up one or the other. In making a relationship and making it develop, therefore, the partners will be subject to group influences and pressures, particularly in the case of intimate relationships, to which we now turn.

4

Beyond attraction: changing the relationship

In Chapter 3 I explored the means by which relationships are intensified, paying particular attention to the changes in behaviour and communication patterns that occur. Many types of relationship begin in the ways described, but then start to take different forms, or to branch into avenues not possible in the other types. For example, dating relationships have many similarities to but also some clear differences from friendships (both involve self-disclosure, for instance, but friendship does not usually involve sex). Also, a dating relationship changes its nature when it turns into a cohabitation, engagement or marriage. These differences are sometimes quite dramatic and bring their own problems, requiring large adjustments from one or both partners whether the partners are heterosexual or homosexual. For instance, when heterosexual dating couples decide to get married they must adjust to the implications that the new relationship will have – marriage, as distinct from dating, is a socially institutionalized relationship, with legal and contractual implications; partners will now live together for the foreseeable future; they will possibly be regarded as failures if they do not do it successfully; they might prepare to have a family. The changes may bring rewards, but they also have to be coped with, as well as having to be brought about and created successfully when desired.

In gay and lesbian long-term relationships there are other problems additional to those encountered by a heterosexual couple who decide to cohabit or marry. Gays and lesbians also have to deal with pressure from society implying that there is something fundamentally wrong with their relationship and with them for engaging in it. (For instance, in the supermarket the day I was writing and thinking about this paragraph, I saw a newspaper claiming 'New drug can cure gays.' Note the word 'cure'.) They do not have the same uncomplicated chances to make their relationship public by using open displays of affection such as holding hands, as these may lead to hostile responses from onlookers, which sometimes may even be violent. As with nontraditional marriages, gays and lesbians also have to work harder at deciding on their roles within long-term relationships than do people in traditional marriages. Two men or two women living together have experienced the same gender-role socializing experiences from society, whereas the two people in a heterosexual couple have not. In short, there are several sorts of 'social script' for heterosexual couples to follow in working out their relationship, and many examples of 'what marriage is like' on television or in magazines. Such scripts do not exist in the same sorts of way for homosexual long-term couples.

In all long-term relationships, partners, whether heterosexual or homosexual, may decide to cohabit, or may decide to engage in sexual intercourse for their first time. A heterosexual couple might decide to start a family; parents may have to face up to their children going to school or leaving home. A person may retire from work and leave all the relationships that were enjoyed there. All of these decisions or events have consequences for the individuals, for the partners and for the relationship, which must be negotiated and carried out systematically and skilfully. Once these special problems are handled, the person's life has to be set back in balance. Adjustments in attitudes towards the partner or to feelings about the relationship have to be set in frame again, against the background of the new developments. Because of their importance to the lives of the people involved, such changes have been closely researched. Evidently they involve a different range of skills from the ones discussed earlier and a range that, even when carried out efficiently, can still

produce stress. High stress scores on the so-called 'significant life events scale' are associated with the decision to
marry, to set up a house or to start a family, as well as arising
from divorce, death of a spouse and loss of children who
leave home. In most people's lives these relationship events
are exacting and in need of careful understanding.

One hidden factor in all of these changes stems from the
fact that there is a concealed pressure that lurks in relationships. Like a germinating seed, the beginning of some relationships is not only rich in promise and hope, but also
pregnant with a whole range of detailed, programmed expectations about the shape and form of the relationship that
will eventually be created – if everything goes according to
plan. Thus an engagement implies very strongly that there
will eventually be a marriage; marriage strongly suggests that
the couple will have children eventually, or at least that they
will have to consider the issue of whether to have children or
not. The early stages of a relationship can predispose or
predict the later stages: for instance, Kelly *et al.* (1985) show
that the style and amount of conflict that occur in premarital
relationships are highly accurate predictors of conflict and
distress in subsequent marriage.

Even when the plan is effectively and smoothly carried
out, it involves the partners in many kinds of change in
activity and in beliefs about themselves, as well, perhaps, as
changes in status, responsibility and duties (as when newly
married couples buy a house, for example). Despite the increasing demands that this may create for them, the partners
are more likely to feel satisfied with the relationship when its
implied 'programme' is completed exactly as expected. On
the other hand, when it is carried out too quickly (as in
whirlwind romances) the partners may have too little time to
make the necessary adjustments, or to create the essential
patterns of activity that the new form of relationship entails.
If the relationship's programmed demands are carried out
too slowly or not realized at all (for instance, when long-term
dating couples realize that one of them does not really intend to get married or that the relationship is 'not going
anywhere') then the partners also experience distress – even
when the relationship is perfectly happy in its present form.

The problem is not necessarily that the relationship itself is unsatisfactory or unenjoyable, but that it does not match up to expectations for the future: the source of the difficulty is the unhappy comparison of reality with hopes.

When people embark on certain sorts of relationship, like engagements, there are highly specific expectancies built into the whole arrangement. For instance, the couple will have the expectancy that they will eventually marry. If it becomes clear that this is going to be delayed, or if one partner seems unwilling to take the plunge, then the relationship becomes pointless, even if it is still enjoyable. Indeed, many courtships break up at around 15–18 months in (S.W. Duck, 1988b), just because one of the partners becomes dissatisfied with the rate of progress towards the expected state; and if the relationship will not change, then it must die.

In other cases the demands implicit in the relationship concern the kinds of activity that partners would expect to enjoy together. For example, friends would expect to share private details and secret knowledge, and to do a variety of activities together as their relationship grows deeper; or a couple may expect to have sex at some later stage. In these cases any problem centres on the ways to bring the changes about at the most agreeable and suitable times, as well as on the most satisfactory manner to execute the decision. In former days such decisions were often structured for a heterosexual couple: sex first took place on the wedding night, perhaps in the presence of a group of formal witnesses who would testify both to the woman's being a virgin beforehand and to her loss of virginity afterwards. Nowadays such activity is usually negotiated in private and can occur at other times or in other forms of relationship.

Researchers have recently begun to look at the ways in which such decisions are taken. I shall look at the research on heterosexual couples regarding such decisions, starting with partners' decisions to engage in sexual intercourse or to cohabit. However, other decisions and other changes are also important in relationships later in life; for instance, the decision to move from being a 'married couple' to being a 'family', and the change from 'family' to 'empty nesters' when grown-up children leave home. I shall look at those later in the present chapter, and shall focus particularly on the skills of coping with the changes, as well as the means of bringing them about.

Researchers have for a long time been interested in the instigation of premarital sexual activity, and have identified several influential factors in isolation (Christopher and Cate, 1985). Approval and frequency of premarital sexual activity are statistically related to such things as religious beliefs, previous sexual experience, age at first intercourse and the sexual behaviour of friends or people in the surrounding networks or friendship groups. None of these statistical findings tells us what we really need to know, however. What researchers have tried recently to discover is the *process* by which premarital individuals decide to start a sexual involvement with a partner. What do people weigh up in their minds when they are deciding such a question, and what influences sway their decisions?

In a study where investigators looked at this question in heterosexual couples contemplating premarital sexual involvement (and not all sexual involvement has anything to do with marriage or eventual marriage, of course), Cate and Christopher (1982) found that there were basically four influences on the decision:

1. The *positive feelings* that partners had for one another, and whether they had discussed these feelings together. For instance, couples who loved one another a lot and felt committed to each other were likely to have discussed their feelings and to have considered the meaning of intercourse for their relationship. If they decided that the meaning of sexual intercourse for the relationship was one that had positive overtones for both of them, gave them a sense of increased commitment and set the relationship further along the track towards marriage, then they were more likely to have decided for intercourse.

2. The *two partners' arousal.* The second most important influence was, naturally enough, found to be the state of excitement, anticipation or arousal before the relevant date where intercourse occurred, coupled with physical

arousal during the date. Partners who felt strong commitment but were not physically aroused simply postponed the activity of intercourse until a later occasion. It is interesting to note that many primitive tribes engage in considerable physical exertion and try to create high arousal and excitement through dance, music, games and ritual exercising during fertility rites which traditionally end in intercourse. Violent physical exercise and dancing can create the necessary state of arousal for intercourse.

3. *Obligation and pressure.* A third feature in the decision was the amount of obligation or pressure exerted by one's partner, one's friends, one's partner's friends and oneself. The respondents in the Cate and Christopher investigation often reported that they were reacting to pressures such as these, although it is very likely that such pressure actually also comes from the implicit demands or expectations in the relationship. Some relationships between young (and even older) people, such as engagements, have a strong pressure for sex in them, partly as 'initiation rites' and partly because it is 'what everybody does' when a relationship gets to that stage. Adjustment to these pressures is often a distressing problem for some couples, who respond to the demands rather than to their own personal wishes. This is particularly true of the males who were interviewed, many of whom reported significant pressure from their friends to have intercourse with the most recent dating partner. (As an aside, we should note that with gay and lesbian long-term couples there are not the same cues from the outside world about when is a good time to become sexually involved. As they do not have official engagements or legally recognized marriages in most countries, and their relationships are frequently not recognized or accepted by others, decisions such as these must be made by the couple based purely on personal and interpersonal dynamics. Nevertheless, there are also sets of norms that apply within the gay and lesbian communities that would also provide benchmarks. Thus, although some such couples may find themselves operating outside (heterosexual) society's norms, many gay or lesbian couples have available a strong normative context

for gay and lesbian relationships, provided by the gay and lesbian community in which they move, such communities, typically, being found in large cities.)
4. *Circumstances.* A large number of the Cate and Christopher interviewees reported that premarital intercourse was a result of circumstantial factors, like the availability of drugs or alcohol, or the fact that the relevant date was a really special event.

The two sexes respond differently to these four inducements, with females reporting a much greater influence of 'positive feelings' in their decision than the males did. Inexperienced individuals also reported that feelings mattered more than any of the other forces, whereas sexually experienced persons were more influenced by arousal level than by anything else.

The Cate and Christopher study makes it perfectly clear that decisions about the first moves in a sexual involvement are not a simple matter. On the contrary, the decisions involve many kinds of pressure and consideration, some of which stem from the nature of the relationship, some from expectations about where it will lead and some from unpredictable circumstances.

In later work, Christopher and Cate (1985) found that heterosexual couples have one of four pathways to orgasmic sex, whatever the surrounding contexts (including those above):

1. *Rapid involvement* couples wasted little time in getting down to it, usually having orgasmic sex (most probably full sexual intercourse) on their first date. This group was only 7 per cent of the total.
2. *Gradual involvement* couples engaged in petting on early dates but did not have orgasmic sex or full intercourse until they were seriously considering becoming an exclusive couple. This group was 32 per cent of the total.
3. The third and largest group, (44 per cent) went for *delayed involvement,* keeping orgasmic sexual activity until they had already become an exclusive couple.
4. The last group, *low involvement* couples (17 per cent of all couples), did not engage in orgasmic sex before marriage.

Christopher and Frandsen (1990) explored the strategies that heterosexual couples used to influence their partners in relation to sexual activity (whether to get more or less of it). They found four general strategies that were used:

1. *Antisocial acts,* where one partner tried to impose his or her will on the other person by such means as ridicule, force, crying, pleading, sulking, insults or becoming angry.
2. *Emotional or physical closeness,* such as acting seductively, telling the partner the extent of love felt for him or her, doing something special for the partner, flattery, or communicating what was wanted by means of hands and other physical means.
3. *Logic and reason* (e.g., compromising, asserting authority, or claiming knowledge about the 'right' level of involvement for people at that stage of relationship).
4. *Pressure or manipulation,* such as being very persistent, using alcohol or drugs, manipulating partner's mood or threatening to break off the relationship – a technique used by men more than by women.

The emotional and physical closeness techniques are those most clearly associated with positive development of the relationship. Only the strategy of emotional/physical closeness led to any marked success in increasing sexual activity, while logic/reason strategies actually decreased its likelihood. Evidently emotion is used by those who want more sexual activity and reason is used by those who want less.

However the sexual side of the relationship is begun, as such relationships mature, the problem shifts from the initial decision and onto the management of sexual desires and patterns and frequency of sex. To a very large extent such relationships will be successful or unsuccessful as a direct result of the partners' abilities and skills in creating the desired patterns of activity, in this respect as in respect of other activities in other relationships.

Most people nowadays reject the naive idea that sexual activities are purely physical events, and research continually demonstrates the truth of the alternative view that they are relationship-based (Yaffe, 1981). As such they reflect the rest of the relationship like a barometer. Sexual difficulties and sexual problems as often stem from relationship problems as from other causes, and relationship stress follows sexual difficulties. In studies of American couples (reported in Markman *et al.*, 1982) it has been found that three out of every five women and two out of every five men who were dissatisfied with their marriage reported no pleasure from sexual activity for about a year before they complained about their marriage. This correlation between sexual dissatisfaction and dissatisfaction with the marriage is found in newlyweds as much as in people who have been married for up to twenty years.

Blumstein and Schwartz (1983), in their major survey of American couples, found that in happy heterosexual couples frequency of sexual intercourse varied considerably, ranging from less than once a month to three or more times a week. Clearly frequency of intercourse in itself is unrelated to a couple's happiness, although one must not forget the famous scene in a Woody Allen film where two partners are seen cross-cut talking to their respective therapists. When asked 'Do you have sex often?', the woman replies 'Constantly, about three times a week', while Woody Allen responds 'Almost never; about three times a week.' Sexual satisfaction is different, then, from frequency of sex.

Cupach and Comstock (1990) explored the quality of couples' communication about sex. Communication about sex obviously allows partners to inform and teach one another about their respective sexual needs, desires and preferences. This is important because a couple's sexual behaviour is largely a matter for them to work out for themselves to their own satisfaction: there are no right or wrong ways to do it, judged from any other criteria. The study showed that satisfaction with the way the couple *talks* about sex is an important influence on the couple's actual satisfaction with their sex lives. Quality communication about sex thus seems to be a vital factor in marital adjustment, even though it does not actually *cause* marital adjustment. With it, you *might* be happy; without it, you will not be.

It seems that sexual adjustment and marital adjustment

are strongly related and the correlation provides further evidence for the point that I made in Chapter 3: the quality of a relationship, whether friendship, courtship, marriage or work, depends largely upon the quality of the activities that take place within it, not just upon feelings about the partner. Feelings and activities are not independent: the former come from the activities that are performed together – or, more importantly, come from the way that people look at what they do together. If partners see themselves enjoying one another's company, they believe more firmly that they like one another. When the activities are enjoyable, feelings about the partner reflect that; when they are not, the feelings change. We used to believe: that the feelings dictate the activities that we perform, but it is not as simple as that – the reverse is equally true.

The above discussion teaches us that developing relationships create demands on the partners to engage in specified sorts of activity in order to 'certify' that the relationship is proceeding normally towards its expected goal or ideal state. However, not all relationships proceed at the same rate, and individuals differ in their beliefs about the speed at which they should proceed. A study of dating couples in America (Peplau *et al.*, 1977) found that some couples who engaged in sexual intercourse within one month of meeting reported that it was due to sexual desire rather than to love, whereas those who waited for six months gave love as the 'cause' of their intercourse rather than just sexual desire. It seems very likely that some couples prefer to delay sex until they feel emotionally close, while others use sexual intercourse as a way of creating greater feelings of commitment and, as it were, make themselves fall in love as a result. The timing of first sexual activity does not seem to affect a couple's perceptions of the closeness of their relationship: both 'early' and 'late' couples report satisfaction to be at about the same level. Equally, 'early sex' is not more nor less likely to lead to the break-up of the couple than is 'later sex'. However, sheer number of sexual partners before marriage does predict likelihood of divorce: the more the marrier had, the higher divorce chances are (Athanasiou and Sarkin, 1974).

Some dating couples decide to go further towards an

institutionalized relationship than is achieved by simply engaging in sexual intercourse. They choose to enter a co-habital relationship, where they live together as if they were married, but without actually going through a marriage cere-mony. National samples of the United States taken before 1977 show that 2–5 per cent of the population was cohabit-ing (Newcomb, 1981).

People choose to live with one another without being mar-ried for all sorts of reasons and, surprisingly, in some 25 per cent of cases have never actually discussed whether to co-habit before they do so. In these cases it just happened, or else it 'just growed', like Topsy: partners spent several nights together, found it generally agreeable and decided to move in together. In cases where the couples do discuss it be-forehand, there are two key influences on the decision. First, partners are influenced by opportunity, as created by such things as the availability of suitable accommodation, the atti-tudes, beliefs and pressures of friends, distance away from parents or authority figures and the attractiveness that they see their partner to have. The second influence is the major one: willingness of the two partners to take advantage of the opportunities that are available. This, naturally, is the major point of discussion between partners, and the decision ul-timately seems to depend on religious beliefs, previous sex-ual experience and the strength of liking or commitment towards the partner.

Where the partners have a low religious commitment they are more likely to cohabit, although, for reasons not yet fully clarified by research, there is an over-representation of Catholics and Jewish women among cohabiting couples (Newcomb, 1981). Cohabitors of both sexes are more experienced sexually and report a wider variety of sexual practices than do people who are not cohabiting. They are also more likely than non-cohabitors to be drug-users, ciga-rette smokers, vegetarians and people who hold nontradi-tional values (Newcomb, 1986).

Some people faced with a decision to cohabit obviously decide to do so whereas others do not. Investigators have been interested in what makes the decision go one way or the other and it seems to come down largely to the way in which the partners see themselves. Cohabitors have a generally more favourable view of themselves and their personality. They see themselves as more intelligent, less controlled by social restraints, less inhibited generally, and more outgoing, attractive and appreciative of art or the aesthetic things of life. One explanation for this is that cohabitation is, relatively, a more uncertain relationship than marriage and the extra social constraints, legal obligations and contractual forces of marriage provide a structure for those who need it (Newcomb, 1981). People who have confidence that, because of their own positive qualities, their relationship will last are probably more willing to consider the uncertain relationship of cohabitation than are those who feel insecure about their ability to retain their partner's affections or commitment. In fact, such fears are justified in both sets of people. Newcomb (1986) showed that when cohabitors eventually do marry, their divorce rate is significantly higher than it is for those who did not cohabit before marrying. This could, of course, reflect the fact that many cohabitants choose cohabitation precisely because they do not want to marry, or because they 'resist bringing the State into their private lives', as a friend of mine put it. In such cases, they may find the institution of marriage an uncomfortable one that soon confirms their worst expectations and leads to their divorcing.

As indicated at the start of this chapter, then, the decision about cohabitation is taken within the framework of the partners' expectations for the relationship, and their ability to hold it together once they take the public step of committing themselves to an unconventional arrangement.

Because cohabitation is not yet a widely accepted alternative to conventional marriage, several investigators have been interested in comparing cohabiting partners with married partners in the expectation of finding differences of lifestyle, or in the patterning of activities that occur in such sorts of relationship (see Newcomb, 1981, for a review). The most influential study found that, contrary to expectations, both married and cohabiting women performed the majority of the household tasks. Overall, there were very few differences between the two groups, despite the fact that cohabiting women see themselves as significantly more masculine (and they see cohabiting men as more feminine) than married persons do. The cohabitors see themselves as more unconventional, but actually operate in a way that does not distinguish them from the traditional role patterns for husband and wife. This is explained by the investigators in the study as due to the tedious efforts involved for the couple in constant reassessment of their behaviour in order to see whether they are acting out the 'right' roles. They too easily find themselves, over a period of time, slipping back into traditional moulds, even though their ideals call for some other line of action.

In coping with both the conventional husband–wife and the unconventional cohabital arrangement, then, the persons' intentions are not enough. The demands of the situation, the pressures on time, the reactions of other people and the extremely powerful constraints exercised by society at large make it rather more difficult for partners to adopt their desired mix of activities than they may have hoped. As indicated in Chapter 1, the effects of a network or surrounding social system can exert a dramatic influence on people's actions in relationships, and the only really effective way of dealing with this problem is to use this knowledge to one's own advantage by surrounding oneself with a network that holds the same values, beliefs and opinions as oneself. Thus cohabital communes are more likely to work out and stick to a nontraditional pattern of relational activities than are cohabital couples who remain in a society that retains its traditional beliefs about role-based activity.

The whole problem stems from the need for any pair to work out ways of running the new form of relationship, to create behavioural strategies and indicators that square up with their feelings for one another, and to cope with the relationship itself, which takes on a kind of life of its own once it reaches a high level of involvement. Partners start by liking one another, then learn to adjust to and cope with one another, and finally have to learn to adjust to and cope with everyone else's and their own responses to the fact that they are now 'in a relationship'. In this way the pair becomes 'socially acknowledged'. Outsiders treat them as a couple rather than as two individuals: where one is invited, the other is implicitly invited too; one partner's friends become the other person's friends. (This is one of the major differences between heterosexual and gay or lesbian long-term couples. As many gay or lesbian long-term couples do not 'come out' to, for example, workmates, they may be regarded, and treated, as though they were not in a relationship.) Such pressures are powerful enough when they are informal but get even stronger once the relationship gets a social seal of approval and turns into 'a marriage'.

FROM LOVE TO COMMITMENT OR MARRIAGE . . . AND BEYOND

I have been discussing the changes that can occur to a relationship both from the inside and from the outside once it is formed, writing mostly about heterosexual relationships, with some few comments about homosexual long-term relationships (partly because the research itself has had less to say about them (Kurdek, 1991)). When people fall in love, so their own behaviour and other people's behaviour towards them changes in a number of ways. So also there is an increase in the partners' belief that marriage (or in the case of homosexual long-term relationships, some form of commitment ceremony) will be a likely result of the courtship. Such beliefs and such inside and outside pressures or influences lead the partners through courtship and make certain patterns of activity more probable than others (for instance, some couples refrain from sex until they are engaged, in the expectation of eventual marriage). The expectations also compel the partners to face up to the business of working out their future roles, planning for marriage and afterwards, and generally fixing their eyes on some point quite distant from the present. This will involve them in charting of their probable route towards marriage, as well as in formation of a time-scale for carrying it out. A line of research on courtship (Huston *et al.*, 1981) has shown that people can be divided into four categories according to the way in which they go about effecting this transition from courtship to marriage.

Whereas the early stages of dating, falling in love and court-ship have a consistent pattern to them, the later stages sepa-rate characteristically according to the one of the four categories that the courtship pattern falls into (see the sec-tion below, 'From courtship to marriage').

Love and courtship

In several studies of heterosexual loving couples (e.g., Rubin, 1974) it has been found that they have a very consis-tent pattern of nonverbal behaviour (as discussed in Chap-ters 2 and 3). This, of course, helps dramatically to communicate their feelings about one another, not only to one another but also to anyone else who sees them. The behaviour serves to signal that they are a loving couple, and the actions of sitting close together, holding hands, touch-ing, talking intimately and so on serve an important signal-ling function at these stages of the blossoming relationship. Researchers talk of 'tie-signs' being used at this point; that is to say, signs that the two people are 'tied' into one unit. Examples of tie-signs are wedding rings, holding hands while walking along the street, wearing one another's scarves or dressing alike. Of course, the existence of marriage and com-mitment ceremonies is itself another example of the strong importance that people attach to public indication of their relationship, over and above the private feelings that they have about one another. For this reason, homosexuals are particularly troubled and stressed by the fact that, as their long-term relationships are not sanctioned by most societies yet, this sort of indicative activity is hard for them, although many do wear rings.

A key point here, then, that is a source of pleasure to heterosexuals who 'can' do it and of pain to homosexuals who 'cannot', is the fact that such behaviour is not simply the result of the feelings that the partners have for one another: it strongly contributes to the sense of belonging to the rela-tionship. It is an essential part of the state of being in love that the two parties feel like a unit. The quality or quantity of the loving behaviour helps both partners – and the outside world – to know that the partners are a unit and in love. Individuals who do not show it satisfactorily will create problems of embarrassment for outsiders who may not know how to treat them – are they really 'a couple', or should outsiders pretend that they are not mutually involved? More important, such individuals will cause their partner dissatisfaction, frustration and, possibly, grief.

The pattern consists first of a much increased level of so-called eye contact – that is, gazing into the eyes of one's partner. As I indicated in Chapter 2, this is not very surprising once we realize that the eyes are the habitual medium for conveying messages of intimacy and liking. They are far more important than words in this respect. Lovers gaze at one another in this way nearly eight times longer than strangers do when they are not actually conversing with one another. The partners are mutually interested in one another, to the exclusion of pretty well everyone and everything else: in the words of the song, 'I only have eyes for you.'

There are some other, more unexpected effects also. One experiment, for example, (K.L. Dion and Dion, 1979) showed that loving couples have a much better memory for random words read aloud by their partner! Furthermore, when their partners are put into a special piece of psychological apparatus (which usually creates the illusion that a person is much smaller than they really are), loving couples do not see it that way. It is almost as if love cancels out the effects of the Hall of Mirrors and distorted reflections of one's partner are instantly corrected by the effects of love.

Once love entices the couple into a working courtship their behaviour 'bottoms out' a little, and the important facts are not so much that they spend more time together (to the exclusion of other relationships), sit closer together, touch one another more, gaze into one another's eyes and self-disclose. The important changes concern the ways in which the partners begin to distribute their time together – the changing amounts of time that they devote to different activities as their courtship develops.

From courtship to marriage
The four types of track towards marriage are, according to Huston *et al.* (1981), as follows:

1. '*Accelerated – arrested*', which starts off very fast, with partners planning marriage within two or three months of meeting, but then not actually carrying out the plan for a year or so after that.
2. '*Accelerated*', which leads to plans of marriage within about five months of meeting and execution of the plan within another five months or so.
3. '*Intermediate*', where the partners do not plan marriage for certain until after about a year or so, and then marry within about eight months after that.
3. '*Prolonged*', where the couple take a relatively retarded and rocky path to marriage.

The last two types of courtship show the greatest problems, with more conflicts and turbulence than the first two, despite the fact that they give partners longest to practise the behaviour that will be required in their eventual marriage.

In all types of courtship there are some common patterns of activity that characterize the growth of the relationship (Huston *et al.*, 1981). For example, although partners spend an increasing proportion of their available time with each other rather than with their other friends, the time is not spent just in the affectionate activities that sustain the relationship, but also in the practical tasks of living. Daily tasks are done together more often than one might expect. It is predictable, on the other hand, that partners would spend more time in leisure activities together. It is found in all the types of courtship that couples do this to the exclusion of leisure activities with other people. In short, the individuals withdraw from their relationships with others and draw towards their partner more exclusively.

There are, however, key differences between the courtship types also. 'Intermediate' courtships show the lowest levels of commitment to one another. The partners show less affection, do not work together so much on tasks and spend more time alone than persons in other courtship types do, including those in the very longest 'prolonged' courtships. By contrast, the partners in both sorts of 'accelerated' courtship report greater closeness and affection, and they work together more closely on tasks, particularly those that are traditionally associated with the female role.

Researchers find that the activities that accompany the growth of a courtship towards marriage are not the same for all couples (Huston *et al.*, 1981). The shortest courtships do not necessarily report more love at the early stages, but the couples do find out faster and better the way in which to work together in the relationship. They cope more rapidly with the problems and everyday tasks that benefit from the cooperative input of both partners, such as joint decision-making and household tasks. By contrast, the long courtships seem to be more full of love and affection: the partners just have greater difficulty getting agreement on how the tasks of life should be performed and by whom. Accordingly, these slowly progressing courtships require the partners to put much more of their time and effort into just maintaining and sustaining the relationship (see the section below on 'Maintaining satisfying relationships'). This probably slows them down by diverting them from the real job in courtship – negotiating and working out how the future marriage will actually be performed.

Complex, committed romantic relationships involve not only the mutual affection and commitment of both partners, but also their ability to mesh their behaviour together satisfactorily in matters like housekeeping, providing and decision-making. They have to negotiate to decide who will be responsible for which parts of the domestic tasks of marriage, and to work out satisfactory ways of acting out the roles of husband and wife. Marital stability depends not merely on affection but on the ability to co-ordinate efforts on such tasks.

In traditional heterosexual relationships, the roles of husband and wife are complementary: they mesh together, although there is no generally ideal way of doing this, and each pair of partners must negotiate their own solution to the problem during courtship and beyond. In nontraditional relationships, such as egalitarian marriages and gay and lesbian long-term couples, the roles are not so clearly defined. It is in the working out of such matters that gay and lesbian long-term relationships run into particular difficulties, since there are no clearly defined complementary roles for such partners to adopt for one another. Indeed, more than this, each person has been culturally socialized and prepared for the same kind of role and some predictable conflicts and relationship management issues arise from that fact (Lawson, 1990). This may be part of the reason why relationship quality in gay and lesbian long-term relationships declines somewhat over a year of being related (Kurdek, 1989), although it also has a lot to do with the fact that the partners constantly get messages from society that gay and lesbian relationships 'cannot last'. There is, as homosexuals are all too clearly aware in conducting their relationships, considerable fear and dislike of homosexuality.

Marital problems are strongly associated with a poor fit between the partners' expectations and beliefs about their respective marital roles (Newcomb and Bentler, 1981). Where partners have a great deal of specialization and demarcation in the household duties and in the types of decision that each partner takes, then marital happiness is generally low. On the contrary, marriages with egalitarian roles are usually better adjusted than those where either partner is excessively dominant and controlling (Fitzpatrick, 1988). So, once again, the research indicates that those partners who successfully work out an agreeable way to distribute their activities will generate a more satisfactory relationship.

Such activities cannot be left to chance and do not simply fall into place if a couple is deeply in love. The activities *are* the relationship, and require the work, time, effort, attention and skill of the partners. It is important that couples who intend to marry give thought to such things, and talk carefully over their beliefs about the marital roles, about the distribution of labour and about the pattern of activities. Even a deeply loving couple's feelings will not make the marriage as happy alone as will the satisfactory creation of complementary roles and ways of behaving in marriage. The couple who are constantly yelling at one another may start to do so through anger, but gradually come to 'fix' in the pattern because they see themselves doing it: obviously, they begin to think, if we shout at one another like that we cannot like one another very much. They perceive themselves to be acting in a way that is inconsistent with close feelings, so they explain their behaviour as caused by dislike. This is exactly the opposite explanation from the one we are used to: we usually think of feelings causing behaviour, but in some cases behaviour causes feelings.

It is thus very important for couples to spend time negotiating and setting up patterns of activity and complementary roles of behaving that will help them to feel that they are close. For men, at least, the rewards of doing so are very significant, even vital in the literal sense. Happily married men have superior mental health, lower suicide rates, greater career prospects and longer lives (Bloom *et al.*, 1978). For women, the picture is not quite so rosy, as is indicated by the fact that women are responsible for the legal initiation of about 75 per cent of all divorces (Hagestad and Smyer, 1982). However, there is some dispute about the meaning of this fact, for it may show that women are less willing to tolerate severe distress or that they are put in unacceptable positions by husbands who are too indecisive to file for divorce themselves.

Most recent research shows that the part of the population most depressed is composed of non-working married women with preschool-age children – just those people so often represented by the media, especially in advertisements, as most fulfilled. This contrasts with the reality where, in most households, women do most of the routine housework and childcare. If they are working too, then being married is more of a strain than being single, whereas for the man it is the other way about.

As noted earlier, though, women are better at coping with intimacy, partly because they rarely concentrate all their intimacy needs into one relationship. They usually have a wide range of friends who are not (as men's friends often are) simply concentrated around the workplace. For this reason women are better at developing intimacy through the activities and behaviour I have been describing, since they have a wider and broader range of experience to draw on. It is certainly the women who handle the development of courtship better and actually take more of the management role. But as with so many other things, it may be the happily married men who ultimately end up getting the greater benefits from this.

As with the kinds of relationship discussed earlier, the research makes it clear that marital satisfaction depends not only on achievement of satisfactory patterns of activity but also on careful attention to communication. Happily married couples talk to each other more than other couples do, convey the clear impression that they understand the other person, show more sensitivity to their partner's feelings, and supplement their speech with a more expressive range of nonverbal signals. In short, they adopt a pattern of communication that conveys understanding and a willingness to open out about their own feelings. Comparable findings sharply contrast distressed and happy families: distressed families have not skilfully created a pattern of communication that stresses interest in the other people's views, sentiments and beliefs. Instead, they are low on the humorous banter and strong emotional support that characterizes the normal and most successful happy families.

From 'married couple' to 'family'

A major change that takes place in the activities of a married couple is brought about by the addition of children. Even during their first pregnancy, couples' experience of their marriage is affected, with 60 per cent of couples reporting greater closeness and focus on family issues (Lips and Morrison, 1986). Clearly pregnancy is a development that ultimately disrupts the patterns of life that the couple has been used to, but in this case probably for the better – at the start, at any rate. What has been said already in this book will prepare us to expect that the change in activities can cause feelings to change also, and will affect the couple's satisfaction with their marriage, with their partner and with themselves. Particularly for the wife, a consistent finding in several studies over many years is that satisfaction with the marriage often declines sharply just after children are born (Newcomb and Bentler, 1981). The wife's satisfaction with herself is also affected.

While these findings are very consistent, some couples emerge from the trough much more successfully than others, and it is becoming clear that it is those couples who create the best patterns of activity that cope best. This seems to mean those patterns where housework and childcare are fairly distributed within the couple. The birth of children affects the way in which a couple can distribute their time, and also the tasks they do together. As I have shown, this can modify their view of the relationship: since they spend less time alone and spend more time doing tasks related to the child, so they come to see themselves as less caring for one another, unless they take the trouble to create and negotiate a more satisfying view of what they are doing. This can be done by the obvious means of forcing more time alone together into their daily timetable; but this is not always possible, and 'special treat outings' can merely throw into sharp relief the fact that they are special, unusual and rare.

A less obvious, but ultimately more successful, way of coping with the problem is to reconstrue the chores and household duties as 'relationship activity'; that is, to grow from seeing them merely as jobs to be done, and to come to see them as indications of the strength of relationship, or opportunities for sharing, and examples of emotional commitment to the marriage and the family. For instance, I know a couple that purchased two ironing boards and irons, so that they could do the ironing together while watching television and so feel that they were both helping the relationship! This relatively subtle psychological shift pulls the activity back into the relationship domain, rather than leaving partners to feel as if it is work done at the expense of the relationship. It is thus a way of preserving the couple's feelings for each other and, incidentally, of strengthening their mutual bond to the child. Accordingly, it creates a smoother transition from marriage to family – a transition that is not simply the result of the birth of the child, but of the negotiation of a newly organized relationship. A 'family' is a relationship that is a psychological creation much more than it is simply a numerical one.

This fact is further illustrated by the relational change that comes later as the children grow. Because the parents are the major agents who turn the child into a social being and help to create its sociable tendencies, skills and understandings, they are very often in conflict with the child's unsociable, selfish, even animal nature. They spend time dealing with the children's conflicts between themselves, with school problems and with disagreements between parent and child over discipline. Those families that pay close attention to this matter as a relationship problem rather than as a discipline problem will be the ones that cope better and adjust to it more successfully. It is necessary to put in hard work to focus themselves away from these issues as routine discipline tasks and onto them as relationship matters, or onto other activities that bring about more positive attitudes to the relationship between parent and child.

According to the most influential studies discussed in Burgess (1981), parents can establish one of three sorts of relationship with their children. They can be authoritarian; that is, they can try to control and relate to their child by stressing the value of obedience, and will use punishment to enforce it. They can be permissive; that is, they exert little control over the child, consult the child about standards of behaviour, and use reason rather than punishment to exercise their childrearing duties. Both of these types of relationship lead, in their own different ways, to disaster. The former produces over-anxious children who are dependent and unduly cowed by authority, rules and social pressures. The second leads to self-indulgent children who show little respect for other people. In short, the relationship that the child experiences itself will affect the range and style of relationship that it is capable of forming with other people later in life (see below). The key piece in the jigsaw is the way in which the child learns through its relationship with its parents to perceive itself.

A third style of parental relationship with the child, the authoritative style, has been shown to be the most successful in respect of its immediate task of inducing proper, suitable behaviour and also in respect of the long-term goal of helping the child develop into an adult capable of establishing good relationships with other adults. In the authoritative parental style, the parent relies on reason and consistency rather than taking each instance as it comes. The child is not consulted, as by permissive parents, but is given firm guidance on the principles that are being used in a given case to exercise control. The general style is caring and supportive rather than indulgent, and this generally promotes a high self-esteem along with good reasoning ability, responsibility and independence in relationships with other people.

As with all other relationships, the good and the bad relationships of parents with children have characteristically different patterns of activity and of communication. Poor parental relationships with children are characterized by an accent on the negative; that is, they tend to focus on failure, to be critical and punitive, and to ignore or underplay the child's successes. A second feature of such relationships is that the parents are very poor observers of the child's behaviour: they do not notice or attend to differences in the child's activities from day to day, and do not recognize such crucial differences as 'failure through not trying' and 'failure despite trying hard'. Consequently they tend to be inconsistent in their use of punishment; in particular, they issue many threats, but do not carry them out. Most important of all, poor parental relationships with children are those where parents are very rarely warm or positive about the children or the children's efforts (Burgess, 1981). This tends to create low self-esteem in the children and to make it difficult for people to motivate them to do things, except by coercion and threat. The children are used to being driven from behind by stick and strap, rather than encouraged from the front by carrot and reward.

In some of the most recent and very exciting work in the relationship field, Hazan and Shaver (1987) have shown that childhood experiences of relationships to parents ('attachment') have strong parallels with the kinds of attachment that persons form as adults – the implication, of course, being that attachment to parents sets the frame for the person's subsequent relationships throughout life. They identify three types of attachment style:

1. *Secure attachment,* based on the fact that the parental caregiver was readily available, attentive and responsive to the child's needs. Secure adults are comfortable in and about relationships.

2. *Anxious/ambivalent,* based on the fact that the caregiver was anxious, fussy, out of step with the infant's needs and so available/responsive only some of the time. Anxious/ambivalent adults are insecure in relationships and find it hard to trust others.
3. *Avoidant,* where the caregiver was unresponsive or rejecting and inattentive. Avoidant adults tend to avoid relationships, immerse themselves in work, and so on.

Most people reflect on these and can readily classify themselves and their partners. However, not so fast! Bartholomew (1990) has recently distinguished two sorts of avoidant style: a *fearful* style, where the person desires contact but is afraid of it, and of commitment and its consequences; and a *dismissing* style, where the person defensively denies the need or the desire for greater social contact. The fearful people see themselves as essentially undeserving of other people's love and affection, while the dismissive people have a positive view of themselves and play down any distress or social needs that they may have.

As more work on this matter builds up, it certainly begins to look as if the parallels between childhood attachment and adult love are rather remarkable, so that you might feel compelled to admit that one may cause the other. A word of caution, though, is derived from the work of Beinstein Miller (1989), which shows that people who deal badly with conflict as adults tend to remember their childhood negatively and recall their relationships with other children as rejecting and unhappy. This raises a chicken-and-egg problem. Does poor childhood attachment make people have poor relationships as adults, or do people with poor adult relationships tend also, for whatever reason, to recall their childhood negatively? Chapter 5 assumes the first of these, but the second is also possible. Indeed, Alfred Adler believed that a person's view of the world was formed by the age of six, and from that time, he thought, our experiences of the world are seen through the frames that we have created: we remember events that fit the frame.

The empty nest
Clearly, a major change in a family's structure and general styles of activity will follow when the children grow up a little

and go to school or finally become independent adults and leave home. In reporting work on the problems experienced by parents when their first child goes to school, Anderson (1985) found that mothers (and, to a lesser extent, fathers) have a bad time for the first month or so that their child goes to school, but then rapidly adapt. It makes the parents feel bad as parents, but (for the mothers) also affects their happiness as spouses. One unwitting consequence, though, is that the *parents'* friendship circles gently expand, as they meet and get to know the parents of children that become friends of their children at school. Actually this has beneficial effects for the child also. Homel *et al.* (1987) show that the involvement of parents in active social networks is related to the child's happiness, social skills and school adjustment. If the parent has a range of dependable friends, the *child* gets happier, more secure and better adjusted – possibly from having a good model to observe.

By contrast, when the children leave school, not only do the parental couple lose the amount of contact that they are used to having with their child, but they have to cope with other incidental consequences. For example, contact with neighbours decreases, particularly with relatively distant neighbours. This seems to be due to the fact that the children and the children's friends serve an important function in linking neighbours together. People who would not normally meet are brought together by the common tasks of childrearing and the common concerns that parents have about discipline, education and employment. Once the children remove this social linchpin, the neighbourly relationships drift apart. This effect on relationship patterns is balanced for many people by a sharp increase in their involvement with club and social activities in middle age. In the years leading up to retirement, people often go through a period of marked expansion of their social activity before retirement, while old age brings about a steady reduction in such activity. It may be partly in preparation for retirement and in response to a feeling of still having much left to give to other people, and partly as a response to the loneliness brought about by the reduction in social activity once children leave home. Since children obviously satisfy many of

121

the relationship needs that parents have, their absence makes the need more acute and the parents set about satisfying them in other relationships. They do this by undertaking different sorts of interest, task and activity, such as taking up painting or joining groups of other adults with similar hobbies.

Another major adjustment that the couple must make to the empty nest is getting used to being alone together once again, and to having only themselves for company in the home. This is another example of all the points made earlier. It is an adjustment to changes in the patterns of behaviour and of communication, rather than to feelings about one another. Yet changes in their feelings are often a direct consequence, and those couples who adjust by spending more of their time actively as 'relationship time' rather than task time, or, worse, just letting it pass unconstructively as wasted time, will be most successful in effecting the adaptations. As with all of the other examples given in this chapter, such adaptive adjustments are important ways of changing relationships, or of coping with change. However, they are also fundamental to the maintenance and sustenance of satisfying relationships, to which I now turn.

Maintaining satisfying relationships
In the earlier sections in this chapter and in Chapter 3 I have focused on the ways in which a relationship is helped to grow, and on the ways in which growth and change have to be shown and represented through the actions of the partners. This is an important feature of the creation of any relationship, for if it does not develop, then the relationship will probably perish. However, once any relationship has reached a level of intimacy that satisfies the two partners, they have to maintain it at that level, keep it in trim and work to ensure that it stays satisfactory for them both. Many relationships perish through the fact that the partners are careless in maintaining it or nourishing it once it has grown to fullness.

In any discussion of maintenance of relationships, it is particularly difficult to specify the behaviours that are necessary in order to keep the relationship going. There are, however, a number of specific strategies that people claim to use effectively to maintain their relationships and there is one overall manner of conducting them that seems to have important effects. Let me take the specific strategies first and then go on to the general style.

Dindia and Baxter (1987) examined the strategies used by married couples to keep their relationship going, and the tactics used to repair the relationship when it got into trouble. Some strategies were as simple as a regular call to one another at lunchtime, or a two-hour period set aside just to talk on a Sunday. There were five sorts of strategy that were particularly important. These were:

1. *Communicative strategies*, such as taking time to talk to one another about 'my day/your day', and sharing feelings and concerns in an open and honest way.
2. *Metacommunication*, or talking about the way to handle a problem, focusing not on the problem itself but on the way they were to deal with it. This is sometimes referred to as 'talk about talk'.
3. *Prosocial strategies*, such as being especially nice, cheerful and warm, and refraining from criticism of the other person.
4. *Ceremonies*, or warm reminiscing about old times, that commemorate, celebrate and help partners enjoy the formation and existence of the relationship.
5. *Togetherness*, or spending time together, doing shared activity, which becomes fun just because it is done together.

Other research has identified a general style, an approach or orientation that is most effective in keeping relationships going (Walster *et al.*, 1978). Essentially, it is based on fairness rather than on the benefits or rewards that a particular person gets out of the relationship. In maintaining relationships, people have a very strong preference for things to be fair, rather than wanting to exploit and get out of them all that they can. When a relationship is not fair for both partners, it hits the rocks extremely hard and the partners employ various correction devices that this section will describe. Investigators have found a resistance on some people's part to thinking of close relationships in terms of fairness, because of a feeling that it is not possible to measure what happens in intimate contexts (Hatfield and Traupmann, 1981). If no measurements can be taken, then it is not possible to evaluate whether everything is balanced, fair and even. However, many people feel that they are able to measure something about their relationships: they can, for instance, form some idea of whether their partner seems to love them as much as they love their partner. People can also tell when they are being let down, poorly treated, ignored, over-indulged, allowed to get away with blue murder, and so on. These vague feelings are all imprecise ways of evaluating the relationship, and the fact that we have the words to describe such evaluations tells us something about the fact that the feelings are very real for the people involved, even if they are not mathematically precise or scientifically valid. People feel as if they can measure fairness in a relationship, and what truly counts to them is precisely the fact that they do or do not feel that they are getting a fair deal. So we should look at fairness in terms of what people think they and their partner are getting out of the relationship. Successful relationships will be sustained when each person ensures that his or her partner feels fairly treated.

We have already come across the idea that the type of relationship and its success are partly defined by the resources that are exchanged in it: by what the partners do for one another and whether they do it for love or money, out of duty, or because they have been promised some attractive service in return. Examples of resources were given earlier as compliments, gifts, advice, services, money, help, and so on. We have also considered the idea that exchanges have usually to be balanced out if they are to survive, but that as the relationship develops and gets closer, so people extend their timespan. They do not expect to receive an exactly equivalent reward immediately in exchange for one that they give. Instead, as the relationship grows, they are more and more prepared to accept longer delays for exchange, different types of 'repayment', and so on. Whereas beginning acquaintances are very attentive to reciprocity, and expect equal repayment fairly soon, this desire diminishes further the stronger the relationship gets (Hatfield and Traupmann,

1981). Indeed, one sign that the relationship is growing well is when the partners notice that they do not feel pressured or obliged to reciprocate every reward or every disclosure that their partner gives.

While this is increasingly true in developing relationships, people still do have a notion of fairness in the long term. We all know that we give up on relationships where we have to do all the work to keep them going, or where friends rarely help us but expect help whenever they themselves need it, and so on. Yet in long-term relationships we are also prepared to extend a kind of social unsecured loan, and to do things for friends, spouses or family that we would expect to be repaid at any time in the distant future, or by some means other than exact reciprocity.

Nevertheless, once the fairness of a relationship starts to feel out of balance, the partners soon revert to focusing on the exchange more closely, and most lovers' tiffs or friends' quarrels are caused by their feeling that the balance is extremely unevenly set. A homely example of such occurrences is provided by statements like 'You haven't noticed that I've been cooking four or five nights a week for the last month – when are you going to get back to doing your half?'

After much debate, researchers like Walster *et al.* (1978) have decided that although there are many sorts of fairness, there is only one that really counts in maintaining relationships satisfactorily: equity. Equity is a particular sort of fairness, as the following example makes clear. If I have £500 to share out fairly between four people who worked on a job, I could give everyone the same amount. Researchers call this *parity.* Or I could give most to the person with the greatest need for the money, and least to the one who was already well-off. Researchers refer to this as *Marxist justice.* Or I could give most to the person who worked the hardest and least to the person who did the least. This is *equity,* and researchers have assumed that people will be happy with their relationships when they feel that their rewards are equitable with their efforts. If they have to put up with a lot in a relationship (e.g., if they have a friend who has very severe changes in mood, has a quick temper and is often irritable), then the amount of love, help, advice or entertainment that they receive from the person will also have to be considerable.

Because there are two people in a relationship, there is an extra factor to take into account in working out what is equitable: namely, what is the general outcome received from the relationship by the person's partner and how it matches up to the person's own outcomes. If a person feels that the partner is getting exactly the same outcome and rewards from the relationship, but is doing less or putting up with less in order to get them, then the person will feel that the relationship is inequitable, even if the rewards are exactly the same. Equally, even if I have to put in an awful lot of effort for very small reward (e.g., nursing a sick friend) I may nevertheless feel that the relationship is equitable because the friend has to suffer so much more to receive the perhaps slightly greater rewards. In this case our rewards may not be equal, but neither are the costs and efforts, and we shall both still feel that the relationship is an equitable one that we wish to preserve.

It should be clear that both the costs and the rewards in relationships can be either psychological or physical. Psychological costs might be things like humiliation and insult; examples of physical ones would be effort, loss of money, and violence. Psychological rewards could be compliments, love and respect; and physical ones might be help in mending a car, or the gift of a book. In considering the equity or inequity of friendships, people will consider both psychological and physical rewards and costs. They can decide that their relationship is equitable, or that they are over-benefited (i.e., receive more than they should) or under-benefited (i.e., receive less than they should).

Just as the rewards and costs can be psychological or actual ones, so can people's responses to inequity (Hatfield and Traupmann, 1981). That is, people may decide to respond to inequity either by actually doing something about it, or by adjusting their psychological attitude to it. For instance, in the last two cases they will be unhappy (guilty when over-benefited, angry when under-benefited) and will try to do something about it, either by leaving the relationship, or by talking to their partner and working to change the relationship, or else by just altering their opinion or evaluation of it

('I have to put up with a lot, but where am I going to find someone who knows so much about my pet love – German medieval history?').

We are probably used to hearing about under-benefit as a cause of bad feelings about a relationship and consequent unhappiness with maintaining it, but over-benefit can have the same negative effects (Walster *et al.*, 1978). For example, where people are showered with goods and attention beyond the capacity to respond, or far beyond what they feel they reasonably deserve, then they may feel so guilty or so uneasy and awkward that they want to withdraw from the relationship either physically (e.g., by leaving) or psychologically (e.g., by treating the other person extremely casually and patronizingly, as if they didn't really care). So generosity and kindness can actually make people want to leave a friendship rather than stay in it, and pairs of friends or loving partners need to achieve equity rather than excessive loving and kindness by one partner alone.

Difficulties, problems or ineptness in conducting relationships equitably can thus lead to the disruption or even the dissolution of the relationship. The practical implications of this are that individuals need to assess the equity of their relationships from time to time, while still recognizing that strict equality of exchange is the mark of a beginning relationship rather than a fully fledged and well-developed one. Since equity means taking account of one's partner's outcomes as well as one's own, this is naturally a good practice anyway, since it involves focusing on the general state of the relationship rather than just on one's own wishes, desires, rewards and efforts. In maintaining relationships, equity is an important factor, therefore. However, there are several other features of maintaining relationships, and these must also be handled with tact and skill – particularly conflict, arguments and tensions.

Conflicts and tensions naturally arise in every sort of relationship from time to time, but recent research suggests that, far from being the destructive force that most of us would predict, conflict can actually help maintain or even develop a relationship if it is managed right. Presumably a conflict that can be resolved actually focuses the two partners on the instability of their relationship, but also upon the benefit that would be lost if the relationship were to die (Lloyd and Cate, 1985). Resolution of the conflict reaffirms the partners' faith in each other, as well as stressing that they have chosen to avoid the consequences of breaking up.

Conflict has been shown to increase quite sharply from the period of 'casual dating' to the establishment of the relationship as 'serious dating'. From then on it levels off, but it is interesting that conflict is growing at the very time when the relationship is growing too. The reason seems to be that there are different sorts of conflict. Beneficial conflict concerns roles in the relationships – the 'who does what' issues. By resolving such matters, the couple can put itself on a much better road to relational success (Lloyd and Cate, 1985). Destructive conflict is simple argument and vituperation. The more of this in a forming relationship, the less likely the relationship is to survive. Canary and Cupach (1988) show that even in such cases the manner of handling conflict is important. Couples who use 'integrative tactics' will produce eventual satisfaction, and couples who use 'distributive tactics' will cause rancour. *Integrative tactics* are such things as looking for areas of common ground rather than focusing on the points of disagreement, expressing trust and liking for the other person even in this moment of crisis, and looking out for the interests of both parties rather than oneself alone. *Distributive tactics* entail competitiveness, the attempt to impose one's own goals on others, and the use of threats, sarcasm and shouting. Even if you win the argument using distributive tactics, you will probably lose the relationship in the end.

A tendency to avoid conflict can be equally destructive if it prevents a couple from dealing with the issue that causes the concern. Effective ways of coping with conflict have been found to be strategies like openly communicating about the distress that is felt as well as about the cause itself, and explaining carefully to the partner at each step the consequences that particular actions have had for one's own feelings (Kaplan, 1976). Willingness to disclose one's feelings is very strongly related to successful marriage and, conversely, there is much more likely to be disruption in a marriage where there is very little mutual sharing of feelings. The same is true of organizational conflict between managers and personnel, between teachers and pupils, and between colleagues at work. Open but controlled expression of feelings about a source of conflict makes it possible for partners to treat the task of healing the rift as a personal, relationship-oriented task, while also allowing each person to rid himself or herself of pent-up resentments. More important, it prevents them from adopting the covert type of conflict that means openly avoiding discussion of some key problem ('ostrich activity') or simply acting as if it does not exist and cannot be discussed ('repressive handling'). The worst form, however, is the 'empty relationship' style where partners speak in an exaggeratedly affectionate way, but deliberately act in ways that show contempt, disdain or irritation (Hagestad and Smyer, 1982).

It is important to note, however, that not all inability to deal with conflict comes solely from efforts to avoid it. Sometimes, as we might expect after reading Chapters 2 and 3, it stems from differences in the partners' beliefs about what is happening, and in their skills at dealing with one another. Acitelli (1987) has shown that husbands typically do not comment on their relationship when they think that it is going well. Instead they feel that talk about the marriage is probably a sign that things are going badly. Husbands, then, see talk about the relationship as a response to a need. By contrast, women's feelings of competence in the relationship are enhanced by talking about the relationship, particularly since women do in fact seem to handle relationships better than men. So wives like to talk about the relationship for its own sake, to 'celebrate' the relationship and enjoy its existence. Thus the two sexes probably approach talk about the relationship in different ways and appreciate its significance differently.

Above and beyond that, Noller and Venardos (1986) demonstrated that couples who were not well adjusted typically did not understand one another's differences in communication very well. They tended to be very confident that they understood one another, when actually they were interpreting the spouse's messages quite differently from the ways they were intended. In other words, unhappy and poorly adjusted couples do not understand one another but do not realize that they do not. Husbands in poorly adjusted relationships are especially bad at this task, and persist in the problem because they obviously see no problem that needs to be solved.

Although the problems of husbands and wives are important and can sometimes be solved by attention to the nonverbal cues that each presents to the other, it is also important to note that husbands are often fathers and wives are often mothers also. The children of those marriages that are poorly adjusted have poor models on which to base their learning about relationships. Since I have already shown here that there is a link between a person's childhood relationships with parents and the subsequent adult ones, we need to know now what else can go wrong with relationships as the child grows up. In order to get a proper run at the issues of breakdown and repair of relationships, I shall consider children's friendships in Chapter 5, since childhood lays the foundations not only for good relationships but also for bad ones.

5

Roots: children's friendships

In the previous chapters I have been stressing that satisfying adult relationships have to be created through behaviour, and that this requires many different skills and abilities. While I have also noted the differences between people's capacities to carry out the necessary skills, I have not yet considered where these differences may arise. The answer, of course, is that they originate in childhood, where the foundations of all adult relationships are laid. Dunn (1988, page 208) concludes that 'early childhood relationships are associated with the quality of later relationships in adolescence and adulthood.'

It is in relationships with parents that the learning begins (see Chapter 4), but relationships with other children continue to provide opportunities for learning. Indeed, these so-called 'peer relationships' offer vital chances for a child to learn about a wider variety of social experiences than those parents can offer (Ladd, 1989). For example, a child learns about cooperating with equals by doing just that, and parents cannot teach it in a vacuum. More than this, peer relationships offer a staging area for a child to develop a sense of its own competence as well as to learn such skills. Not only is childhood a place to learn fundamental skills of competency, it is the main area where basic social skills, including the management of conflict, can be developed (Ladd, 1989). Against this background, the child also develops its sense of security and support, as well as learning, from its interactions with peers, many lessons that feed in to the child's eventual development of a self-concept and beliefs about its own abilities.

It is in childhood and adolescence that the child begins to acquire an important *range* of friendship skills and that these are first practised and developed. Each skill has to be picked up and polished, not only as an essential ingredient of later friendship abilities but also at a time that is right and useful for the child's conduct of its own relationships with its peers. There are thus two problems for the child: first, learning to relate in a way acceptable to its peers at the time; second, learning the skills of friendship that will be a good grounding for relationships in later life.

Childhood relationships are, of course, important throughout the whole time of childhood, and they can exert strong influences on the development of character and personality, as is well known. It is perhaps less well known that childhood relationships affect educational achievement, and there are some researchers who believe that intelligence itself can be affected (Asher and Gottman, 1981). The relationships in childhood can affect a child's understanding of complex problems and influence the development of its comprehension of relationships between objects, between concepts and between people, as well as having a predictable effect on the child's happiness. For example, unpopular children perform poorly at school, experience learning difficulties and drop out of school in much greater numbers than their popular peers (Putallaz and Gottman, 1981).

The most significant aspect of relationships in childhood, however, is the fact that they clearly shape adult relationships and the child's ultimate willingness to engage in them. In childhood, some children experience such difficulties with relationships, or are so unpopular, that the consequent resentment makes them generally hostile and resistant to intimacy, or else hopelessly dependent and over-sensitive. These effects can be very far-reaching and are only just being fully realized (Ginsberg *et al.*, 1986; Berndt and Ladd, 1989). Unpopular children are more likely to become juvenile delinquents, to be disgracefully discharged from the armed services, to have higher rates of emotional and mental health problems in adulthood, and to be at higher risk of schizophrenia, neurosis and psychosis (see Putallaz and Gottman, 1981).

It is also quite clear from the depressingly small amounts of research work that are funded to investigate children's friendships that the socially withdrawn, socially incompetent and aggressive child soon becomes the socially inept adult social casualty (Ginsberg *et al.*, 1986). Conventional wisdom, via the media, tells us that the most famous mass murderers of almost every country (e.g., Christie, the Black Panther, Blue Beard, the Michigan Murderer, the Boston Strangler, the Stockton Schoolyard Rifleman, and others) have invariably been found to have had abnormal social experiences in childhood. The media portray them as having been left without adult help or guidance when they ran into difficulties with their peers, whether the people in the same school classes, same age cohort or same playgroups. They are usually depicted as loners, quiet, withdrawn and unsociable people, often dominated by selfish parents or hounded by thoughtless classmates. The implication seems to be that if friend-making had been properly learned – or if they had been helped to learn it – their violent, destructive and unusual personalities might have turned out in a more rewarding and acceptable form, although the present state of support for research on these issues does not keep step with conventional wisdom.

The drama of this picture may have been a little overstated, but the broad brush strokes of the claims are borne out by many different studies (reviewed in Ginsberg *et al.*, 1986). More important, though individually less dramatic, is the fact that the personalities of large numbers of people which go wrong in only minor ways do so from similar causes and roots, and I shall have them in mind for the rest of the chapter.

The extent of this problem has not previously been fully appreciated because the consequences of poor relations in childhood are hidden, and are only just beginning to be brought clearly and obviously into the light. Research on these issues has been a long time coming, but there are now several important research programmes and books on them. Even things like truancy and delinquency are still often viewed as problems in their own right rather than as possible consequences of inability to form proper friendships at school. Yet research in prisons for the especially dangerous and the criminally insane has shown that many violent offenders have developed peculiar and abnormal ideas about friendship. For example, they often show attitudes that are characteristic of retarded or arrested social and relational development (Howells, 1981). Moreover, British and American work on alcoholics casts up, time and time again, cases of adults who turn to excessive drinking because their relationships are not satisfactory, and as children they have not learned to put them right (Orford and O'Reilly, 1981).

It is necessary at the outset, therefore, to stress that there exist many forms of the bad results of poor childhood relationships. Unpopularity can be created by such oddities as an uncommon first name, unattractive physical appearance or atypical racial origin; while factors such as classroom size, organization of desks, cloakrooms and teaching materials, and the personality of the teacher can also be influential in children's friendship patterns (Asher and Parker, 1989). Nevertheless, far and away the most important influence is the faulty learning that the child does about friendship or the negative experiences that they have with their peers.

Learning to make friends – and *how* to make friends – is something that everyone has to do in the early years in the family, at play and at school (Schneider *et al.*, 1989). Friend-making ability is *absolutely not* instinctive or genetically programmed, nor is it something that is inherited. Rather, it is something that comes about through, and in the social experiences of, childhood and adolescence. It is something that has to be acquired, learned carefully and practised.

This raises the interesting question of why it is all treated so casually by society and politicians. We all believe that it is absurd to expect children and adolescents to develop academic or intellectual knowledge without help and guidance, but when it comes to something equally important – the ability to get on with other people – we leave them to do it on their own. Despite the fact that it is one of the most important, far-reaching and continuous lessons of children's lives, it is at present a lesson that we leave, irresponsibly in my view, to chance alone. It is a lesson, therefore, in which accident and coincidence have a persistent, uncorrected influence and where they can turn and twist a personality for life. It is a lesson that some people learn well, some grasp with difficulty but eventual success, and some learn so poorly that it afflicts their adult relationship with a virulent social canker. Yet it remains true that with equal consistency governments and educators underfund and ignore the research on children's relationships. At present politicians seem quite happy to allow the seeds of a whole field of later social problems to be fed and watered by inadequate or threatening playground experiences.

The problems result from faulty learning of many different sorts of friendship skills. For instance, a child has to feel and express intimacy, respect others' rights, cooperate, keep and share secrets, manage disputes, aid others, gain inclusion into others' activities and play, and become accepted by peers. Children need to develop the ability to share, to think of things from the other person's point of view and to develop critical skills in the choice of friends. They also learn, from peers, the ways to *really* get by in school, the art of insults, the sorts of pranks that are fun for everyone, the kinds of mischief that are enjoyable and not too harshly punished. In short, they learn from peers where lines can and should be drawn (Asher and Parker, 1989). Also, of course, later in life they begin to learn about sex from peers.

Friendship involves, as we have seen, a reasonable level of self-esteem, an understanding of the meaning of fairness and cooperation, ability to use and comprehend nonverbal behaviour, recognition of the activities that suit a particular level and style of relationship, trust, intimacy, self-disclosure and an ability to reciprocate – and that is an incomplete list. To some extent children pick these items up separately, practise them, consolidate them and go on to the next one, since many new intellectual abilities are developed along the way and they promote new curiosity as well as new social abilities. Failure to pick up one element may, however, create problems in moving on to the next one, or may 'throw' the whole process of learning.

Nevertheless, in general terms, children learn four types of skill from all of this (S.W. Duck, 1989):

1. *Social skills,* such as were covered in Chapter 2.
2. *Interpersonal competence,* or the way to handle other people without disruptive conflict.
3. *Communication competence,* or the ability to communicate skilfully and persuasively.
4. *Relational competence,* or the ability, specifically within close relationship contexts, to handle themselves skilfully when dealing with such things as intimacy, privacy and trust.

What, then, do children need to learn from and about friendship at different ages? How does it shape their view of themselves, their comprehension of life, and their future relationships? In addressing such questions I shall pay particular attention to the research that has identified effective training or correctional strategies for cases where things are going wrong.

THE CHILD'S FRIENDSHIP WORLD

The term 'childhood' covers a considerable span of years. Much that can be said of its beginning will not still be true of its ending in adolescence, and friendship is a good example. Many aspects of friendship change during childhood, both in terms of children's thinking about friendship and in terms of their behaviour with and to their friends as they grow more mature. One item which is consistently being shaped and moulded in early childhood is the child's view of itself (self-image) and of its value or acceptability to other people (self-acceptance).

Psychiatric theorists have often noted that people who cannot accept themselves cannot accept others; in other words, people with a poor self-image or low self-acceptance will tend to be hostile or rejecting towards other people (A. Adler, 1929). They are nervous of entering close relationships in adulthood, and are mercurially unstable or unpredictable when they feel that they are becoming vulnerable. For example, when their relationships become intimate they may become irrationally agitated and even violent (Howells, 1981). Such people find adult relationships difficult, unpredictable and explosive. Since they cannot handle intimacy easily, they also find it hard to enter friendships, or react wildly and oddly when later 'cornered' into intimacy. Most normal, but untrained, outsiders will not understand why such a person acts this way, and will not be able to give the encouragement that is needed – which makes matters worse.

It seems clear that the parent who devotes energy to creating in the very young child a favourable self-image is doing that child at least as much good as a parent who devotes time to teaching the child to read at an early age. There are, after all, several types of social advantage. Good education is only one of them; good social relationships are another. For this reason a wise parent will draw the child's attention to its competences, growths of learning, increasing capacities and skills in a way that makes it aware of its ability to cope in a variety of situations. Such assistance need not be uncritical, but should stress the successes more than the failures. It will give advice, guidance and the rewards of attention once the child attempts new or difficult tasks, whether these be physical, intellectual or social. Encouraging the child to notice its successful interactions with adults and with other children is a useful way of protecting and improving its self-image, thus increasing self-esteem.

Edwards and Middleton (1988) have shown some very subtle ways in which this is done in normal family life. They studied the ways in which mothers looked through photograph albums with their children and found that this seemingly trivial and insignificant act actually has some important consequences for the child. The conversation that arose during the browsing often focused on the child's sense of belonging to a secure family, as well as helping to locate the child in the family biography. Relationships to other people were often dwelt on and so were aspects of the child's history and identity. Pictures are often worth a good deal in helping the child to get a sense of itself.

While the child's sense of self-acceptance most probably originates in the very first years of interacting with parents, there is considerable scientific controversy over the question of whether such effects can be reversed or undone (La Gaipa, 1981). Once the child goes to school, for instance, it encounters a whole new range of people and new situations which it may find so different from home that it shows a completely different range of responses – perhaps more confident ones. On the other hand, however, it is necessary for children to learn some basic social skills before they go to school, where they have to meet and befriend other children on their own initiative rather than at their parents' prompting (Kafer, 1981). If for some reason, such as low self-esteem, the child has not yet learned the appropriate skills for friendly behaviour with other children, then school probably just exposes the child to a wider range of social learning experiences that end in failure. A lot depends on how the child responds to the inevitable rejections that all children receive. Children with high self-esteem are better prepared to let rejection just wash over them, and try again. Others with low self-esteem tend to withdraw, make fewer and fewer attempts to initiate other friendships, and so become isolated. On the other hand, another ineffective strategy is to become noisy, rebellious, boastful and, ultimately, a nuisance to teachers and classmates: this attempt to attract notice also leads to isolation.

The first unsuccessful strategy for dealing with rejection, then, leads to hesitancy in starting off friendships and to lack of interest in gaining acceptance by other children. The second is simply an incompetent way of attempting to gain acceptance. In their own way each of them protects the child from further problems of rejection. Kafer's (1981) research shows that the first kind of strategy protects the child from encountering rejection: it simply enables the child to avoid rejection because it avoids both the situations where rejection can be expressed, and the people who will express it. The second strategy is more subtly based. Investigators believe that the incompetent attention-seekers are actually less perceptive, and that they constantly misinterpret other people's behaviour so that they do not see rejection as rejection. It is as if they come to live in a fantasy world where they misperceive a slap in the face as a subtle kind of welcome. This is less painful for them than it would be to recognize that they are truly being rejected.

Such defensive strategies are complex ways for the child to protect itself from having to recognize that it is really disliked. They are psychological defences against a feeling of inadequacy. In some sophisticated psychological way, the defences help the child to compensate for the fact that it fears dislike and rejection, or feels inadequate in social settings. The child therefore protects and defends itself by coming to avoid situations that would confirm its inadequacy, or else by coming to misperceive such confirmation when it occurs. The root cause of both of these strategic twists of psychological development lies in self-esteem. A child who acquires a low self-esteem and low self-acceptance will be an incompetent relater, will be poor and inadequate in its relationships with other people, and will need to develop such defensive strategies for coping with rejection.

The child's self-esteem level is set on track very early, and perhaps responds predominantly to the influence of parents and family. The parents' beliefs, especially the mother's beliefs, about friendship are important in shaping the child's social life. Rubin *et al.* (1989) show that mothers' beliefs play an important role in the mothers' efforts to teach their children to be sociable and also in the ways in which they respond when the child has problems with relationships. If the mother thinks that friendship ought 'just to happen', then she will not direct the child towards good friendship experiences; if she thinks that the child needs help (or if she has read this book!), then she will encourage, support and provide opportunities for the child to learn about friendship and to develop the right skills.

After such influences wane as the child gets into the social world of school, much of its other detailed learning about relationships is derived from social experiences with friends, peers or other children. It is, after all, such people that the child spends most time with throughout the decade-and-a-half of growing maturity, and it is a peer who will eventually become its romantic partner. If the early relationships with parents sour or spoil the basis on which such relationships will be formed, considerable efforts may be necessary to correct the child's behaviour in play with other young children.

However, its behaviour reflects its internal beliefs: people behave in particular ways because they believe that they are effective or appropriate ways to act, or that they serve some deep, possibly unconscious, purpose. If these internal beliefs are wrong or twisted by reactions to some horrible experience, then the behaviour will be wrong or twisted in consequence. Accordingly, the proper place to direct corrective energy is towards the beliefs that make the child do what it does; towards the expectations that it has about friendship; towards the concepts and notions that it has concerning cooperation and friendliness. A useful addition to such work is the coaching of disturbed or incompetent children in the other behavioural skills of friendship. I shall look at these ideas in turn.

When children begin to play with one another they are usually under the supervision of an adult, and their activities are to a very large extent restricted, constrained and determined by that fact. Once they get old enough to be independent initiators of play (when they can independently form and carry out desires to go round and play with neighbours' children, for example), their actions in friendship also change. Of course, their desires for friendship and social contact will be shaped to a large extent by their level of self-esteem, but assuming that they do seek friendship, then their behaviour and beliefs change in characteristic ways.

Very young children are not naturally social and, as parents of toddlers (say of 18 months) will know, two such children do not so much play with one another as play in each other's presence. They do not cooperate; they do not share things, act together or play jointly. However, they do prefer to be with another child rather than be left alone, and gradually they come to act cooperatively, to acknowledge each other and to enter into the wonderful world of joint fantasy and shared imagination that 4-year-olds can enjoy.

If children in the first stages of development desire friendships with other children and are capable of creating them, friends are defined by their proximity (La Gaipa, 1981). That is, a friend is someone who lives nearby or who is met fairly frequently. (Even later in school careers, proximity has a powerful effect in children's friendship choice, and teachers may not always be aware that by rearranging classroom seating they may be tacitly interfering with the children's social structure.) A friend is a momentary playmate, is valued for its possessions, toys or physical characteristics and is assumed to think in exactly the same way as the child itself or to enjoy exactly the same activities. At a later stage (from about 4 years) children get better at differentiating their own viewpoint from that of their friend, but they do not yet recognize the necessity of give-and-take in relationships (La Gaipa, 1981). The friend is valued and appreciated for what he or she can do for the individual. It is not until about the age of 6 that the child begins to understand that cooperation, reciprocity or 'turn-and-turn-about' are important for friendship. Nevertheless, children still see their own self-interest as being most important in the friendship, and are not truly or genuinely concerned about mutual interests or the friend's needs.

From about the age of 9 the child begins to shift towards a more objective and less self-centred view (La Gaipa, 1981). Friendship is seen as collaboration with other people in the furtherance of mutual common goals or interests. However, the research also shows that children of this age regard friendship as a possessive and exclusive relationship, which means that a 'best friend' cannot really have other friendships too and still remain a best friend. The final stage of recognizing the friend's autonomy and rights to other relationships does not truly come until about the age of 12 (La Gaipa, 1981). A 12-year-old comes to respect the fact that one person cannot fulfil all of his or her personal and psychological needs in one exclusive relationship, and that independence is not only acceptable but desirable.

Thus the child's understanding of the purposes of friendship is one that develops dramatically and changes fundamentally during the growth toward maturity. One thing that the research makes clear is that essential learning about friendship concepts can be as haphazard as it is far-reaching in its personal significance to the child (Asher and Parker, 1989). Just as there are children who are intellectually advantaged in any schoolroom, so there are some who are relatively advanced in their understanding of friendship –

and equally, some who would benefit from greater attention and help with the social learning that they need to complete. As yet, this important feature of their development is left in the lap of the playground gods, despite the fact that it will ultimately affect the child's friendships and social behaviour in ways that may outweigh other intellectual changes and developments.

The point here is that the child's understanding of social action changes and develops, from one where other children are simply responsive objects in their social world, to one where joint activity can be enjoyed. At early ages an interest in joint activities permits children to explore the world more effectively. Such activities also start to give children someone to measure themselves against, and with whom to form impressions of the limits of their own abilities and capacities. That is, they help to develop further and clarify the detail of their level of self-esteem, whether high or low. There is not much point in parents trying to encourage very young toddlers to be sociable: they simply do not properly understand what is meant by 'sharing' or by 'playing with' another toddler. However, placing them in situations where they have access to other children can increase their social potential, although not by much. The early stages are ones where self-esteem is a better focus of parental attention. In other respects the growth of understanding cannot be forced, and nature has to be allowed to run its course, while the child develops its conception of the meaning of friendship. Such development largely parallels its development in other conceptual areas, like problem-solving and reasoning.

This is not to say that even at nursery school the signs of problems cannot be perceived and dealt with (Manning and Herrmann, 1981). At very young ages, children's difficulties with friendship can be spotted by observant adults and correctional guidance, training or treatment can be started. For example, a problem child is particularly noticed by teachers as one who very rarely initiates a conversation with them, or who quarrels and fights often, fails to cope with opposition from other children in a satisfactory manner and makes overly demanding approaches to other children. Such children are noticeably unhappy or liable to sharp changes in

142

mood. Something more serious actually lies behind this troublesome behaviour. The pattern may mean something as grave as the onset of a clinical or psychiatric disorder, or merely the beginning of a development towards deviancy of some kind. Relationships at nursery preschools in the 3–5-year-old range are thus likely to affect the child's whole future just as much as the relationships with parents do; but they depend on different things and concern different areas of development – particularly, at these ages, developments in beliefs about friendship.

Such developments are quite dramatic (La Gaipa, 1981). Very young children (2–4 years) describe other people and their value as friends in terms of concrete characteristics (e.g., 'Jane is my friend because she lives in a big house'). Later, in early childhood, children use more personalized descriptions (e.g., 'John is my friend because he is tough'), but do not use psychologically evaluative descriptions of the sort familiar to adults (e.g., 'John is a friend because he is a nice, helpful, thoughtful person'). By later childhood (say age 8 years), friends are seen as people who share joint activities, provide help and support against enemies, are able to produce practical assistance and often provide physical benefits. Here is the first time when the admiration of a friend's character begins to feature in children's descriptions of friends. It is only right at the point where childhood turns into adolescence (around 12 years) that friendship notions start to focus on intimate sharing, secrets, private knowledge, trust and loyalty, genuineness and acceptance of the friends, warts and all.

The notion of disliking is also something that undergoes dramatic transformations with age (Gaebler, 1980). At the earliest ages dislike is expressed through behaviour, not through words: rejection and avoidance are the clearest methods. Children of about 5 will be able to express dislike for others, but do not give specific or satisfactory reasons (e.g., 'I dislike him because I do' – a circular definition or, at best, something like 'I dislike her because she's horrid'). At this age, and right up until about 8 years, the reasons that children give for disliking someone are not direct opposites of the reasons that they give for liking someone. They dislike people who fight or are rough, while they like people who give them sweets or play with them. Liking and disliking are not strict logical opposites for 8-year-olds (Asher and Parker, 1989). For this reason a child's likes and dislikes may not be particularly stable until mid- to late childhood, when the concepts begin to 'set' and the child forms a more complete and robust idea of the nature of friendship and its opposite. Once the ideas set – in the period of later childhood and adolescence – the learning that must then be done falls more squarely into the behavioural area rather than that of concepts or beliefs: that is, the young adolescent must start to learn and practise his or her newly acquired ideas about friendship.

All the same, there are several significant changes even in a younger child's behaviour towards other people as the child gets older, and these are so systematic as to amount to a relatively normal pattern, worth spending time considering here. One curiosity that may be important psychologically is that from about 4 up to the age of 10 (and even a bit beyond in most cases), a child's friendship choices and the child's comments about friends and friendship are predominantly in relation to same-sex friends, and in relation to people the same age as itself (La Gaipa, 1981). Before the age of 4 the child has little enough idea of friendship (or of sexual differences if it comes to that: it takes time for them to appreciate that biological sex is a fixture and cannot be changed at a whim or by dressing in the clothes of the other sex). After the age of 10 the problem of creating and managing friendships with the opposite sex begins to be more significant. Of course, during adolescence such problems take up a large percentage of the person's time, although most girls begin to get concerned about them well before most boys do.

So children probably learn most about friendship with same-sex people before the turmoil of adolescence takes them into the market-place of significant relationships with the opposite sex. In the first stages their friendship choices are not particularly stable, and loyalty to a friend is not much prized. Friends are people who do things for you, or give you things like sweets, as far as a 6-year-old is concerned. If someone unexpected does this for you one day, then they are pretty instantly crowned 'a friend', and will as soon lose that crown tomorrow if they do not repeat the performance.

The apparently pointless rough games, quarrels, making up and changes of allegiance are also quite important training grounds for children to do early learning about the management of relationships in general. Smith (1989) has shown that 'rough-and-tumble play' is important in children's learning about social relationships, and, rather like the apparently rough games of young lions or other animals, is more ritualized and less dangerous than it might appear to the adult who has grown old enough to have forgotten what it was like. It is necessary for the child to learn for itself how to handle conflicts (Hartup, 1989), since this ability is in itself influential on the child's social acceptance and rejection by others. Skilful children learn to use 'softer' sorts of conflict style with friends than they use when disagreeing with children who are not friends. Conflict and competition are natural occurrences in the child's world and should not be avoided or prevented. Rather, the child should not only be taught that conflict and competition are an inevitable part of social life, but should be educated in good ways of handling them, such as seeing them as providing an opportunity to bargain rather than a time for war. To bargain with someone is at least to recognize that they have a legitimate point of view, and that can be a valuable exercise in the child's lessons about taking other people's perspectives.

Well-meaning parents, then, are probably ill-advised to keep breaking up fighting children unless danger is imminent. More useful is not the outside influence of an adult, but advice and guidance subsequently about how the child should have handled the disturbance, the importance of considering other people's views, and the desirability of using means other than force to resolve disputes. But such advice must be made appropriate to the age of the child and to the child's development of understanding about friendship. Emphasis on sharing and cooperation will be more clearly understood, and hence more readily accepted, by an 8-year-old than will emphasis on loyalty, trust or the non-violation of confidences.

What else do children learn? As well as concepts relevant to friendship, they are learning, as they grow older, the various activities that are important in the actual conduct of social relationships. What really matters is not simply how a child views friendship, but rather the ability to perform the activities of friendship in a way that is consistent with such views and with the general views held by other children. It is important that they learn what to do, what to say and the value of cooperation, as well as how to quarrel and make up. They must also learn something along the way about their own social assets and their value to other people. They learn how other people characteristically respond to them and this can have an important effect on their view of themselves (their self-image), which can in turn influence their willingness to risk friendly or sociable activity.

Over and above this, the child is learning something about the nature of the social world and how to operate in it while it is increasing in social understanding and interpersonal skills (La Gaipa, 1981). As the understanding and concept of friendship mature, so are children's friendships more stable and persistent, although even at the ages of 10–13 the friendships are still predominantly with same-sex partners. At this time (early adolescence) the child becomes more concerned about the reliability of a friend, the psychological and emotional support that a friend provides and the confidences that are shared. Increasing emphasis is placed on the talking over of problems with friends. As adolescence gets under way, there is a sudden surge of interest in the character, disposition and general psychological make-up of other people. Until adolescence the individual's understanding of motivation is very primitive and there is little grasp of the complex reasons that people have for their actions. People's moods and dispositions are only crudely comprehended, and such things as another person's emotional stability play a very small role in the child's choice of that person as a friend or not.

The research also shows that children who are withdrawn or socially disabled usually also have a distorted view of friendship or else one that is far below what is appropriate for a child of their age (La Gaipa and Wood, 1981). Thus a child of 9 may have a 'friendship age' of 7. It is not surprising that the child then finds it hard to make friends with children its own age and so become socially withdrawn (since there are usually physical and social barriers against befriending children outside their own age group). Such notions of friendship do not seem very clearly related to intelligence, and even bright children can be backward in friendship terms. What seems to matter is the experience and the range of opportunities that they have had to play with other children, perhaps even before they went to school.

When parents or teachers suspect that a child has relational problems – which may come to light in obvious ways through persistent complaints from other children, or in less obvious ways through work problems, refusal to participate in games, or instability of moods and sleep patterns – the first requirement is a diagnosis of the level of the problem. If the child has general problems related to self-esteem then the correct solution to the problems lies in one place, while if they are simply slow to develop appropriate concepts about friendship it lies in another. If, on the other hand, the problem is centred on poor enactment of friendship skills and behaviours then the solution lies in the sorts of social skill training programme and coaching effort that have been successful in the United States, and which are discussed below. However, before such drastic steps are taken, the parents and teachers should ask themselves what they can do to help. In an influential manual published in 1917, Beery urged mothers to create opportunities for the child to get together with other children (e.g., at picnics or barbecues) and to help the child to 'have a royal good time'! As we saw in Chapter 1, this may or may not help if the problem is really caused by deficient abilities to deal with other children in the first place.

The most important but by far the simplest answer is that parents and teachers should pay attention to the child's relationships with other people – with adults as well as with other children. It is important that the child draws useful lessons not only from quarrels but also from satisfactory interchanges. Even with an unproblematic child, the thoughtful parent will always underline the principle that a given inter-change might demonstrate (e.g., the benefits of sharing, the importance of cooperation with friends, the values of loyalty and trust, and so on). To some extent the child will find this unsatisfactory on its own because most of its practical experi-ence will be derived from play with other children when parents are not there to see. However, just as with other sorts of learning and training, the point is to get the child to think for itself in new situations, using the principles that the par-ent or teacher is trying to instil.

Another point must also be made: not all children pro-gress in social knowledge at the same rate. While the child will probably benefit from playing with very slightly older children who are more advanced, this is not necessarily the case. The research shows that children prefer friends who are at their own level of social development (or slightly above) but not usually at a markedly lower level (La Gaipa, 1981). Thus while the less developed 'normal' child may benefit from playing with the more developed child, the discrepancy may be large enough for the more advanced child to become uncomfortable, and so to turn the experi-ence into a negative one for the underdeveloped child. In the case of children with social problems, this pattern can work well in reverse; that is, older children with social prob-lems sometimes benefit from play with younger children (Furman, 1984). It appears to give them experience of leadership and control that they would otherwise not be able to get.

When the manipulation of such contexts for friendship is guided and co-ordinated by experts the effects are often very good. Several programmes in America have been devoted to exploring this particular avenue for social improvement (Berndt and Ladd, 1989; Schneider *et al.*, 1989). In one type of case, problem children or socially retarded children are introduced into carefully composed and structured groups, and that experience itself helps them. In other cases they are carefully observed at play and are then 'debriefed' or talked through the experience by a trained researcher in a way that focuses them on their successes and on the points that they could improve (Asher and Gottman, 1981). Such training in sensitivity to the effects of their own behaviour seems to be particularly effective with children, but requires expert handling. A third method of intervention is to draw up a dictionary or conceptual map of the child's ideas about friendship and to retrain the child where such concepts are found to be inadequately developed (La Gaipa and Wood, 1981). These all work quite well once the child's problem has been correctly assessed.

Other techniques involve cooperative learning, where pairs or groups of children, including at least one with social problems, are encouraged to work together to learn. The hope is that the necessary cooperation will help to bring the normally rejected child back into the group. However, results from such experiments have been inconclusive and the desired cooperation does not always occur (Furman and Gavin, 1989). It may not always happen that *other* children's perceptions of a child with social problems can be ignored or assumed to be easily changed just because the problem child's behaviour is changed by one of the above techniques. Even when re-educated, the rejected children may still be disliked by peers and may never get the chance to *show* their peers that a change really has occurred. For this reason, some very recent techniques now involve the child's peer group as well (Berndt, 1989) and provide opportunities for these other children to witness, accept and respond to the change that has been brought about by the re-education of the 'target child'. Without such social engineering, the re-educated child otherwise simply gets the old responses and treatment that it used to get. Of course, it soon goes back into its shell, with self-esteem lowered again and the improvement programme's benefits largely nullified.

The root problem of childhood unpopularity often is deeply related to self-esteem, and may require psycho-therapeutic intervention in severe cases. In less severe cases, and in any case where the parent wants to avoid future problems, the parents and teachers should help children to obtain or retain a reasonably high self-esteem by pointing out their successes in relationships, and helping to defuse or minimize the effect of negative social experiences. They should also make conscious efforts to encourage the child to

Friends, for Life

think about friendship and to try to ponder its principles. They can help children refrain from aggression and should encourage them to develop positive social contacts in pre-school groups so that when they go to school they are among peers who are familiar. Children need encouragement with their social conceptual development just as much as with aspects of their intellectual development.

Given that researchers place great emphasis on the learning and development of conceptual understanding of friendship, their next most important concern is the behaviour of friendship, particularly the nonverbal behaviour that is involved. There are consistent differences between popular and unpopular children not only in what they know or believe about friendship, but in how they conduct it and bring it to life. Popular children are more inclined (and better able) to initiate play with other children, and presumably they become popular because of this (Asher and Parker, 1989). It just might be vice versa, although other studies suggest that once children are coached in the skills of starting play and friendship, their popularity increases.

There is generally thought to be a parallel between the behaviour of unpopular children and the behaviour of new-comers. That is, newcomers to a school show a particular style of behaviour for a while; unpopular children show it most of the time (Putallaz and Gottman, 1981). For instance, newcomers stare the other children in the face when they play, and so do unpopular children; by contrast, acquaintances and friends look more at what they are playing with, or look around the room. As I indicated in Chapter 2, looking at someone's face (as distinct from gazing at their eyes, specifically) is a usual way of expressing basic friendliness to new acquaintances, though it can be interpreted as hostility or dominance when it turns to a prolonged stare. In this case, it demonstrates the fact that the relationship is an uncertain, starting one.

Unpopular children are constantly signalling to other children that their relationship is an uncertain one, therefore. Unpopular children communicate ambivalence in other ways: they turn their backs on other children more often, they stand still rather than joining in the movements of other children, they 'automanipulate' more – that is, they play with their hair or scratch themselves, for example. All of these behaviours are signs of doubt, insecurity and anxiety, and they are just as noticeable to other children as they are to observant adults (Putallaz and Gottman, 1981).

The most useful diagnostic difference between children who know how to be friends and those who do not is the specific problem known as 'hovering'. In hovering, the child lurks on the edge of a group, shows indecision about entering and joining in, decides to join in too late when the others are moving on to something else, and adopts a pleading, whining style of talking. Hoverers also show lower ability to concentrate, higher rates of daydreaming, and more frequent episodes of staring out into space. Such children are clearly disturbed. Furthermore, the behaviour is typical of some abused children and may indicate that such children 'invite' abuse in this way (perhaps partly explaining why often only one child in a family is abused). It has even been shown in some cases that when such an abused child is removed to a 'safe' foster home, the foster parents may also abuse the child, or request that it be removed because they cannot cope. It is therefore very important to spot the development of hovering and to do something about it. When the child is very young, parents and teachers may feel inclined to do little about it, but this can be an extremely unwise attitude, given the consequences that can follow from poor relationships in early childhood.

The basic problem here is a complicated one and it really lies beyond the layperson or concerned parent to put it right: what must be corrected and improved is the isolated or unpopular child's whole strategy for behaviour in friendship. Their behavioural strategy requires meticulous examination and systematic reconstruction. There are now several programmes for conducting such interactions, and although they are still at the experimental and development stage, success rates are very encouraging (Berndt, 1989). A simple four-week programme is enough to bring about behavioural changes that significantly increase the child's popularity (Asher and Parker, 1989). The programme consists of expert instruction about the initiation of friendly behaviour and entry into a group (e.g., participation, cooperation, helping, proper communication and nonverbal skills), opportunities to practise the skills and strategies in groups, and a review with the coach. The effects are not merely immediate, but also prolonged. In follow-up studies a year later the previously unpopular children were showing continued progress and had retained their newfound popularity, by altering the general style of their behaviour.

Successful entry into a group is certainly a skill that needs practice when it is underdeveloped, but it is not the whole story. The child has to know what to do when it is accepted into the group, and has to adopt an effective strategy for staying in. Unpopular children are often bossy and demanding, disagree more than most with other children and get into argumentative struggles, and talk about themselves much more often (Putallaz and Gottman, 1981). In short, they attempt to force the other children to pay attention to them, to the exclusion of other tasks, games and people. (In this respect they are very like adult bores.) Programmes designed to remove this poor strategy can focus the children on ways of being more rewarding to other children rather than demanding attention from them. In some cases the changes are minute but extremely effective. For instance, unpopular children are very specific in their instructions to other children and give no alternatives, while popular children cite a general rule and then offer alternative ways of fulfilling it. An example of the unpopular style might be 'You can't move your counter now', while the popular child might say 'You can't move your counter until you throw a six.' Although these differences seem extremely small, they actually build into the pattern that causes popularity and unpopularity.

In summary, unpopular children have low self-esteem, more psychological defences against rejection, poorly developed understanding of the meaning of friendship, an immature style of attempting to enter a group, and a poor and unacceptable behavioural strategy for conducting the activities of friendship. However, an emerging view in the recent research (T.F. Adler and Furman, 1988) is that social problems arise not just because of one child's characteristics, but because of problems in the *two* children who make up a pair (or 'dyad', as the researchers call them, from the Greek for 'two'). Some of the problems in children's social relationships come, as it were, from two gears of different sizes trying unsuccessfully to mesh together. The fault does not lie so much in either gear alone as in the fact that the two of them just do not fit one another. Essentially this proposal puts the emphasis on *communication* between two people and the sequences of their behaviour together. This is an interesting approach that will most likely be useful in the future. Since the emphasis falls on communication, it is not really very different from the focus that I have taken here, where the individual's style of communication has been highlighted. However, it does emphasize that it takes two to communicate – and as long as the children as individuals know how to do it, their likelihood of being consistently rejected by everyone is diminished.

The differences between popular and unpopular children are often so seemingly trivial that they can easily be missed, yet they make the difference between success and failure in childhood relationships and, ultimately, as an adult in society.

GROWING FROM CHILDHOOD TO ADOLESCENCE

The social learning and relational education of childhood are predominantly focused on friendships with other children of the same sex. It is only later in development that opposite-sex friendships become acceptable, desirable, important and worth the risks of trying. Up until the age of 12 or so, there is considerable group pressure not to play with (or express liking for) the opposite sex, and it is usually only popular children who risk it until quite late on. Adolescence thus brings not only intellectual, social and sexual changes: it also brings several changes of emphasis in relationships. All of the changes have sweeping consequences for friendship, both in adolescence itself and also in later adulthood, since it is in the turmoil of adolescence that many new inadequacies of friendship can be acquired and stamped in.

153

Many reasons can be found for the changes and for their consequences. First, the development in understandings about friendship continues and grows (Kon, 1981). Second, the adolescent begins to become capable of forming friendships in different ways from the ones that younger children find to be important. Specifically, adolescents are increasingly concerned about the character of their friends, and place great emphasis on loyalty and trust in friendship. Third, adolescents begin to develop the adult concern over finding support for their personality and have to nourish the skills of detecting it and exploring its extent, as discussed in Chapters 2 and 3. Errors and embarrassments in this task are as likely as successes with these entirely new experiences.

Fourth, the adolescent becomes much more independent and responsible for the conduct and success of friendship. This requires the skills of forming and stage-managing relationships to a much greater extent than previously, in childhood. An additional dimension is provided by the fact that many such relationships are not only with the opposite sex but are sexual in nature. There begin the many complications of dating and courtship, the problems of handling sexual desires and restraints, and the difficulties of creating satisfactory relationships with members of the opposite sex (see Chapter 4). Finally, the difficulties of maintaining all sorts of relationship become much more significant once the child's time-span turns into the adolescent's and there is a greater appreciation of the fact that friendships last, sometimes for life.

For all these dramatic reasons, early, middle and late adolescence are true test-beds for later adult relationships and are likely breeding grounds for many sorts of personal disturbance that can persist right through adulthood. One important point here is that adolescence is really the first time that people become clearly aware of differences in the degrees of friendship that can exist. A child will simply distinguish best friends from friends and the others – but an adult is able to distinguish many other, more subtle, different degrees of friendship, types of friend (e.g., workmate, personal friend, neighbour) and stages in the growth of friendship. Thus adults know that friendship progresses from first encounters with strangers, through casual acquaintanceship, to close friendship – and that it really takes time. Younger children tend to believe that friendship is all or nothing, and they have little idea about a slow process of getting to know someone. As far as they are concerned, you either are a friend or you are not.

One of the changes in later childhood and early adolescence is the more sophisticated view of the growth of friendship through different grades, and of the way these grades are based on what we know about the other person – how well we know them, indeed. Younger children do not think, as adolescents begin to do, about how much they know about someone and what they have yet to learn. Especially, children and adolescents are different in that the adolescents begin, as part of this change, to pay attention to other people's personality. They gain an increasingly sophisticated view of the fact that people do have inner characteristics, personalities, moods, wishes, desires, motivations and intentions. Therefore, they begin to make increasing use of this realization in the conduct of their social lives in general and their friendships in particular.

This, of course, means that they start the long business of making a personal dictionary of personality, or creating their own theory of what makes people tick (S.W. Duck, 1975). This means finding out the sorts of terms that best describe other people's characters, and testing out or becoming familiar with the use of these terms. They must try out their own abilities as judges of character and learn to find friends who really do have the qualities that they admire, as well as finding those people who can offer them the personal support that they need.

These choices are also an early part of learning the process of managing and assuming greater personal responsibility for the conduct of one's personal relationships. Indeed, one source of conflict with parents is often the growing desire to choose and develop one's own friendships for oneself rather than through parents. As this is an especially potent time for learning, mistakes are made – just as they are later – but because at this age it is especially important to the adolescent, strong stands are often taken and conflicts with parents usually result. Since it is important to adolescents to develop some control over their relationships, and since they do not yet do so on the same basis as adults, these conflicts may appear to parents to be irrational obstinacy. To the adolescent they are seen as fundamental to their independence. Both viewpoints are correct. Consequently, adolescents also begin to talk to other adolescents rather than to parents about their concerns (Rawlins and Holl, 1988). In particular, one style that they adopt is to talk to other adolescents rather than to parents about the things that they did wrong.

Boys, furthermore, are very likely to form into or join gangs at the early points of adolescence, causing their parents alarm, although girls' cliques usually do not (Kon, 1981). However, these gangs and cliques are the basis for subsequent growth of normal sexuality, since they give the young person a 'safe' base from which to run the risk of forming first relationships with the opposite sex. In important ways they also act as rulemakers for normal behaviour. This is because, between them, the members create a 'theoretical' approach to relationships (in terms of beliefs, ideas and hopes) that actually builds the foundations of their relationships with the opposite sex later on. Parents who discourage their children from joining such gangs and cliques are probably preventing them from establishing the basis for normal adult relationships at the proper time.

It is a well-known feature of adolescent relationships that they characterize a time of movement (Kon, 1981). First, there is movement away from parents and adults in general towards their peers as the point of reference. For adolescents, the people in their age group gradually but significantly become much more central torchbearers of opinions and standards, with the ideas of parents and adults being rejected or derogated, almost as a matter of duty. Secondly, there is, as mentioned above, the movement away from predominantly same-sex friendships towards relationships and friendships with the opposite sex. These changes have their psychological effects as well as their relational ones. Adolescents who are deprived of casual, friendly interactions with their peers are going to have trouble developing a normal personality at a normal rate, since personality testing and growth are major results of adolescent friendship and gang membership. If such developments do not take place, then it becomes increasingly difficult for the adolescent to enter relationships that require that development first; and so a vicious circle is entered.

These are obvious and clear movements, but there are some less obvious ones too; for instance, the subtle movement, mentioned above, from pair friendships to gang or clique friendships (La Gaipa, 1981). Instead of having the one, two or three best friends of a normal child, normal adolescents rapidly absorb themselves into larger clusters, which provide many sorts of psychological support and guidance or prescription. Each gang develops its own views about what should be done and what should not, and its own attitudes about relationships with other people, especially the opposite sex. These gangs and cliques introduce the adolescent forcibly to different features of friendship, since they often exert sanctions upon members of the gang who do not form the right sorts of friendship or the right number.

Equally, the cliques present the individual with the forceful social implications of place in the hierarchy of the group. Gangs and cliques invariably evolve a structure which can develop or restrain the individual's growth. For instance, the leaders and high status members of the gang or clique are always the first ones who are 'permitted' to start friendships with the opposite sex, while low-status members are ridiculed or ostracized if they attempt such friendships. Particularly, the male adolescent must therefore prove himself to his same-sex peers before they will tolerate his attempting to find companions of the opposite sex.

Thus, besides the other things being learned by the adolescent are the significance of status, the force of group pressure, the significance of disobeying the group rules or norms for behaviour, and the tragic interrelationship of status and success with opposite-sex friends. Partly as a result of direct influence from the group, and partly as a consequence of indirect cues from media such as television, comics and pop-group fan clubs, the adolescent begins to be 'shaped' with respect to beliefs about the types of other person who are most desirable as friends and the degree of emotional involvement that should be expected or displayed in friendship.

The adolescent is also continually developing and evolving a more sophisticated language of friendship, and a broader and deeper system of concepts to apply to relationships with other people and what to expect or extract from them. In particular, the adolescent develops the idea that people are not simply sources of gratification of the person's own needs but have requirements and needs of their own (La Gaipa and Wood, 1981). The normal adolescent thus changes from demanding of others to being demanded of, and from being provided for to providing for others. Because this requires a dramatic shift in perspective, and because it brings the adolescent face to face with his or her ability to provide for others' demands, it is usually experienced as complex, confusing and threatening. Instead of concerning themselves with what other people can offer them, adolescents must find what they have to offer other people. This can generate confusion, alienation and the severest self-doubts. It is one of many reasons why adolescents discuss and argue about friends and friendship more than children do.

When the lessons are not learned
This can all be summed up very simply: first, the adolescent learns to expect different things of friends from those that children expect; second, the adolescent learns that different people are significant in defining friendship (i.e., peers are the 'reference group' now, not adults); third, the adolescent learns to communicate differently to friends and learns to learn about friendship and its development through stages.

The biggest risks are that the adolescent does not complete all of these lessons satisfactorily. Of course, the differences between levels of social development in children that were mentioned earlier do not simply disappear because the child has become an adolescent. Some adolescents are more socially advanced than others of the same calendar age. Significantly, adolescents, particularly girls, begin to show a preference for same-sex friends who are older, while children almost invariably choose friends of the same age as themselves, give or take a few months. Adolescents hardly ever (about 4 per cent of all cases) pick same-sex friends who are significantly younger than themselves – say in the year below them at school (Kon, 1981). When it comes to dating, as distinct from friendship, girls get into a pattern which will persist into adulthood, that of dating boys or men who are somewhat older than themselves (Shaver *et al.*, 1985). Boys date girls younger than themselves, by and large.

For the same reason that it is beneficial for younger children to play with slightly older children, the adolescents probably find it rewarding to have same-sex friendships with slightly more advanced adolescents because these, as it were, show them the ways in which they should grow psychologically. That is to say, adolescents who form friendships only with younger persons may be retarding themselves developmentally, or may be slightly socially retarded in the first place. It should be a useful sign that something is amiss when parents and social workers notice their adolescent showing a distinct preference for friendship with markedly younger persons of the same sex.

Mildly retarded social development is only one reason why an adolescent may develop friendships that are not only ultimately unsatisfying, but are also predictive of probable dissatisfaction with later adult relationships (La Gaipa and Wood, 1981). For one thing, adolescence brings to fruition the curse of an inadequately supportive family or a disturbed childhood where trust in other people could not be established. Individuals who have no history of basic trust in relationships with other people will have more than the usual uphill struggle to establish friendships based on the criterion of trust in adolescence: they have little encouragement to draw on from past experience. Equally, many disturbed and socially withdrawn adolescents have already acquired a highly negative view of the value of social relationships, and are very wary of other people (La Gaipa and Wood, 1981). They tend to 'use' them, and are primarily help-seekers rather than help-givers – which, of course, makes them less attractive to their partners and so less likely to be invited into relationships with other people. Other adolescents are difficult to relate to because they maintain an immature or aggressive style of behaviour that other people find unattractive or hard to cope with. These adolescents are likely to find it hard to maintain friendships, while the 'users' are likely to find it hard to develop them in the first place.

Just as popular and unpopular children show characteristic differences in ability to begin and continue relationships, so disturbed and normal adolescents show characteristic differences in their approaches to the development and maintenance of friendship (La Gaipa and Wood, 1981). Normal adolescents focus on the possibilities of self-development through friendship; that is, they do as described earlier, and select friends who help them to develop their personality. By contrast, disturbed adolescents focus on their perceptions of their own inadequacy and on doubts that the friend really values them. For instance, they have excessive doubts about their own personal worth as friends for other people, and assume that other people are their friends out of pity. Accordingly, a normal adolescent focuses on the skills and abilities of the other person, while a disturbed adolescent focuses questioningly on the other person's genuineness. Such suspicion and doubt are sure to make it harder for other people to relate to the disturbed adolescent, and hence will increase the doubts about genuineness.

As in the case of unpopular children, so too with adolescents it is the case that the warning signs can be picked up by observant adults and used to help the adolescent towards a more satisfactory use of the skills of friendship. It must be honestly admitted that psychological research has not been funded here as it ought to be, and the number of correctional programmes is correspondingly underdeveloped. Programmes in Canada have been concerned with the problem of integrating the disturbed adolescent into the normal group and have explored the ways in which disturbed adolescents are perceived by normal adolescents (La Gaipa and Wood, 1981). We can be sure, however, that a root problem is the disturbed adolescents' beliefs about friendship and the behaviour that they base on the beliefs. Intervention programmes based on those that are successful in children would also work in the case of disturbed adolescents. They would require modification to suit adolescent needs and are probably beyond the skills of most schools.

It is disturbing to have to admit that education of children and adolescents about friendship has been relatively under-researched, despite the importance of both childhood and adolescence as seed-beds for society's future problems. I believe that politicians reflecting on this might provide more funds for researchers to explore what goes wrong with children's relationships, and to build upon what we know about child development in order to prevent children's problems turning into adult ones. (Chapter 6 looks at deficient adult relationships.) This is an area where prevention is better than cure. It is best to catch possible problems early, before they have burned themselves irresistibly into the individual's psyche. There seems little reason to doubt that our society's social and psychological 'casualty departments' are unnecessarily full of lonely people who could be helped by training programmes. Such training programmes, based on a clearer idea of what actually does go wrong when childhood (and adult) relationships fail, are beginning to be devised. They show the promise of being able to put satisfactory relationships within the grasp of more and more people who are unhappy as a result of their poor childhood relationships.

6

Poor relations

Many people are not completely satisfied with their relationships. For some of us this is because of job or life circumstances that take us away from loved ones, such as commuter marriage partners, long-distance lovers, divorced parents separated from their children, or military personnel on active duty away from home. Other people have poor relationships for a variety of reasons that are not so circumstantial, and they may need to be helped out in other ways. I will look here at both of these sorts of relationship difficulty and also at the ways in which relationships break up and can, perhaps, be rescued and repaired.

RELATING ACROSS THE MILES

A strong message of this book has been that there are complex processes behind close personal relationships and that they do not 'just happen'. There are several special sorts of relationship that I will briefly consider here, in order to show how these processes work to advantage. I will deal here especially with long-distance relationships, and the special relationship problems of divorced parents or service personnel posted overseas or away from their families.

Despite the growth in the number of long-distance relationships in recent years, whether so-called commuter marriages or other relationships where partners are regularly separated by large distances, there have been few studies of the special character of such relationships. Those that have been done are instructive, particularly since some of them show that for the separated pair of friends or intimates, the issue of break-up is a constant one. Miller (1990), for example, explored the metaphors that long-distance partners used to describe their relationships, and also attended to the ways in which they talked about the communications that took place between them. In all the forms of communication the partners used many 'boundary markers' to do with time, change and finality. In other words, they were highly conscious of the fragility of their relationship and felt that it was tenuous and uncertain.

In a way this is curious and in another way understandable. Given that most of the partners contacted one another extremely frequently, they were probably doing more relating than do people who live in the same house – at least insofar as the discussion of feelings was concerned. What they lacked was the daily, routine interactions 'about nothing' that are increasingly showing up in research as important to relationships. In short it seems that those are the *most shaky* relationships where the relaters spend their time doing the intensely emotional things that older research used to think was the essence of relating. In fact what is more important is the interconnection of daily activity and events (S.W. Duck, 1986). People in long-distance relationships therefore seem to be happier when they spend a little less time telling each other how much they care and a little more time relating those important 'unimportant activities' of the day. This can never recapture the spontaneity of doing this face to face as the day unfolds, but more closely resembles the communication patterns of those partners who work in separate places and do not meet until the evening to 'share their day'.

Other adults have long-distance relationships that are rather special in nature: with their children. For instance, service personnel posted overseas or sales representatives on frequent business trips may see their children only infrequently, while individuals serving time in prison may not see them much at all. Some grandparents or divorced parents likewise live a great distance from their (grand)children and have to maintain most of their contact through telephones and letters. For all of these people the relationship with the children needs to be conducted with thought and care.

It requires a special sort of parenting skill to do this without making the children feel guilty, since children like to receive letters but are less enthusiastic about writing them, and need encouragement. Frequent contact nevertheless allows the parent to ensure that the child remains attached and feels loved and cared for. Letters are an important source of contact, since they can be stored and kept in a secret place for future rereading in a way that telephone calls cannot. A significant element of this is consistency in the timing. The children appreciate a regular letter rather than an infrequent one, and can come to rely on the consistently timed relationship more securely.

It is also interesting to the child to find out details of where the adult is or what the adult is doing or thinking or feeling (those important 'unimportant activities' again), so that he or she can hold a strong image in mind while reading the letter and keep psychologically involved with the life of the adult correspondent. Valuable to include, too, are stories about the writer and the family, memories of what things were like when the writer was their age, the pranks that the writer was involved in and the times he or she got into trouble. Other strategies are to involve the child by asking questions or setting games and tasks to be answered in the reply. In short, the more the letters resemble everyday conversation and the interactions that would happen if the writer and reader were together, the better they work.

ALL THE LONELY PEOPLE . . .

Voluntary separation from children deprives persons of particular relationships, but some social difficulties deprive people of *all* relationships, like it or not. As this book has continually pointed out, the absence of satisfying relationships directly causes all sorts of illness, both psychological and physical. In addition, it can cause stress indirectly. For instance, it is found that loners tend to adopt a pattern of work that creates health problems, often overworking and hence developing illnesses that are presently known to derive from stress (S.W. Duck, 1986, page 216). The point here is a simple one: while nurses and social workers may attempt to cure stress patterns directly, the actual problem can often be disguised: friendship difficulties or social problems.

Another way to sum up this state of affairs is to say that there is absolutely no doubt that while good relations have a powerful positive effect on people, it is depressingly clear that poor relations have an equally impressive negative effect. Yet although psychosomatic effects in medicine have been known for some time, it is only quite recently that people have looked at the influence of personal relationships in the equation. It is as if we all knew that the mind could affect the body, but that we have only just realized the ways in which personal relationships affect the mind and thereby the body. Recent research has done a good job of isolating the factors that matter most in the equation (Hobfoll, 1988).

What I have been trying to emphasize in this book is that likeability and unlikeability cannot be explained just in terms of the attractive or unattractive qualities that someone has. People who are ugly, arrogant, silly, diseased or foolish often have many friends. For instance, Socrates was notably ugly and yet had a large following – so large, in fact, that the state became concerned and put him to death for corrupting the youth of Athens. Julius Caesar was high-handed, bald and lecherous and yet his soldiers would follow him anywhere, including, illegally, across the Rubicon. Martin Luther suffered from various unpleasant digestive problems but was nevertheless massively influential.

The deep causes of likeability and unlikeability are to do with performance, behaviour and action. The force that makes or breaks a relationship comes from the behaviours and interpersonal social action of the persons involved. In short, people will tolerate an ugly extravert, but not a beautiful social cripple. This is a good thing: it means that professionals like nurses and social workers can actually foster ways to help such persons to try out and experiment with new ways of conducting their relationships.

It should now be clear that there are very many different reasons why someone may behave incorrectly in relationships. For one thing, as Chapter 5 showed, a person may retain an immature understanding of what an intimate relationship is. Quite simply, he or she may mistake the activities involved (e.g., by sharing only goods but not secrets, or providing physical assistance but never psychological support, when these reactions are appropriate only to childish relationships). He or she may have failed, as an adolescent, to learn the fundamental

165

importance of trust and confidence-keeping in relationships. Such people have a poorly developed idea of what relationships mean to normal adults, and they will do the wrong things simply because their guiding principles are faulty. They may get on very well with children, but adults will find them hard to cope with and hard to get close to. As indicated in Chapter 5, such problems can be dealt with, once people know how to recognize them and learn what they mean.

A second reason why someone may behave ineptly in relationships, especially as these are first getting off the ground, is also to do with problematic development as children – but a different sort of developmental problem. Because of early experiences many people develop low self-esteem. Such people are usually afraid that others will not like them and they become suspicious of other people, especially those who are nice to them. Their concept of friendship may be perfectly all right, but their self-esteem refuses to allow them to believe that other people feel genuinely positive or that close friendships are really possible for them. Also, many women develop low self-esteem from early childhood because they receive messages that they are worth less than other types of people – men or boys. (Women in the United States, for example, are still paid only 66 cents for every dollar that a man earns doing the same work.) It takes hard work as an adult to break free of those internalized messages, and the continuous ones from the media and the wider society combined with low self-esteem can turn into a self-fulfilling prophecy, as we saw in Chapter 2.

A third reason why people may behave incorrectly in relationships could be that they lack the skills of relating outlined in Chapters 2–5. This reason is much more common than most people realize, partly because it can take highly specialized forms. By this I mean that some people may suffer from 'skill deficit' only in some types of relationships (e.g., with the people in whom they are sexually interested) and not in others (e.g., with children or people in whom they are not sexually interested). Other people may be skilled at beginning relationships, but may lack the skills to develop them or, worse, to sustain and keep them. Some are good at establishing friendships but not sexual relationships, and vice versa. Yet others may be very good at establishing quick, superficial relationships with strangers, but unable to cope with lasting, deeper and more personally intimate relationships. For instance, they may feel threatened, vulnerable and exposed when they begin to realize that their friend is getting to know their personality well; they fear that the friend may not like what is discovered.

It is difficult to know which of these deficits is the most frustrating for the persons involved. Obviously all of them are significant, all of them cause major psychological and emotional distress, and each of them is differently caused and requires different treatment, some of which can be carried out by the person alone and only some of which requires special counselling. To help draw this distinction, compare these two letters I have received. One, from 'Alfred', shows how disturbing it is to be unable to start friendships (and also, I believe, shows us some of the reasons why Alfred had no friends. Look at the short, sharp sentences and the off-putting style):

> Dear Dr Duck,
> I'm in need of help and would like to know if you can help me. I'm 25-years old and totally unable to make friends with other people. I find it difficult to talk and what to talk about. I become very nervous and self-conscious. All my communications are short, straightforward. What I think is known as small talk. Up to now, I haven't mixed with people because of being unable to talk. I don't have any friends. Beside being born a quiet, shy chap, I had a very religious, sheltered life. Because of this I become very self-conceited and pompous. Please can you help me. Thanks.
> Yours sincerely,
> 'Alfred'

The other letter was from 'Madge', and her complaint was about poor development of relationships. She shows a sensitivity to the problems, while being unable to find solutions:

> Dear Dr Duck,
> I am one of those people who does not seem able to make friends and I get so disheartened at times because I do not know how to change this. I meet people at the office and I enrolled in Adult Education evening classes, I joined a knitting circle and a year ago in conjunction with another woman, started a local women's group to give myself the opportunity of meeting people. Somehow I never seem to get past the initial stage of getting to know them, I dry up at asking questions about themselves for fear they think I am prying so that doesn't make me feel very easy in their company. I try to be friendly and obliging towards people, nevertheless, in the hope that I can cover up my unease. It

gives me such an inferiority complex that I now stammer slightly too. Unfortunately, my husband is a very quiet person who does not feel the need for company very often so I don't really make friends through this source. We have a lot of acquaintances through our work and neighbours, etc., and I do try so hard to get on with everyone but I don't ever seem to get to know them any better. The few people I do get to know don't seem to want to get very friendly, maybe it is because they don't really find me their type of person? I don't know. I know through these sources that people see me as a friendly, lively and confident sort of person and it baffles me all the more that I can't make friends. I am a hypersensitive person and find myself very aware of the subtle changes in people's moods towards me and I find it confusing when people 'go off' me for no apparent reason. I appeal for your help, Dr Duck, and would very much appreciate a reply.

Yours sincerely,
'Madge'

I believe that these two letters make some important points about poor relations. They emphasize the value, when relationships are unsatisfactory or go sour, of examining the *processes* that happen in them. New hairstyles, new clothes and plastic surgery are less helpful than a new way of looking at the problems, and at new ways of behaving. For instance, recent studies show that many people with relationship difficulties blame themselves rather than looking at the situation they are in, and how it might limit their opportunities for relationships. Yet there are many natural limits to growth of relationships, and they should be borne in mind as a way of keeping a proper perspective on relative 'success' and 'failure' in friendships. The next section considers a few of these, and shows that there are many causes of relationship problems that are little to do with the people themselves (e.g., effects of time of the year (really!), career development, chance, coincidence), and they certainly do not create a situation that is permanent and unchangeable.

'WHERE DID I GO WRONG?'

People usually demand explanations for their relationship's break-up, and they are soon satisfied with some very unrealistic answers. It is all too natural – but not necessarily right just because it is natural – for people faced with a dissolving relationship to focus on themselves and ask themselves over and over again, 'What's wrong with me?' and 'Where did I go wrong?'. The answers are more than likely to be 'Nothing' and 'You didn't.'

It is a very well-known finding in psychology that people actually prefer personal explanations for things rather than external, situational or circumstantial explanations. We all like to blame persons rather than chance; we all tend to see things in personal terms rather than in terms of 'It just happened.' So personal sorts of explanation are given for the most unlikely occurrences. The first time this tendency was examined was over forty years ago when two researchers, Heider and Simmel, showed a cartoon of triangles and circles moving around the screen (Heider, 1958). Observers preferred to describe it in personal terms: 'The triangle is *chasing* the circle, and the circle is *running away* because it is *afraid.*' There is every reason to believe that this human tendency prevails in poor relations, too, as people look for scapegoats (whether themselves, their partner or some third party).

Although human beings have enduring tendencies to look for people to blame, or for persons rather than circumstances as the main cause of events, researchers have, for a long time, regarded this as a fundamental error, particularly in respect of friendship and other relationships. There are many other reasons why relationships fail or do not reach their full potential, and many of them have little to do with the people personally. For instance, two friends may simply live too far away for the best relationship to be conducted. If my best friends live in Michigan and I live in England, then there are naturally going to be some dissatisfactions and some constraints in the relationships, even if they are as enjoyable and satisfying as possible in the circumstances.

To take another example, there are some natural limits to relationships created by norms or public standards, as we saw in Chapter 2. The relationships possible between a teacher and pupil, boss and worker, or Queen and subject, are naturally limited by expectations about what is proper in the circumstances, even if, given a different set of circumstances, these two same people could get into a deeply fulfilling relationship. As a third instance, recall from Chapter 4 that individuals may have different expectations about the future of the relationship (one of them may be thinking that it will become 'serious' and one may not, for example). These differences may disrupt the relationship for reasons that do not reflect badly on either partner personally.

Breaking up is hard to do, but not always your fault
Having made it clear that people tend to over-personalize the ending of relationships, let me first go through some of the beliefs about relationship endings that are commonly held – along with some of the surprises that research has cast up.

The first point is that the ending of relationships is usually tainted with self-accusations and guilt. It is perfectly normal but misguided for people in a troubled relationship to start asking awkward questions about it. They start to ask themselves questions about the partner and the relationship itself, most likely, and to ask whether they really need it and why. Unfortunately, because it is usually very difficult to answer this sort of question even when a relationship is going well, answers are particularly unsatisfying, especially when worked out alone. The reasons for liking someone are hard enough to state verbally, even when there are no doubts that good reasons exist. Yet if there are any doubts at all then good and persuasive reasons for staying in the relationship are even harder to find.

As soon as one begins to think for one rather than for two, it can get clear that relationships have lots of drawbacks, especially in relation to time that must be shared, extra chores because there are two people around rather than one, and having to reach agreement about things together where one person could decide more quickly alone. Also, as soon as individuals focus on a relationship, the lack of equity and fairness in exchange can soon become apparent (and is seen out of all proportion). It is easy to forget that in a properly developed relationship strict equity would not be expected anyway. So it is naturally very easy to give inequity as the reason for a poor relationship, whether it actually is or not.

Plenty of research has shown that the tendency to give personal reasons for a break-up is common, even if simplistic (see Weber *et al.*, 1987). Human beings tend to overlook the possible influence of their personal style of behaviour, rather than specific events. For instance, a large amount of research has shown consistent gender differences in approaches to relationships and their dissolution (e.g., Hill *et al.*, 1976), and sociological research suggests that this gender difference comes from socialization in early life. Females are much more vigilant in relationships; that is, they watch the progress of relationships more carefully, are more concerned about the development of them, are more aware of disruptive undercurrents, think more often of the possibility of a relationship's ending and are more likely to give sophisticated and complex accounts of the break-up of a relationship than men are. In heterosexual dating and courtship, the female partner is directly responsible for breaking the relationship in about 80 per cent of cases, but this is probably because women monitor relationships more closely than men and detect sooner that the trouble is probably final. Females fall in love more slowly and yet fall out of love more quickly than men, as we saw earlier.

There are also some other influences on courtship and friendship that people would not usually suspect, namely, time and the calendar. For example, in the northern hemisphere at any rate, more marriages break up in February than any other month. Also, British counsellors and social workers report every year that the period around and just after Christmas is one where marriage and family disturbances suddenly increase, probably because people are looking for stereotyped family harmony and togetherness, but it does not really reflect their true feelings for one another. The media portrayals of festive closeness and seasonal conviviality simply, in many instances, contrast with the reality. Evidently the season of goodwill does not extend universally to one's next of kin!

Another influence of time is that the biggest risk time for heterosexual courtships is around 15–18 months (S.W. Duck, 1988b). Many more are reported to run into trouble about this time than would be expected by chance. It seems likely that this is the sort of length of time that it takes most people to 'notice' the relationship, and to see that there is a clear expectation that it will end in marriage. When the partners come to the realization (and, possibly more important, when outsiders do too, and begin to put pressure on them to clarify their intentions), the partners need to decide what their intentions really are. Presumably, then, there are many couples who decide that the time is not right, that it would be too early to commit themselves, that their careers are not well enough clarified – and a whole host of other reasons for deciding to call it off rather than live out a hopeful but misleading life.

Other subtle temporal reasons for break-up can also be found. For instance, the break-up of marriage will usually be blamed on the behaviour of one of the partners in the marriage, or upon the partners' behaviour with one another (sexual incompatibility, arguments, and so on). But it is a remarkable fact that a very substantial number of marriages break up about 8–10 years in. Researchers have tended to explain this in terms of the length of the relationship and the strains that are created, but this misses one key point: after 8–10 years of marriage most people (given the age at which people tend to marry in the first place) are approaching the early mid-30s and are thus entering one of the well-known periods of psychological turmoil known as an 'identity crisis'. At this point in life, the individual begins to feel the disappearance of youth, the greater fixity of life's probable career, and the closing of opportunities that would have still been open five years ago. (For example, in some professions people are regarded as too old to join after the age of 28 – in computing, officer training in the armed services, banking, and so on. People beyond this age are thus forced to recognize that certain paths and opportunities are now irrevocably closed.) It seems likely that many such people feel uneasy with their personal position, and simply give vent to this in the easiest place: their marriage or their personal relationships.

In *developing* friendships there are some hidden effects of 'length of time in the relationship' also, which are relevant to break-up. After about 4–6 months of friendship, people begin a very dramatic increase in the testing out of their relationship (McCarthy and Duck, 1976). For instance, they may have found that their friend is very similar to themselves in many attitudes and they begin to wonder if the similarity is sincere. So they apply a test and start trying out a few of their more outrageous views, just to see if the other person disagrees. If so, then they may conclude that previous agreements were genuine rather than merely ingratiating, but if the partner just goes along with these outrageous views too, then it may be necessary to assume that the previous agreements were truly baseless also. In any case, these tests are just that: tests. A relationship that does not pass the test at this stage of development will be allowed to drift away, and that is a perfectly natural result of applying the test in the first place.

People at this stage try other tests, too. For instance, they may try to find out whether their partner is likely to be stimulating, is capable of broadening them out in attitudes or opinions, or knows about things they have no knowledge of (Wright, 1984). Such tests are valuable ways of finding out the future value of a friendship but, of course, many relationships fail the test and break up. People begin to assert themselves more, to 'be themselves' rather than be polite in the friendship, seek out areas of disagreement and attempt to resolve them vigorously. It does not always work, and so the relationship crumbles. So, again, relationships can head towards the rocks because of the way everyone starts to behave in a relationship of that length. It is not really 'personal' if the relationship does not survive the test. That, after all, is the purpose of the test in the first place – to see if the relationship can survive and is worthwhile for both partners to pursue. It is as healthy and beneficial for dying relationships to be discarded at this stage as it is for healthy ones to be continued.

I have found other apparently wild effects of the calendar among students (S.W. Duck and Miell, 1986). In their first academic year at college (starting in the autumn, of course), the Christmas break at the end of the first term seems to cement more of their college friendships than would be expected. The students go home looking forward to seeing their old school-friends, but get appalled and dismayed at the changes that have taken place in themselves and their friends at home. They find it harder to relate to them than they had expected, and come back to college in January feeling bursts of relief at meeting their college friends again. Students are not the only ones who find it hard to keep up relationships with old friends from way back. Meetings between such people are often hollow and the greater joy is usually to be found at the beginning and end of the meeting rather than in the middle.

All this serves to make the point that relationships often break up from the influence of strange and unlikely impersonal causes that people overlook. Few people stare at their partners and think 'Hmmmm! February again – perhaps we ought to break it all off', but for some reason this is what seems to happen! Recognizing these strange effects, people whose relationships break up may be able to keep a sense of perspective and not punish themselves as a first step. It may well be that their behaviour did contribute to the break-up in a major way, but this should be a conclusion in context. In order to cope with the break-up it is obviously intelligent to accept its ending or identify, as far as possible, the real causes of it, rather than to thrash around in speculative self-reproach. Equally, the first step towards repairing a relationship is to identify as clearly as possible the true mix of personal and situational causes in the problems with the relationship.

How and why do relationships break up?

There can surely be no-one who has *never* experienced a broken romance, a lost friendship, a disrupted work relationship or a family argument. Relationships break up all the time and enemies are as natural a part of the social environment as are friends. Rivalries are as common as is turmoil within established relationships. These in themselves do not prophesy the inevitable end of the relationship. Break-up is a complex and extended process that can be corrected as it happens.

Let us start at the beginning, with rivalries between people who do not know one another very well, and then work through the break-up process to look at the ways in which close partners go through it.

In interesting recent work, Buss and Dedden (1990) have begun to explore the ways in which human beings derogate one another as a part of their biological make-up. Based on the work of sociobiologists, who see humans as concerned about their ability to pass on their genes, even in their social behaviour, this work assumes that even attempts to put down other people will be based on concern over genetic matters. These authors believe that members of the same sex will 'bad mouth' one another in predictable ways. Women, they claim, will imply that other women are 'genetically unreliable', while men will cast other men as sexually unsafe bets for genetic transmission. In other words, women's derogatory remarks will try to suggest that a man could never be sure that a rival woman's children would be his, while men will imply that a woman could not even count on *having* children if she got involved with the derogated target male. Sure enough their study found that women claimed rival women were either frigid, slept around indiscriminately or had a sexual disease (and, interestingly, did not take showers), while men claimed that the other man had a prior commitment to another woman, went in for violent attacks on other women and, almost inevitably, had an incapacitating sexual disorder anyway.

Derogation of others is usually a part of breaking up also, but in close relationships has other forms besides these above. Indeed, telling tales about the partner is something that starts late in the break-up process. At the start of it, partners are most often rather keen that other people do *not* find out about their relationship problems and they go to considerable lengths to conceal their troubles. Naturally this usually means that when the troubles surface in public, they are at an advanced stage of development and it may be too late for anyone to help (in addition to the fact that it takes everyone by surprise and they are occasionally angry at not having been kept informed or allowed to try to help).

Take a look at Figure 6.1. It depicts the processes by which people break up their relationships, according to a review of the research that I have done. There are five phases to the process.

The first phase (*breakdown phase*) is entered when one or both partners feel that things are not going as well as they should. They probably do not mention it to anyone in a serious way at this point. Life has its ups and downs after all. It may not even bother them all that much, especially if they can explain it as due to partner's illness, mood-altering medication (such as some hormone treatments), the fact that there has been awful weather lately, they are both tired, there are a lot of debts, or other exterior forces that just make every day feel like a Monday morning. The determination of whether the next stage of the dissolution process gets activated depends on the way this phase resolves itself. Not every instance of a breakdown in communication or a reduction in the level of enjoyment in the relationship leads to its death. Partners each decide, on the basis of the evidence before them, whether they are fed up enough or not. If one of them is, then that person proceeds almost imperceptibly to the next phase, the intrapsychic.

The *intrapsychic phase* is basically an internal grumbling phase, but it occasionally spills out. At this point the aggrieved individual merely feels that things have been going badly for long enough, or at a serious enough level, that he or she is concerned and wants to feel some self-pity or even let off steam. 'I don't get as much out of this relationship as I put in' is a thought that begins to creep in here. 'My partner has a bad attitude to the relationship' is another. In this phase the purpose of the grumbling is to get sympathy or to feel sorry for oneself. It is not at all to leave the relationship; indeed the person may get a perverse pleasure from staying in the relationship to demonstrate what a saint he or she is. However, other outsiders might get to hear about all this. Close personal friends may be complained to, or impersonal third parties such as hairdressers or bar servers may be enlisted to sympathize – basically people who will not tell the partner.

The point is that the person wants to let off steam only, to be told that he or she is right to be irritated and to feel aggrieved, and wants to be given the support of other people who see it the same way. Well, of course they would if they get only half the story – an important point. This is the reason why relationship therapists generally will work only with both partners in a troubled relationship. There is research to show that doing therapy with only one partner can increase the risk of divorce.

In the intrapsychic phase, then, the point is *not* to let the partner know about it: that might spoil the 'agony'. Yet if this steam-letting does not release the tension or solve the problem properly for the person, then there will be gradual or swift movement to the next phase. Let me emphasize again that there is no inevitability about this. In some cases the satisfaction or support received at the intrapsychic phase will be adequate to relieve the situation, or perhaps to give the complainer an objective view that will cause a re-evaluation of the problem and a return to normality. If people discussed with each other (instead of with outsiders) during the intrapsychic phase, they would have a very good chance of saving the relationship before things get out of hand. In fact the best thing that a friend can do, if cast in the role of comforting ear, is to persuade the complainer to speak to the partner and try to work things out before they get worse (S.W. Duck, 1984).

Poor relations

BREAKDOWN: Dissatisfaction with relationship
↓

| Threshold: I can't stand this any more |

↓

INTRAPSYCHIC PHASE
Personal focus on partner's behaviour
Assess adequacy of partner's role performance
Depict and evaluate negative aspects of being in the relationship
Consider costs of withdrawal
Assess positive aspects of alternative relationships
Face 'express/repress dilemma'
↓

| Threshold: I'd be justified in withdrawing |

↓

DYADIC PHASE
Face 'confrontation/avoidance dilemma'
Negotiate in 'our relationship talks'
Attempt repair and reconciliation?
Assess joint costs of withdrawal or reduced intimacy
↓

| Threshold: I mean it |

↓

SOCIAL PHASE
Negotiate post-dissolution state with partner
Initiate gossip/discussion in social network
Create publicly negotiable face-saving/blame-placing stories
 and accounts
Consider and face up to implied social network effects, if any
Call in intervention teams?
↓

| Threshold: It's now inevitable |

↓

GRAVE DRESSING PHASE
'Getting over' activity
Retrospection: reformulative post-mortem attribution
Public distribution of own version of break-up story

Figure 6.1
A sketch of the main phases of dissolving personal relationships. (Reprinted from S. W. Duck (1982), 'A topography of relationship disengagement and dissolution', in S. W. Duck (ed.) *Personal Relationships 4: Dissolving personal relationships*, Academic Press: London. Reproduced by permission.

The *dyadic phase* is the tough one, though, when one confronts the partner with one's dissatisfactions. Several things can happen at this stage. First, the problem may be acknowledged by the partner and both of you may agree also to work to correct it. Alternatively, one may find that the partner is dissatisfied also, or that the partner is blissfully unaware of one's own unhappiness, or that the partner has a good excuse; and any one of these might be a shock. One will find that the partner has a totally different recollection of key events and circumstances, different explanations for them, different attitudes about their importance, and so on; and that will be a shock. One is, finally, quite likely to find that the partner has a few views about oneself that will be shocking also.

In short, the dyadic phase is an essentially confrontative phase and forces the partners, if not into conflict, at least into negotiation and re-evaluation of the future of the relationship. Not only are such confrontations hard in themselves, but the very conflictive nature of the exercise means that partners are faced with managing conflict as well as trying to resolve the problem. It is a difficult time that calls upon the fullest resources of the couple. It is at this phase that couple-therapy would be most useful, as everything is out in the open between the partners and the couple can renegotiate their relationship.

However, the outcome is not certain. Not all conflicts result in the break-up of the relationship: in fact, being able to solve conflicts satisfactorily is one of the most important skills for any couple to develop, because some sort of conflict is inherent in relationships. After some of the discussion that takes place at this phase, many couples decide to work at the relationship, to correct things that they had not realized that their respective partner found troublesome and to start anew with fresh vigour and involvement. Others may see the writing on the wall and begin to prepare for the eventual dissolution of the relationship. If that is what is foreseen, then the couple will begin to move inexorably to the next phase: the social.

The *social phase* is the point that makes or prevents the dissolution of the relationship: it is the phase where the troubles in the relationship are openly discussed with third parties by both of the partners. Whereas the intrapsychic phase is one where the individuals select out 'safe' confidant(e)s who are sure not

178

to report to the other partner or may not even know him or her, at the social phase the essence of the matter is to gain alliances with others who *do* know the partner and can be persuaded to take sides. The social phase is where friends, relatives and neighbours become involved. There are two parts to this phase. In the first part, the network of associates tries to reconcile the partners and may act as go-betweens, messengers or healers. When this fails, as it most often does, then the network starts to take sides, to make its positions clear and to make judgments about the partner and the relationship.

At this point persons may find out, for example, that their parents never really liked their partner, or that a close friend actually thought that the other person was right and oneself was wrong. One also has to deal with the pain and embarrassment that the network members may feel about the relationship breaking up. After all, they may have treated the two of you as a pair for a long time and now they have to come to see you as separate individuals again. Many of them find it awkward to have to take sides, for it is very difficult to remain neutral when two people are going at one another hard and when you know both of them. As will become clear, the essence of this phase is the emergence of a socially acceptable story about 'who is to blame', and the efforts of the partners are devoted to getting the people in their personal networks to accept their version of what is going wrong. At this point, there is much gossip transmitted, many rumours, several allegations, and stories of the doings of the other person that put them in a bad light, while one's own activities are given a lick of attractive paint. But too late: the slide to the final, grave-dressing phase begins, and this time, break-up is utterly inexorable.

The *grave-dressing phase* is the last and sometimes the longest phase of a break-up: the time when the death of the relationship is acknowledged and the story of its birth, life and ending is created for all to see, like a gravestone – the phase, in short, where the partners adjust to the break-up. The purpose here is to satisfy oneself, and the people that one meets and knows, that there is a rationale to the ending of the relationship, just as there was to its existence (S.W. Duck, 1991). There is also an important, subtle issue that surfaces here. The ending of the relationship must be accounted for in such a way that it does

179

not deny the future possibility of other relationships for the teller, while also giving a good account of the ending. One has to present a story about the relationship that 'credits one's social face' and casts one in a good enough light for other people to find it acceptable to enter into relationships with one in future. It is no good admitting that one is a selfish relater who just does what suits and then drops partners for others at whatever time is convenient! No-one would want to get into a relationship with someone like that in future.

Hence the classic 'ending story' has to be along the lines of 'I entered the relationship with both eyes open, knowing that my partner had some faults as well as attractions. I worked at it – we both did – but the difficulties were too great for us and I decided that, for both our goods, we should end it.' Of course there are many variations on such a basic line, but the elements of it are usually present in most break-up accounts. The story presents one as no fool (or else an *honest* fool who was deceived by a sly and devious partner), as someone who will work at relationships, but who is a realist and recognizes when to call it a day. Such stories may be tilted one way or the other depending on the extent to which one wants to blame the ending on the treachery and bad character of the other person or on an honest inability to get along together.

Interesting work has also uncovered the general structure of ways in which people describe their burst relationships in the grave-dressing phase (McCall, 1982). A very elaborate system of metaphors applies to relationships and these have an important role in convincing people that their relationship has ended or should end. For example, people who saw themselves as fellow travellers along life's highway might come to see themselves as reaching a parting of the ways; people who saw themselves as providing each other with support, like timbers, come to think of the collapse of the relationship. There is also a whole dictionary of metaphors related to coupling and uncoupling: 'getting hitched', 'stuck on one another', 'magnetically attracted', and so on, which imply that, once connected, two people can simply become disconnected, or the connections can become restraining – bonds can become chains. Finally, once people begin to want to leave relationships they use a characteristic style of language to describe the relationship, such as images of confinement ('I felt smothered', 'I was cooped in', 'It was like being in a cage').

Such differences of language and description are more significant than we normally appreciate, since they build in a special sort of perspective that indicates exactly how the relationship is to be seen and approached. They therefore give an observant person an immediate clue about the best strategy for counsel. Someone who uses imagery based on bonding is tacitly complaining that the closeness or lack of closeness in the relationship is the trouble, rather than anything else. Someone who complains of confinement is tacitly admitting that social pressures are the force that keeps the relationship together rather than strong emotional bonds. It is important for such professionals as nurses, social workers and counsellors to pay close attention to such 'trivial' clues, since they identify the person's focus on the problem.

As is clear from the above, then, the ending of relationships is a complex set of processes, not a simple action. It can last for quite a while after the separation of the partners, because of the need to formulate and often reformulate one's account of the ending and the placing of blame, if any. In the case of divorcees with children to think about, such things are likely to continue for quite a while, and there will be 'ending stories' for the children as well as for oneself and other people. It is, however, possible to maintain a friendly relationship with ex-spouses as long as one recognizes the importance of the give-and-take that is necessary in the creation of ending stories.

Another point should also be made: not all relationships that break up are to be regretted. Many people learn not only how to avoid breakdown of relationships when they wish to, but also how to welcome it when it is best to do so. Obviously there are cases where people sit down together, at the dyadic phase, and make a rational and calculated decision to break up the relationship because this truly is best for both of them. This is not because just one of them is now thoroughly unhappy or dissatisfied with the relationship, but because they both agree that they have reached the limits of what they can provide for one another; or perhaps they feel that the relationship is stifling their personal growth, or simply that it has gone as far as it is going and is now dead. Some behaviours may kill relationships too, such as violence. Couples often find that they cannot work out a satisfactory future relationship when violence has been part of it in the past. For these couples, the dissolution of the relationship is almost certainly the better outcome.

When couples have decided to split up, social workers or couple-therapists can help them to do so in a way that is less damaging for each of them. For instance, any of the above may indicate that it is better to assist the person out of the relationship rather than to stick a big adhesive plaster over the problem. So some endings of relationships can actually be good, normal and beneficial, as this helps the partners to grow and stops their being suffocated. Even when a break-up is not mutually arranged, I do not want to suggest that this necessarily shows that the partners must be unattractive or inadequate. Nor do I wish to suggest that any ending of relationships is necessarily a bad reflection on the personal worth of the individuals concerned: they may just be doing something inappropriately, without realizing it, which can be corrected, either by themselves personally, by their friends and acquaintances or by counsellors.

MAINTAINING AND REPAIRING RELATIONSHIP

The above model of relationship break-up emphasizes that it is a process with many parts, some of which switch in at some times and others at other times. For this reason, relationships can go wrong in many different ways and from many separate causes. In attempting to repair relationships, helping professionals would be guided by this research not to expect one simple technique or comfort to work for all relationships that are in trouble. The first problem in such cases, then, is to identify the phase that the partners have reached in the break-up and to deal with the problem in a manner appropriate to that phase.

If a person seems to be in the intrapsychic phase, identified above, then help is needed with 'ventilation'; i.e., spelling out the dissatisfactions with the relationship or with the partner and letting off the necessary steam. However, reality demands also a dispassionate and objective consideration of the ways the person may appear from the point of view of the partner in the relationship. Counsellors often, therefore, encourage the complainer to describe realistically the probable intentions and thought processes of the other person. What is intended to be achieved by the behaviour? What could the person really be trying to do, assuming that he or she is essentially an honest person with sensible motives? The complainer is thus often nudged to see the partner's behaviour more positively.

On the other hand, the complainer could also be nudged to evaluate the elements of his or her own behaviour that may cause difficulty to the partner, or to focus on the benefits of the relationship as well as the difficulties. One of the techniques that couple-therapists use early on in therapy is to ask each person to think about the changes that he or she could make to himself or herself as a way of improving the relationship, rather than homing in on the changes that the partner 'should' make. This can help to change the person's perspective away from simple blaming and towards thoughtful problem-solving.

Such methods are best used after the person has been encouraged to 'unload the baggage' about the relationship, by describing feelings about the relationship so that the person does not feel frustrated or that the listener is not hearing his or her complaints. It may even help if the person is encouraged to list the partner's pleasing behaviours and advantages. Finally, the counsellor may lead the person to think about the real difficulties of leaving a relationship, with all the consequences that that may hold. This can be very useful for individuals in a relationship as it makes them aware of the realities involved in a possible break-up.

At the dyadic phase the pair of partners is basically on its own and yet is faced with a welter of difficult problems, one of which is simply handling the conflict. As we saw in Chapter 4, there are integrative tactics that focus on the interests of *both* partners and which work best in conflict management. It is also important at this phase that the couple is counselled to read each other attentively and to ensure, by frequent checking, or summaries or statements of what is being 'heard' (See Chapters 1 and 2), that the real messages of the other person have been registered. Remember from earlier chapters that one major problem with seriously distressed married couples is that they (especially the husband) tend to overestimate the accuracy with which they have understood one another. A frequent problem at this stage is that the couple enters a 'cross-complaining cycle' (Gottman, 1979), where one person answers an accusation by reciprocating – simply making an accusation back against the partner, as children do in the playground (*'You* did *this'*; 'Well *you* did *this*, so there'). Also common and equally problematic is 'kitchen-sinking', where irrelevant complaints are attached to relevant ones and the whole relationship is evaluated, rather than the specific behaviours or difficulties that caused the original strife.

In brief, the couple often finds it difficult to focus on the issue and to hear one another's points of view while trying to integrate the two of them to reach a solution that is satisfactory to them both. Simple anger is very normal and healthy, but its expression needs careful management.

The social phase is essentially where the partners try to get support for their own viewpoint and may even be helped by outsiders to deal with their issues. These can be counsellors, friends or support groups. The main goals of repair here (S.W. Duck, 1984) are to enlist the support of others who will make one feel that one is right, to obtain help in understanding what is going on in the relationship (by comparing one's experiences with other people's) and perhaps to obtain support and comfort during the process of break-up itself, if that is what occurs. Often this is done by helping the person to construct a satisfactory grave-dressing that makes them feel better about themselves, the past relationship, the reasons for the break-up and the future that lies before them, now that the old relationship is done.

COPING WITH PERSISTENTLY POOR RELATIONS

Occasional relationship problems are bad enough, but some people have poor relationships all the time. What can be done for individuals whose relationships are persistently unsatisfactory? Several answers have already been outlined, and I shall focus here on the psychological adjustments that are possible before I look at the changes in behaviour that are effective.

First, consider the idea that someone feels isolated or feels that his or her relationships are unsatisfactory. When we explore what this actually means, it refers to feelings that result when there is a discrepancy between two ideas that a person may have about relationships (Perlman and Peplau, 1981). One of these ideas is a belief about the number of satisfactory relationships that they achieve or actually have, and the other is the level of desire or aspiration that they have for other people's company. Each of these will be different for different people, and what counts is the way in which each person sees them tying together. For instance, some people have a generally low desire for other people's company, and so would not feel lonely if in fact they had very few satisfactory relationships. Other people with higher aspirations would feel terribly lonely with exactly the same number of friends as this first person.

People's desires for company and their perceptions of relationships are both changeable from time to time. Borys and Perlman (1984) showed that a person's feelings of loneliness increase when they feel badly about themselves from some other cause. In this case, people who had just been defeated at racquetball felt more lonely than people who had won. As another example, young people, such as students, feel lonelier at weekends than at other times (Perlman, 1986), presumably because their *expectations* that the weekends will be fun-filled and lively are not consummated. The number of friends that they have would obviously be identical whether the day is Saturday, Wednesday or Monday, but on Saturdays their expectations, desires and aspirations increase. On some days even normally sociable people just want to be alone, and do so without getting morbid or upset. The problem and the pain arise only when the discrepancy between beliefs about one's actual number of relationships and one's desired number of relationships is intolerably large and persistent.

Research has uncovered two psychological strategies that are effective in coping with such discrepancies (Rook, 1988; Marangoni and Ickes, 1989). The first is a 'behavioural approach'; that is, it involves adjusting one's behaviour. For example, a person may go out to create more relationships by meeting more people or may visit existing friends more often and for longer periods of time. Alternatively, one might try a so-called 'cognitive approach' and adjust one's attitudes or beliefs about the problem. For example, the person may realize that underestimates have been made and there are more friends out there than first thought, or that existing friendships are actually very satisfying. As a mix of these two strategies, the person may make so-called 'surrogate relationships', by buying a dog, talking to the television newscasters, watching the relationships played out on television soap operas or replaying memories of successful relationships from the past.

These methods can be very successful in relieving loneliness, each in its own way. In some methods of coping, people adapt their attitude to the whole concept of friendship. For instance, they begin to see themselves as self-sufficient, independent 'loners'. They may also create an image of themselves in their own minds as independent, or someone who is happiest with one very close friend or with a single intimate partner, and insist that this person provides all the psychological company they need. There is also the tendency for people to derogate other persons as friends ('You can't trust people, they always let you down') or to sublimate by nonsociable means like writing lots of letters to national organizations or, in extreme cases, by hallucinating about imaginary friends, visitors from outer space and contacts with spirits. Finally, they may simply take steps to alleviate the negative impact of loneliness, by becoming 'sad passives' who overeat, watch too much television, take drugs, get drunk, overspend on their credit card or commit suicide.

These extreme responses have actually confused many people for a long time. For instance, it used to be noted that many alcoholic husbands reported poor sexual relationships with their wives and everyone jumped to the obvious, but wrong, conclusion: too much alcohol hinders sexual performance. But it was also known that alcoholics often reported difficulties with other relationships, too, and again people jumped to an obvious but wrong conclusion: that this was because alcoholism makes you difficult to live with. In fact, when researchers began to look into it a bit more deeply, they found that poor interpersonal relationships had often *preceded* the alcoholism (Orford and O'Reilly, 1981). Many leading researchers now believe that at least some alcoholics turned to alcohol as a refuge and anaesthetic against the effects of social isolation or chronically unsatisfying friendships. As in many other instances, the social isolation is a consequence of poor performance in friend-making, and part of the cure for some alcoholics is to be found in improved relationships.

Equally, many family therapists base their therapy on the premise that although the individuals in the family may appear to have psychological disorders or difficulties, it is the relationships within the family and between the individuals that provoke or aggravate them (Orford and O'Reilly, 1981). Families containing children labelled difficult or individuals regarded as disruptive are now often treated as a family system rather than as if they were a lot of outsiders in a group with just one difficult member. The poor relationships in the family can often be bad enough to provoke one individual to burst out in dramatic ways in order to let somebody outside know that the family needs help. Some therapists regard the person identified as the patient as a sort of messenger for the family as a whole. The answer is to treat and 'cure' the family, not just the individual. For instance, an individual's disruptive behaviour may be partly determined or reinforced by the reactions of other family members, and it is no use giving therapy to the individual if the family merely reacts to the individual in the same old way once he or she returns from the therapy. The answer is to examine and investigate the patterns of activity and styles of interaction in the family as a whole – to take the family as a system with a malfunction rather than to isolate one component. This can lead to changes in relationships between all the members of the family and may, for example, bring a distant father back into close contact with the rest of the family.

Further examples of people helped by relationship counselling are found in unlikely places: prisons. Many forensic psychologists point to the fact that violent offenders often have a history of unsatisfactory relationships – of chronic faulty performance in friendships and difficulties in other personal relationships (Howells, 1981). This is particularly true of 'one-off murderers' (who, contrary to popular belief, are much more likely to kill a friend or family member than a stranger) and so-called 'murder-suicides', who kill someone very close to them (their spouse or child, most probably) and then kill themselves. In these cases it is commonly found that they are people who are 'overcontrolled'. That is to say, they do not express their emotions, but bottle up their anger and cannot show affection except extremely (e.g., in violent sexual passion).

These people are usually men who have learned to express a narrow range of emotions due to being trained in the traditional male sex role, which emphasizes 'strength' and suggests that expression of emotion is unmanly. In this case the man may find that anger is the only emotion that he is truly aware of. These persons can be helped in therapy by being taught to see what is behind the anger, thereby learning to experience and express a fuller range of emotions. Without treatment, such people often 'burst' in unexpected ways, and other people are shocked because they do not see it coming in the gradual ways that would be expressed by people with normal ways of showing different degrees of emotion in their relationships.

When these overcontrolled people are treated for relationship difficulties, their other symptoms subside (Howells, 1981). Such treatment usually involves training in normal expression of emotions. However, it may also be the case that such persons inadvertently create the relationship bed that they lie on, and this style needs changing, too. For example, someone who is persistently aggressive and competitive may inadvertently organize other people to be hostile towards him or her, thus making the perceptions of hostility actually realistic. Such organizing can readily be altered once the person is brought to the full realization of the effects of his or her own behaviour on other people in the situation.

As a final example of the unlikely consequences of relationship problems, I recall reading in the local paper a story entitled 'Sex attack youth (18) jailed for six years.' In essence, an 18-year-old youth had threatened two women with an air pistol and attempted to embrace them – an act that the papers and prosecution represented as a 'sex attack'. In his defence the youth argued that he had no girlfriends, found relationships difficult and only wanted someone to talk to. He claimed to have taken the pistol along in order to make the girls talk to him. He was rightly found guilty of assault and jailed for six years. Nonetheless, I have often wondered if he is not really serving time partly because he did not know how to make friends or attract the opposite sex in the usual, understandable and acceptable ways. If he receives no relevant guidance in prison, presumably his female victims will be no safer when he is released. In fact he may learn a lot from his fellow prisoners about other ways to attack and demean women. There is a prevalent myth in our culture that says that women like men to be sexually aggressive towards them. This can lead to many problems in relationships where the man believes he is doing what is expected of him when in fact he is not. In prison this incorrect but 'macho' image is particularly likely to be portrayed, admired and transmitted to the other inmates.

The 'bottom line' suggestion from all these areas of social casualty is that, in many cases, they stem indirectly from poor relations that both precipitate and follow other sorts of disturbance in people's behaviour. Until now, the connections have not been properly realized. A cure for the relationship disorders would help us on the way to curing the rest – a conviction that is increasingly shared by workers in a variety of helping professions.

Several of the foregoing are extreme examples, or concern only persistently poor relations. Unfortunately, everyday relationships also often go sour or have difficulties, and repairing relationships that are seriously disturbed is not a simple job. It is one that is only becoming clearer through recent investigations, although its far-reaching consequences have been clarified more easily. In each case there are techniques for people to help themselves, techniques for them to help other people, and more formal techniques for intervention by counsellors and other agents of society.

Epilogue

The future of relationships

People of every historical age have looked back and claimed that the past was the place where friendships were truly wonderful, and that present ones fall short of such perfection. Even in first-century Rome, the poet Horace (Odes, III, vi, 46) took the view that everything had gone downhill since his grandfather's day!

The same tendency exists today. Everyone thinks that intimacy (like the quality of life, language, family holidays or beer) has deteriorated since the last century when relationships were blissfully idyllic. We have all heard, too, the cliché that people nowadays are becoming 'alienated' as a consequence of an increasingly industrialized and technological society that has somehow spoiled the friendships and intricate dependencies that were possible in an essentially agricultural social system. We all decry the decline of friendship (even though no one has ever been able to put their finger on the sorts of test and measurement that would be necessary to prove it), and we all look longingly to the past. Our age thus shares many of the disappointments and idealized hindsights of previous ages. Of course, someone in a hundred years' time may look back on the videotapes of the 1990s to show that, compared to those of the late twenty-first century, our friendships are deep and significant.

I hope that in the future friendships are going to be more satisfactory for the people who, in our own age, were stigmatized as social failures. In my dreams I see a fundamental shift in attitudes to friendship (and to friendship deficiency) comparable to the shift in attitudes about the causes of illness that took place in the later Middle Ages. No longer will lonely people be blamed as if they were sinners being punished by God, as physically sick people often were then. They will be taught in childhood how to help themselves and if they need further help to perform properly in friendships, then it will be readily available without stigma.

In the best of all possible worlds, greater attention will be paid to the family and its role in society, as several prominent politicians, such as Congresswoman Pat Schroeder in the United States, have recently urged. However, I believe that such interest will not be restricted only to the role of the family in society as some 'stabilizing force', but will extend to concern over the operation and development of happy families. The creation of good parent–child relationships and the extension of this outside the home to include children's social and relational development are also becoming exciting possibilities, as the research unravels the mysteries of loneliness, social rejection, and the processes of relating.

I do not believe it is too unrealistic to predict that our descendants will come around to the view that unsatisfying relationships are not only personally distressing, but are ultimately socially harmful and worth preventing. They will reject the simplistic idea which contends that lonely people have only themselves to blame. The lonely are not solely responsible for their 'deficiency', any more than children who cannot play the piano are solely to blame for theirs. By recognizing that attitudes towards people and relationships are learned and shaped in childhood, we can also see that they can, like other types of learning, be improved by the use of proper techniques and proper education.

IMPROVING RELATIONSHIPS

I have already discussed many specific ideas about improving relationships in each of the previous chapters, and I want to raise only general policy issues here.

A major need is for problems with the family, friendship and personal relationships to be brought forward for discussion. For too long the stigma of 'failure' has been attached to unhappy relationships, and when divorce is seen as the equivalent of personal failure (rather than due to faulty process, coincidence or chance), then people getting divorced have extra social burdens to carry. This has encouraged people to seek ways out of their difficulties which help them to disguise the true problem. When a person begins to feel the pain of loneliness it is presently more socially acceptable to take a few drinks, become depressed or write to a problem page rather than to seek real help! Except in marriage guidance or couples/individual therapy, not all of which are openly 'accepted' in all countries, there are few general and legitimated relationship clinics where people can take the problems to be dealt with openly and constructively. Relationship problems as a whole are not recognized as important, although in the United Kingdom the agency 'Relate' has begun to take up this challenge, and in the United States it is becoming much more common for couples and families to seek therapy to help them work through difficult periods in their relationship. Attitudes have not yet changed, nonetheless, and such agencies are seen by many people as a last resort, rather than the sort of service that ought to be approached initially.

Strangely, in the United States, major health insurance companies will pay for clients to go for individual therapy, but will not pay for couples or families dealing with relationship problems or parenting issues. It is highly likely that a family would send a 'problem child' to see an individual therapist because their insurance company will pay – but then find that desired changes do not occur in the child, because the problem was a family problem in the first place. Many families who eventually seek, and have to pay for, family therapy are doing this only after finding that several attempts at individual therapy for the 'problem individual' have not helped. Perhaps the future will bring a change of heart to the insurance companies, if only because they begin to see that the money they are paying for the individual therapies is essentially money down the drain in many cases.

Another kind of approach is provided by women's (and more recently also men's) consciousness raising groups and encounter groups. These all help people to cope in various ways but often are the kinds of help sought rather late in the day. It is better to have this state of affairs than no help at all: but far better would be the creation of an atmosphere where people are less afraid to visit someone to discuss the problem. A beginning could be made with the recognition of the general extent of the problems and the growing resources available to resolve them. Once people can be encouraged to bring their relationship problems to legitimate resource centres, as they now take physical problems to a doctor, then counselling programmes can begin to play an effective role in reducing the social problems that stem from relationship difficulties.

It is the knowledge of the far-reaching social consequences of relationship distress that makes the basis for such a plea. I have shown throughout this book the previously unforeseen and unrecognized joys of relationships and also the unhappy consequences of their disturbance. I have also shown that the root cause lies not in some inherent and incurable unattractiveness of the persons involved but in the poor training or imperfect conduct of their relationships with one another. Poor conduct, like poor health, poor diet or bad exercise programmes, can be treated, and may be cured by the sorts of means indicated, whether by the person's own good sense or by formal intervention and guidance.

So-called loneliness intervention programmes also now exist (W.H. Jones *et al.*, 1984) and are a practical possibility for solving many difficulties, from shyness through dating anxiety to social isolation. Loneliness intervention programmes have their first impact by being respectable and available. Their major value lies in the fact that distressed persons referred there do not regard themselves as anything more of a failure than someone does who catches flu and seeks medical advice. But a second value of legitimized loneliness intervention programmes lies in their specific abilities to change lonely people's inappropriate friendship behaviour and to redirect ineffective attitudes about the person's own value and esteem. They focus on the training of the social skills outlined in Chapter 2, on conversation and communication skills (Chapters 1 and 3), and on attempting to increase a person's self-esteem by generally reducing anxieties about social interaction. It may even be necessary to make fundamental psychological readjustments to a person's beliefs about social rejection (for instance, in the case of distressed children or adolescents) by giving them new ways of interpreting themselves and their experiences.

It is perhaps understandable that people find it very hard to accept that relationships do have such far-reaching social consequences, just as many people cannot bring themselves to accept that relationships can be improved by training. As I noted earlier in the book (Chapter 1), I am not denying that friendship is an art as well as a skill, and that even mastery of its basic mechanical elements is not the whole story. The skill of a Yehudi Menuhin is not reducible to a set of mere mechanical movements, although it may be possible to *describe* it in terms of such movements. I am saying that relating, too, has some essential component skills, but that it can be supplemented by other skills.

How is this possible? Several research scientists now claim to have techniques that predict liking, many of which are based on compatibility studies using personality measures. The most effective are those that are not based on simple similarity but take account of the many ways that personality can be measured and the relative importance of the different aspects of personality that matter at successive points in a growing relationship (S.W. Duck and Craig, 1978). Also important are tests of interactional compatibility that are based on management of conflict, ability to compromise and attention to self-disclosure as detailed elsewhere in this book (Sprecher, 1987; Canary and Cupach, 1988).

The value of some of the long-term studies of friendship development has been in their indication of the changing influence over time of different factors in liking as relationships grow (Griffin and Sparks, 1990), and some of the more sophisticated techniques put us within an ace of telling at first meeting who will get on well in what circumstances, and for how long. For instance, using one of these systems my research team was able to predict which set of students would be able to survive a year as room-mates and which would not (S.W. Duck and Allison, 1978). Other researchers (for example, Huston *et al*, 1981; Kelly *et al*, 1985; Sprecher, 1987) have developed techniques that predict certain aspects of couples' later relational behaviour based on particular measures of their early behaviour in the relationship, as detailed in other chapters here.

In relation to work productivity and other settings, however, the research has not yet been properly tested and many opportunities to develop good predictions of effective cooperation are being lost. Since we now know more not only about personality compatibility but, more importantly, about the ways in which people negotiate and create working relationships, the opportunities exist for practical exploitation of the research in the context of industrial work team selection. For example, it is now possible to match up apparently compatible pairs of people, to observe their acquaintance style in a brief exercise and thus predict their ultimate success in a particular type of relationship (Miell, 1984; Miell, 1987; Miell and Duck, 1982).

One step beyond that is the fact that the future success of a marriage will soon be predictable by the advanced techniques currently being tested. Certainly, although precise statements of probability have not yet been made or tested fully, many key bases for such predictions have been explored. Research teams in the United States have now devised methods for charting the progress of courtships and classifying their main features as we have already seen in Chapter 4 (Huston *et al*, 1981). Other workers have been tying this in with our knowledge about divorce, and it is only a matter of time before the two teams are able to show the relationship between courtship, the way a courtship is conducted and the probability of eventual divorce (Ponzetti *et al*, 1991). One ultimate use of such research is to develop these scientific procedures to the point where they can offer valid advice to engaged couples about the probable future of their marriage and the ways in which they must change in order to maximize its chances of survival. Marital therapy and marriage guidance is all very well once the marriage hits the rocks, and can be a useful lifeboat even before then, as many couples come to therapy early in a relationship to obtain help to manage conflict or deal with the pernicious effects of traditional sex-typing. All the same, it is probably better for everyone if the rocks can be charted before the journey begins.

At present, this is really all that people are doing when they have trial marriages of 'living together without the certificate', and again, they are merely being unscientific and intuitive. As we saw in Chapter 4, those who cohabit and then marry actually stand an increased chance of eventual divorce! This is unsatisfactory, unreliable and full of room for improvement once more accurate techniques are freely available.

The future of friendship as well as of marriage could also be tested in like manner now we are finding out so much more about how it works. We can now assess the likely compatibility of two people by means of scientific personality techniques, and, at the other end of the problem, my own research team has been looking at ways of making the most out of the basic compatibility that exists between two people. For instance, using theories about friendship development and structured acquainting methods we have been able to devise ways of helping people to find out about one another in great depth in a short time (Miell and Duck, 1982). Essentially, the technique is based on ideas given in Chapter 3, and it involves the persons taking carefully selected areas of their own personality and talking about them with their partners. As experimenters we use advance pre-testing to ensure that partners will find that they are similar and compatible in these areas hence the discussion will produce some attractive and rewarding discoveries, and the partners end up liking one another as well as feeling that they know each other well. If we merely left them to their own devices, who knows whether they would ever pick up on the right areas to explore? They might even end up focusing on differences and end up disliking one another, when a different strategy, a different sequence of discussions, can produce an opposite result. The sequence of discoveries is the important thing, we have found, and that further knocks on the head the idea that it is someone's characteristics or properties that make them attractive or unattractive to someone else. It is not. It is the way and the order in which these are disclosed and discovered that count.

However, these are not the only areas where such work on friendship is significant, although they are important. From the point of view of its social value, the most important place to apply this research is in medicine. Medical research in the next twenty-five years will pay more attention to the strong connections between lack of friends and physical illness. Psychosomatic medicine has already explored the ways in which physical illness can result from mental states; it has also shown the effects on mental state that are caused by relationships and relationship problems. We are only just starting to find out that friendships are probably better than an apple a day at keeping us away from the doctor. But more than that, we are also finding out how friends can actually reinforce a doctor's influence on the patient by encouraging him or her to keep to prescribed advice, and so on. Studies now show that support from network members makes patients keep to their prescribed regimen of drugs better than they will do on their own (see S.W. Duck with Silver, 1990, for a discussion).

RELATIONSHIPS AND SOCIAL POLICY

The major area for development lies in the field of relationship education. There are presently no systematic attempts to deal with this feature of our children's development into adults and this verges on the irresponsible. At present children and adolescents probably learn quite a bit from entering relationships that are doomed to failure, but the pain associated with such learning is still pain and it can last a long time. It could be reduced or prevented without removing the essential learning experience, if only schools would begin to take the learning of social and personal relationships seriously. For instance, it is still common to find in children's storybooks and magazines the most extraordinary accounts of human friendships, just as there are vast amounts of hidden implications about racial differences (golliwogs, etc.) and sex differences that promote views now thought to be unsatisfactory. Serious consideration of such things is truly a matter of social policy, in the manner that has been used in relation to sex discrimination and the undesired effects of portrayal of males and females in such places. So, too, is the issue of displaying and describing friendship in children's stories in a way that maximizes a child's chance to learn theoretical lessons that can be practised in the playground. For instance, we need to be sure that the basis for friendship in children's stories is not portrayed at a level that they are not prepared for. We now know that it would be absurd to expect a 5-year-old to get anything from a friendship story describing trust, loyalty and secret-sharing (except they may get confused!). This is not the basis for their own friendships, and it may be no use telling them stories where it is shown to be one.

A more directly practical advance would be the bringing of friendship into the school curriculum. Encouraging children to write about it, think about it, play act it and do projects on it can help them to become more aware of its importance and can help them in their development. A member of my research team did just this and tried out a number of ways of making children more sensitive to the nature of friendship (Brydon, 1982). He used such techniques as a project where children mapped out their friendships and indicated by coloured pins and wire the relationship between friendship choices and housing position: in this way they are given a graphic picture of the influence of housing on friendship. Adolescents have also been encouraged to write essays and poems about friendship or even to act out relationships and then discuss them. Without fail they report this as a useful and valuable experience that helps them to come to terms with friendship. In these ways the children and adolescents are encouraged to think about friendship, to feel that it is a legitimate focus for their attention and to see that it is a proper subject for public discussion.

At present, females are taught to be interested in relationships and males are taught to be more interested in instrumental styles of relating. This means that as adults, both men and women often expect women to be the main caretakers of relationship. Relationships are also seen as something that 'only females should worry about', and therefore 'not a serious issue'. When men can start to take them seriously and teach their sons to do the same, we will have made some progress. Furthermore, increased attentiveness would help the sensitive teacher or educational worker to spot potential social problems and nip them in the bud. Children with inefficient ideas about relationships or immaturity of approach to friendship with other children could be more effectively identified and reserved for more intensive care and guidance.

Although childhood and adolescent friendships are the most pressing areas for making good use of the scientific research, there are other profitable avenues where it can be used. For instance, we have now found out a great deal about the relational factors that influence satisfaction with buildings and living accommodation. The size of the community created by a building can be functional or dysfunctional, helpful or unhelpful. For example, in a communal residence the inhabitants prefer to have six people sharing a small kitchen than to have a larger community (say twenty-five) sharing a larger and better equipped one. Community feeling can also be influenced by very minor building design points to do with location of postboxes and lifts, so as to lead to increased opportunity for meetings and for greater community atmosphere. The purpose of these bits of metal is not simply the literal one of accepting letters and getting people from one floor to another: they have a social function, too. The most efficient arrangement of amenities from the building point of view may be the least acceptable from the social point of view.

A similar idea can be extended to such apparently purely administrative matters as the arrangement of visiting times in hospitals. It used to be thought that the visit itself was the desirable thing for the patient and that times should be chosen on grounds of efficiency for hospital staff. Now the idea seems to be that patients should be allowed visitors whenever the visitors turn up, except for times that are maximally inefficient for the staff. (Incidentally, such times include the doctors' round times. As evidence that scheduled and threatening visits can be fatal, let me add by the way that coronary patients have more heart attacks in the period just before consultants' rounds than at any other time during intensive care.) On the other hand, friendship researchers have shown convincingly that, from the patient's point of view, the most satisfactory relaxing and 'healing' arrangement is neither the tight schedule nor the random access system (Perlman and Peplau, 1981). The visits are most valuable and most satisfying for patients who can control arrangements themselves and when they know in advance when a visitor will come. Patients who could make up their own schedule of visits reported feeling better even if the visits were actually shorter or less frequent than those allowed to patients who had their visits scheduled for them. Proper thought about such issues alone can contribute substantially to patient recovery.

In addition to the implications of friendship research for educational policy, building design and hospital management, we should attend to a final area: the friendship implications of the growth in unemployment. As I showed earlier, many of a person's friendships are made at work – mostly because of the opportunity provided by meeting there. If opportunities for work continue to contract, and more people become unemployed, so they will lose these occasions for social contact and their friendships will fall into decay. We can expect, then, that loneliness, alcoholism and violence will increase sharply as a result. We can also see that families will be forced to spend more time together under one another's feet and that, as already happens during the extended public holidays (particularly at Christmas), this will increase irritation with one another, and lead to increases in family disturbance or even divorce. A hidden cost of unemployment will thus emerge: social casualties from decreased friendships will begin to fall back more and more onto the state's rescue services. At present people are naively blaming such consequences on the loss of self-respect that follows redundancy. That is only part of it: the other part is a relationship problem. An alternative would be to encourage families to focus on relationships and learn to manage conflict more effectively in healthy ways, instead of pretending that the conflict is not there. That way they may come to enjoy spending more time together!

What else can be done? It will not be adequate merely to

create unstructured opportunities for lonely people to meet (e.g., by building social centres), although this will help. Many people will be isolated by unemployment because at present they probably establish friendships only through work and because the work-place structures their meetings with other people. The work thus subtly pushes them along in their friendships. Take away work and its structure, and you throw such people back on their own abilities to create relationships. They will need a great deal of help in such circumstances. The kinds of help required will be twofold: first, many people will need some sort of replacement structure for the relationships that the lost workplace used to make; second, many people will need the help of intervention programmes outlined earlier.

And so we come full circle, and conclude that the value of such programmes will be of inestimable value to our societies in the years to come. Governments can set them up with ease once research on social and personal relationships begins to receive deserved recognition for its potential, as it has done in the last ten years in the academic world. It is a practical study with far-ranging usefulness. It has already shown the vast number of apparently unrelated affairs into which friendships intrude, and where they can affect the conduct of life for good or ill. It promises the possibility of genuine advances in the quality of life for a vast number of people. Whatever else happens in the next twenty-five years, it is clear that idle curiosity about relationships will be replaced by the more systematic knowledge accumulated by research into relationships and how they may be improved.

References

Acitelli, L. K. (1987), 'When spouses talk to each other about their relationship', *Journal of Social and Personal Relationships* (5), 185–99.

Adler, A. (1929), *What Your Life should Mean to You*, Bantam: New York.

Adler, T. F., and Furman, W. (1988), 'A model for children's relationships and relationship dysfunction', in S. W. Duck (ed.) with D. F. Hay, S. E. Hobfoll, W. Ickes and B. Montgomery, *Handbook of Personal Relationships*, Wiley: Chichester.

Ambert, A.-M. (1988), 'Relationships between ex-spouses: Individual and dyadic perspectives', *Journal of Social and Personal Relationships* (5), 327–46.

Anderson, S. A. (1985), 'Parental and marital role stress during the school entry transition', *Journal of Social and Personal Relationships* (2). 59–80.

Argyle, M. (1978), *The Psychology of Interpersonal Behaviour (3rd edn)*, Penguin: Harmondsworth.

Argyle, M. (1981), 'The social psychology of long term relationships', Report to Social Science Research Council, Oxford University.

Argyle, M. (1986), 'Long term relationships', Paper to the Third International Conference on Personal Relationships, Herzlia, Israel, July.

Argyle, M. (1987), *The Psychology of Happiness*, Penguin: Harmondsworth.

Argyle, M., and Henderson, M. (1984), 'The rules of friendship' *Journal of Social and Personal Relationships* (1), 211–37.

Argyle, M., and Henderson, M. (1985), *The Anatomy of Relationships*, Methuen: London.

Argyle, M., Furnham, A. and Graham, J. (1981), *Social Situations*, Cambridge University Press: Cambridge.

Arkin, R., and Grove, T. (1990), 'Shyness, sociability and patterns of everyday affiliation', *Journal of Social and Personal Relationships* (7), 273–81.

Asher, S.R., and Gottman, J. (eds.) (1981), *The Development of Children's Friendships*, Cambridge University Press: Cambridge.

Asher, S. R., and Parker, J. G. (1989), 'Significance of peer relationship problems in childhood', in B. H. Schneider, G. Attili, J. Nadel and R. Weissberg (eds.), *Social competence in developmental perspective*, Kluwer: Amsterdam.

References

Athanasiou, R., and Sarkin, R. (1974), 'Premarital sexual behaviour and postmarital adjustment', *Archives of Sexual Behavior* (3), 207-25.

Ball, R. E., and Robbins, L. (1984), 'Marital status and life satisfaction of Black men', *Journal of Social and Personal Relationships* (1), 459–70.

Bartholomew, K. (1990), 'Avoidance of intimacy: An attachment perspective', *Journal of Social and Personal Relationships* (7), 147–78.

Baxter, L. A. (1987), 'Symbols of relationship identity in relationship cultures', *Journal of Social and Personal Relationships* (4), 261–79.

Baxter, L. A., and Dindia, K. (1990), 'Marital partners' perceptions of marital maintenance strategies', *Journal of Social and Personal Relationships* (7), 187–208.

Baxter, L. A., and Wilmot, W. (1984), 'Secret tests: Social strategies for acquiring information about the state of the relationship', *Human Communication Research* (11), 171–201.

Baxter, L. A., and Wilmot, W. (1985), 'Taboo topics in close relationships', *Journal of Social and Personal Relationships* (2), 253–69.

Beinstein Miller, J. (1989), 'Memories of peer relationships and styles of conflict management', *Journal of Social and Personal Relationships* (6), 487–504.

Bell, R. A., Buerkel-Rothfuss, N., and Gore, K. (1987) ' "Did you bring the yarmulke for the cabbage patch kid?": The idiomatic communication of young lovers', *Human Communication Research* (14), 47–67.

Berg, J. H., and McQuinn, R. D. (1989), 'Loneliness and aspects of social support networks', *Journal of Social and Personal Relationships* (6), 359–72.

Berg, J. H., and Piner, K. (1990), 'Social relationships and the lack of social relationships', in S. W. Duck (ed.) with R. C. Silver, *Personal Relationships and Social Support*, SAGE: London.

Berndt, T. J. (1989), 'Contributions of peer relationships to children's development', in T. J. Berndt and G. W. Ladd (eds.), *Peer Relationships in Child Development*, Wiley: New York.

Berndt, T. J., and Ladd, G. W. (1989), *Peer Relationships in Child Development*, Wiley: New York.

Berscheid, E., and Walster, E. H. (1974), 'Physical attractiveness', in L. Berkowitz (ed.), *Advances in Experimental Social Psychology, vol. 7*, Academic Press: New York.

Bloom, B., Asher, S., and White, S. (1978), 'Marital disruption as a stressor: A review and analysis', *Psychological Bulletin* (85), 867–94.

Blumstein, P., and Schwartz, P. (1983), *American Couples*, Morrow: New York.

Borys, S. and Perlman, D. (1984), 'Gender differences in loneliness', *Personality and Social Psychology Bulletin* (11), 63–74.

Bradburn, N. (1969), *The Structure of Psychological Well-being*, Aldine: Chicago.

Brydon, C.F. (1982), 'Children and adolescent friendships', Paper to Social Science Research Council Programme, Lancaster, July.

Bull, R. (1977), 'The psychological significance of facial disfigurement', Paper to International Conference on Love and Attraction, Swansea, Wales, September.

Burgess, R. L. (1981), 'Relationships in marriage and the family', in S. W. Duck and R. Gilmour (eds.), *Personal Relationships 1: Studying Personal Relationships*, Academic Press: London.

Burgoon, J. K., and Koper, R. J. (1984), 'Nonverbal and relational communication associated with reticence', *Human Communication Research* (10), 601–26.

Buss, D., and Dedden, L. A. (1990), 'Derogation of competitors' *Journal of Social and Personal Relationships* (7), 395–422.

Byrne, D. (1971), *The Attraction Paradigm*, Academic Press: New York.

Cahn, D. (1990), 'Perceived understanding and interpersonal relationships', *Journal of Social and Personal Relationships* (7) 231–44.

Canary, D., and Cupach, W. R. (1988), 'Relational and episodic characteristics associated with conflict tactics', *Journal of Social and Personal Relationships* (5), 305–25.

Cate, R., and Christopher, F. S. (1982), 'Factors involved in pre-marital sexual decision-making', Paper to International Conference on Personal Relationships, Madison, WI, July.

Cheal, D. J. (1986), 'The social dimensions of gift behaviour', *Journal of Social and Personal Relationships* (3), 423–39.

Check, J. V. P., Perlman, D., and Malamuth, N. M. (1985), 'Loneliness and aggressive behaviour', *Journal of Social and Personal Relationships* (2), 243–52.

Chelune, C. J. (1979), 'Measuring openness in interpersonal communication', in G. J. Chelune, (ed.), *Self-Disclosure*, Jossey-Bass: London.

Chown, S. M. (1981) 'Friendship in old age', in S. W. Duck and R. Gilmour (eds.), *Personal Relationships 2: Developing Personal Relationships*, Academic Press: London.

Christopher, F. S., and Cate, R. M. (1985), 'Premarital sexual pathways and relationship development', *Journal of Social and Personal Relationships* (2), 271–88.

Christopher, F. S., and Frandsen, M. (1990), 'Strategies of influence in sex and dating', *Journal of Social and Personal Relationships* (7), 89–106.

Cupach, W. R., and Comstock, J. (1990), 'Satisfaction with sexual communication in marriage: Links to sexual satisfaction and dyadic adjustment', *Journal of Social and Personal Relationships* (7), 179–86.

Daly, J. (1990), 'Competent conversation', Paper to the Iowa Ideas Forum, University of Iowa, February.

Davis, J. D. (1978), 'When boy meets girl: Sex roles and the negotiation of intimacy in an acquaintance exercise', *Journal of Personality and Social Psychology* (36), 684–92.

Davis, K. E., and Todd, M. (1985), 'Assessing friendship: Prototypes, paradigm cases, and relationship description, in S. W. Duck and D. Perlman (eds.), *Understanding Personal Relationships*, SAGE: London.

Derlega, V. J., Winstead, B. A., Wong, P. T. P., and Hunter, S. (1985), 'Gender effects in an initial encounter: a case where men exceed women in disclosure', *Journal of Social and Personal Relationships* (2), 25–44.

Dickens, W. J., and Perlman, D. (1981), 'Friendship over the life cycle', in

References

S. W. Duck and R. Gilmour (eds.) *Personal Relationships 2: Developing Personal Relationships*, Academic Press: London.

Dillard, J. P. (1987), 'Close relationships at work: Perceptions of the motives and performance of relational participants', *Journal of Social and Personal Relationships* (4), 179–93.

Dindia, K., and Baxter, L. A. (1987), 'Strategies for maintaining and repairing marital relationships', *Journal of Social and Personal Relationships* (4), 143–58.

Dion, K. K., and Berscheid, E. (1974), 'Physical attractiveness and peer perception among children', *Sociometry* (37), 1–12.

Dion, K. L., and Dion, K. K. (1979), 'Personality and behavioural correlates of romantic love', in M. Cook and G. Wilson (eds.), *Love and Attraction*, Pergamon: London.

Douglas, W. (1987), 'Affinity testing in initial interaction', *Journal of Social and Personal Relationships* (4), 3–16.

Duck, K. W. (1982) in a personal communication.

Duck, S. W. (1975), 'Personality similarity and friendship choices by adolescents', *European Journal of Social Psychology* (5), 351–65.

Duck, S. W. (1977), *The Study of Acquaintance*, Teakfields, Saxon House: Farnborough.

Duck, S. W. (1982), 'A topography of relationship disengagement and dissolution', in S. W. Duck (ed.), *Personal Relationships 4: Dissolving Personal Relationships*, Academic Press: London.

Duck, S. W. (1984), 'A perspective on the repair of personal relationships: Repair of what, when?', in S. W. Duck (ed.) *Personal Relationships 4: Dissolving Personal Relationships*, Academic Press: London.

Duck, S. W. (1986), *Human Relationships*, SAGE: London.

Duck, S. W. (ed.) (1988a) *Handbook of Personal Relationships*, Wiley: Chichester.

Duck, S. W. (1988b), *Relating to Others*, Open University Press: London/ Dorsey/Brooks/Cole/Wadsworth: Monterey, CA.

Duck, S. W. (1989), 'Socially competent communication and relationship development', in B. H. Schneider, G. Attili, J. Nadel and R. Weissberg (eds.), *Social Competence in Developmental Perspective*, Kluwer: Amsterdam.

Duck, S. W. (1991), 'The role of theory in relationships loss', in T. L. Orbuch (ed.), *Relationship Loss*, Springer Verlag: New York.

Duck, S. W., and Allison, D. (1978), 'I liked you but I can't live with you: a study of lapsed friendships', *Social Behaviour and Personality* (6), 43–7.

Duck, S. W., and Condra, M. B. (1987), 'Stimulus deficient communication: An investigation of the Goldman effect', unpublished MS, University of Iowa.

Duck, S. W., and Cortez, C. A. (1986), 'The heart is a lonely hunter', unpublished MS, University of Iowa.

Duck, S. W., and Craig, G. (1978), 'Personality similarity and the development of friendship', *British Journal of Sociology and Clinical Psychology* (17), 237–42.

Duck, S. W., and Gilmour, R. [eds.] (1981), *Personal Relationships 3: Personal Relationships in Disorder*, Academic Press: London.

Duck, S. W., and Lea, M. (1982), 'Breakdown of relationships as a threat to personal identity', in G. Breakwell (ed.), *Threatened Identities*, Wiley: Chichester.

Duck, S. W., and Miell, D. E. (1982), 'Toward an understanding of relationship development and breakdown', in H. Tajfel (ed.), *The Social Dimension: European Perspectives on Social Psychology*, Cambridge University Press: Cambridge.

Duck, S. W., and Miell, D. E. (1986), 'Charting the development of personal relationships', in R. Gilmour and S. W. Duck (eds.), *The Emerging Field of Personal Relationships*, Lawrence Erlbaum Associates: Hillsdale, NJ.

Duck, S. W. (ed., with R. C. Silver) (1990), *Personal Relationships and Social Support*, SAGE: London.

Duck, S. W., Cortez, C. A., Hurst, M., and Strejc, H. (1989), 'Recalled parameters of successful and unsuccessful first dates as a function of loneliness,' Paper to the Annual Convention of the Speech Communication Association, New Orleans, November.

Duck, S. W., Rutt, D. J., Hurst, M., and Strejc, H. (1991), 'Some evident truths about communication in everyday relationships: All communication is not created equal', *Human Communication Research* (in press).

Dunn, J. (1988), 'Relations among relationships', in S. W. Duck (ed.) with D. F. Hay, S. E. Hobfoll, W. Ickes, and B. Montgomery, *Handbook of Personal Relationships*, Wiley: Chichester.

Edwards, D., and Middleton, D. (1988), 'Conversational remembering and family relationships: How children learn to remember', *Journal of Social and Personal Relationships* (5), 3–25.

Fitzpatrick, M. A. (1988), *Between Husbands and Wives: Communication in Marriage*, SAGE: Newbury Park.

Frankel, A., and Morris, W. N. (1976), 'Testifying in one's own defense: the ingratiator's dilemma', *Journal of Personality and Social Psychology* (34), 475–80.

Furman, W. (1984), 'Enhancing peer relations and friendships', in S. W. Duck (ed.), *Personal Relationships 5: Repairing Personal Relationships*, Academic Press: London.

Furman, W., and Gavin, L. (1989), 'Peers' influence on adjustment and development: A view from the intervention literature', in T. J. Berndt and G. W. Ladd (eds.), *Peer Relationships in Child Development*, Wiley: New York.

Gaebler, H.C. (1980), 'Children's friendships: The interaction of cognitive and social development', unpublished PhD thesis, University of Lancaster.

Gerstein, L. H., and Tesser, A. (1987), 'Antecedents and responses associated with loneliness', *Journal of Social and Personal Relationships* (4), 329–63.

Ginsberg, D., Gottman, J. M., and Parker, J. G. (1986), 'The importance of friendship', in J. M. Gottman and J. G. Parker (eds.), *Conversations of Friends*, Cambridge University Press: Cambridge.

Glick, P. C. (1979), 'Children of divorced parents in demographic perspective', *Journal of Social Issues* (35), 170–82.

References

Goodwin, R. (1990), 'Dating agency members: Are they 'different'?', *Journal of Social and Personal Relationships* (7) 423–30.

Gotlib, I. H., and Hooley, J. M. (1988), 'Depression and marital distress: Current and future directions', in S. W. Duck (ed.) with D. F. Hay, S. E. Hobfoll, W. Ickes and B. Montgomery, *Handbook of Personal Relationships*, Wiley: Chichester.

Gottman, J. M. (1979), *Marital Interaction: Experimental Investigations*,. Academic Press: New York.

Griffin, E., and Sparks, G. (1990), 'Friends forever: A longitudinal exploration of intimacy in same sex friends and platonic pairs', *Journal of Social and Personal Relationships* (7), 29–46.

Guthrie, E. R. (1938), *The Psychology of Human Conflict*, Harper: New York.

Hagestad, G. O., and Smyer, M. A. (1982) 'Dissolving long-term relationships: Patterns of divorcing in middle age', in S. W. Duck (ed.), *Personal Relationships 4: Dissolving Personal Relationships*, Academic Press: London.

Hartup, W. (1989), 'Behavioral manifestations of children's friendships', in T. J. Berndt and G. W. Ladd (eds.), *Peer Relationships in Child Development*, Wiley: New York.

Hatfield, E., and Traupmann, J. (1981), 'Intimate relationships: A perspective from equity theory', in S. W. Duck and R. Gilmour (eds.) *Personal Relationships 1: Studying Personal Relationships*, Academic Press: London.

Hays, R., and DiMatteo, R. (1984) 'Towards a more therapeutic physician–patient relationship', in S. W. Duck (ed.), *Personal Relationships 5: Repairing Personal Relationships*, Academic Press: London and New York.

Hays, R. B. (1984), 'The development and maintenance of friendship', *Journal of Social and Personal Relationships* (1), 75–98.

Hays, R. B. (1989), 'The day-to-day functioning of close versus casual friendship', *Journal of Social and Personal Relationships* (7), 21–37.

Hazan, C., and Shaver, P. R. (1987), 'Romantic love conceptualised as an attachment process', *Journal of Personality and Social Psychology* (52), 511–24.

Heider, F. (1958), *The Psychology of Interpersonal Relations*, Wiley: New York.

Helgeson, V. S., Shaver, P. R., and Dyer, M. (1987), 'Prototypes of intimacy and distance in same-sex and opposite-sex relationships', *Journal of Social and Personal Relationships* (4), 195–233.

Hill, C. T., Rubin., Z., and Peplau, L. A. (1976), 'Breakups before marriage: The end of 103 affairs', *Journal of Social Issues* (32), 147–68.

Hinde, R. A. (1979), *Towards Understanding Relationships*, Academic Press: London.

Hinde, R. A. (1981), 'The bases of a science of interpersonal relationships', in S. W. Duck and R. Gilmour (eds.), *Personal Relationships 1: Studying Personal Relationships*, Academic Press: London.

Hobfoll, S. E. (1988), 'Overview of section on community and clinical', in S. W. Duck (ed.) with D. F. Hay, S. E. Hobfoll, W. Ickes and B. Montgomery, *Handbook of Personal Relationships*, Wiley: Chichester.

Hobfoll, S. E., and Stokes, J. P. (1988), 'The process and mechanics of social support' in S. W. Duck (ed.) with D. F. Hay, S. E. Hobfoll, W.

Ickes, and B. Montgomery, *Handbook of Personal Relationships* Wiley: Chichester.

Homel, R., Burns, A., and Goodnow, J. (1987), Parental social networks and child development', *Journal of Social and Personal Relationships* (4) 159–77.

Honeycutt, J. M., Cantrill, J. G., and Greene, R. W. (1989), 'Memory structures for relational escalation: A cognitive test of the sequencing of relational actions and stages', *Human Communication Research* (16), 62–90.

Hopper, R., Knapp, M. L., and Scott, L. (1981), 'Couples' personal idioms: Exploring intimate talk', *Journal of Communication* (31), 23–33.

Howells, K. (1981) 'Social relationships in violent offenders', in S. W. Duck and R. Gilmour (eds.), *Personal Relationships 3: Personal Relationships in Disorder*, Academic Press: London.

Huston, T., Surra, C., Fitzgerald, N., and Cate, R. (1981), 'From courtship to marriage: Mate selection as an interpersonal process', in S. W. Duck and R. Gilmour (eds.) *Personal Relationships 2: Developing Personal Relationships*, Academic Press: London and New York.

Johnson, M. (1982), 'Social and cognitive features of dissolving commitment to relationships', in S. W. Duck (ed.), *Personal Relationships 4: Dissolving Personal Relationships*, Academic Press: London.

Jones, E. E., and Gordon, E. M. (1972), 'Timing of self-disclosure and its effects on personal attraction', *Journal of Personality and Social Psychology* (24), 358–65.

Jones, W. H., Hansson, R. O., and Cutrona, C. E. (1984), 'Helping the lonely: Issues of intervention with young and older adults', in S. W. Duck (ed.), *Personal Relationships 5: Repairing Personal Relationships*, Academic Press: London.

Jourard, S. M. (1971), *Self Disclosure*, Wiley: New York.

Kafer, N. (1981), 'Interpersonal strategies of unpopular children: Some implications for social skill training', Paper to University of Lancaster, Department of Psychology, November.

Kaplan, R. E. (1976), 'Maintaining interpersonal relationships: A bipolar theory', *Interpersonal Development* (6), 106–19.

Kelly, C., Huston, T. L., and Cate, R. M. (1985), 'Premarital relationship correlates of the erosion of satisfaction in marriage', *Journal of Social and Personal Relationships* (2), 167–78.

Kerckhoff, A. C. (1974), 'The social context of interpersonal attraction', in T. L. Huston (ed.), *Foundations of Interpersonal Attraction*, Academic Press: New York.

Koestner, R., and Wheeler, L. (1988), 'Self presentation in personal advertisements: The influence of implicit notions of attraction and role expectations', *Journal of Social and Personal Relationships* (5), 149–60.

Kon, I. S. (1981), 'Adolescent friendship: Some unanswered questions for future research', in S. W. Duck and R. Gilmour (eds.), *Personal Relationships 2: Developing Personal Relationships*, Academic Press: London.

Kurdek, L. (1989), 'Relationship quality in gay and lesbian cohabiting couples: A one year follow-up study', *Journal of Social and Personal Relationships* (6), 39–59.

Kurdek, L. (1991), 'The dissolution of gay and lesbian relationships', *Journal of Social and Personal Relationships* (8), 265–278.

Ladd, G. W. (1989), 'Towards a further understanding of peer relationships and their contributions to child development', in T. J. Berndt and G. W. Ladd (eds.), *Peer Relationships in Child Development*, Wiley: New York.

La Gaipa, J. J. (1977), 'Interpersonal attraction and social exchange', in S. W. Duck (ed.), *Theory and Practice in Interpersonal Attraction*, Academic Press: London.

La Gaipa, J. J. (1981), 'Children's friendships', in S. W. Duck and R. Gilmour (eds.), *Personal Relationships 2: Developing Personal Relationships.* Academic Press: London.

La Gaipa, J. J. (1982), 'Rituals of disengagement', in S. W. Duck (ed.), *Personal Relationships 4: Dissolving Personal Relationships*, Academic Press: London.

La Gaipa, J. J., and Malott, O. (1989), 'What to do with mother, dear', Paper presented to the International Network on Personal Relationships Conference, Iowa City, May.

La Gaipa, J. J., and Wood, H. D. (1981), 'Friendship in disturbed adolescents', in S. W. Duck and R. Gilmour (eds.), *Personal Relationships 3. Personal Relationships in Disorder*, Academic Press: London and New York.

Lawson, J. M. (1990), 'Management issues in gay and lesbian relationships', unpublished MS, University of Iowa.

Lea, M. (1989), 'Factors underlying friendship: An analysis of responses on the acquaintance description form in relation to Wright's friendship model', *Journal of Social and Personal Relationships* (6), 275–92.

Leary, M. R., Rogers, P. A., Canfield, R. W., and Coe, C. (1986), 'Boredom in interpersonal encounters: Antecedents and social implications', *Journal of Personality and Social Psychology* (51), 958–75.

Leatham, G., and Duck, S. W. (1990), 'Conversations with friends and the dynamics of social support', in S. W. Duck (ed.) with R. C. Silver, *Personal Relationships and Social Support*, SAGE: London.

Lips, H. M., and Morrison, A. (1986), 'Changes in the sense of family among couples having their first child', *Journal of Social and Personal Relationships* (3), 393–400.

Lloyd, S. A., and Cate, R. M. (1985), 'The developmental course of conflict in dissolution of premarital relationships', *Journal of Social and Personal Relationships* (2), 179–94.

Lynch, J. J. (1977), *The Broken Heart: The medical consequences of loneliness*, Basic Books: New York.

Mangham, I. L. (1981), 'Relationships at work', in S. W. Duck and R. Gilmour (eds.), *Personal Relationships 1: Studying Personal Relationships*, Academic Press: London.

Manning, M., and Herrmann, J. (1981), 'The relationships of problem children in nursery schools', in S. W. Duck and R. Gilmour (eds.), *Personal Relationships 3: Personal Relationships in Disorder*, Academic Press: London and New York.

209

Marangoni, C., and Ickes, W. (1989), 'Loneliness: A theoretical review with implications for measurement', *Journal of Social and Personal Relationships* (6) 93–128.

Markman, H. J., Floyd, F. and Dickson-Markman, F. (1982), 'Towards a model for the prediction and primary prevention of marital and family distress and dissolution', in S. W. Duck (ed.), *Personal Relationships 4: Dissolving Personal Relationships*, Academic Press: London.

McAdams, D. (1988), 'Personal needs and personal relationships', in S. W. Duck (ed.) with D. F. Hay, S. E. Hobfoll, W. Ickes, and B. Montgomery, *Handbook of Personal Relationships*, Wiley: Chichester.

McCall, G. (1982), 'Becoming unrelated: The management of bond dissolution', in S. W. Duck (ed.), *Personal Relationships 4: Dissolving Personal Relationships*, Academic Press: London.

McCarthy, B., and Duck, S. W. (1976), 'Friendship duration and responses to attitudinal agreement-disagreement', *British Journal of Social and Clinical Psychology* (15), 377–86.

Mehrabian, A., and Ksionzky, S. (1974), *A Theory of Affiliation*, Lexington Books: Lexington, MA.

Menges, R.J. (1969), 'Student–instructor cognitive compatibility in the large lecture class', *Journal of Personality* (37), 444–59.

Miell, D. E. (1984), 'Cognitive and communicative strategies in developing relationships', unpublished PhD thesis, University of Lancaster.

Miell, D. E. (1987), 'Remembering relationship development: Constructing a context for interaction', in R. Burnett, P. McGee, and D. Clarke (eds.), *Accounting for Relationships*, Methuen: London.

Miell, D. E., and Duck, S. W. (1982), 'Similarity and acquaintance: The role of strategies', Paper to International Conference on Personal Relationships, Madison, WI, July.

Miell, D. E., Duck, S. W., and La Gaipa, J. J. (1979), 'Interactive effects of sex and timing of selfdisclosure', *British Journal of Social and Clinical Psychology* (18), 355–62.

Miller, L. (1990), 'Metaphors in long distance relationships', unpublished MS, University of Iowa.

Montgomery, B. M. (1984), 'Behavioral characteristics predicting self and peer perception of open communication', *Communication Quarterly* (32), 233–40.

Montgomery, B. M. (1986), 'Flirtatious messages', Paper presented to the Third International Conference on Personal Relationships, Herzlia, Israel, July.

Morton, T. L., and Douglas, M. (1981), 'Growth of relationships', in S. W. Duck and R. Gilmour (eds.), *Personal Relationships 2: Developing Personal Relationships*, Academic Press: London.

Murstein, B. I. (1976), *Who Will Marry Whom?*, Springer: New Nork.

Newcomb, M.D. (1981), 'Heterosexual cohabitation relationships', in S. W. Duck and R. Gilmour (eds.), *Personal Relationships 1: Studying Personal Relationships*, Academic Press: London.

Newcomb, M. D. (1986), 'Cohabitation, marriage and divorce among adolescents and young adults', *Journal of Social and Personal Relationships* (3), 473–94.

References

Newcomb, M. D., and Bentler, P. (1981), 'Marital breakdown', in S. W. Duck and R. Gilmour (eds.), *Personal Relationships 3: Personal Relationships in Disorder*, Academic Press: London and New York.

Noller, P., and Venardos, C. (1986), 'Communication awareness in married couples', *Journal of Social and Personal Relationships* (3), 31–42.

Norton, R. W. (1988), 'Communicator style theory in marital interaction: Persistent challenges', in S. W. Duck (ed.) with D. F. Hay, S. E. Hobfoll, W. Ickes, and B. Montgomery, *Handbook of Personal Relationships* Wiley: Chichester.

Notarius, C. I., and Herrick. L. R. (1988), 'Listener response strategies to a distressed other', *Journal of Social and Personal Relationships* (5), 97–108.

Orford, J., and O'Reilly, P. (1981), 'Disorders in the family', in S. W. Duck and R. Gilmour (Eds.), *Personal Relationships 3: Personal Relationships in Disorder*, Academic Press: London and New York.

Parks, M. R., and Barnes, K. J. (1988), 'With a little help from my friends: The role of third parties in the initiation of interpersonal relationships', Paper to the Annual Convention of the Speech Communication Association, New Orleans, November.

Patterson, M. L. (1988), 'Functions of nonverbal behavior in close relationships', in S. W. Duck (ed.) with D. F. Hay, S. E. Hobfoll, W. Ickes, and B. Montgomery, *Handbook of Personal Relationships*, Wiley: Chichester.

Peplau, L. A., and Perlman, D. (1982), 'Perspectives on loneliness', in L. A. Peplau and D. Perlman (eds.), *Loneliness: A sourcebook of theory, research and therapy*, Wiley: New York.

Peplau, L. A., Rubin, Z. and Hill, C. T. (1977), 'Sexual intimacy in dating relationships', *Journal of Social Issues*, (33), 86–109.

Perlman, D. (1986), 'Chance and coincidence in personal relationships', Paper presented to the Third International Conference on Personal Relationships, Herzlia, Israel, July.

Perlman, D., and Peplau, L. A. (1981), 'Toward a social psychology of loneliness', in S. W. Duck and R. Gilmour (eds.), *Personal Relationships 3: Personal Relationships in Disorder*, Academic Press: London and New York.

Peterson, C., Seligman, M. E. P., and Vaillant, G. E. (1988), 'Pessimistic explanatory style is a risk factor for physical illness: A 35 year longitudinal study', *Journal of Personality and Social Psychology* (55), 23–7.

Pfeiffer, S. M., and Wong, P. T. P (1989), 'Multidimensional jealousy', *Journal of Social and Personal Relationships* (6), 181–96.

Phillips, D. P. (1972), 'Deathday and birthday: An unexpected connection', in J. M. Tanur (ed.) *Statistics: A guide to the unknown*, Holden Day: San Francisco.

Ponzetti, J., Zvonkovic, A., Cate, R. M., and Huston, T. L. (1991), 'Reasons for divorce: A comparison of former partners' accounts', *Unpublished manuscript*.

Putallaz, M., and Gottman, J. M. (1981), 'Social skills and group acceptance' in S. R. Asher and J. M. Gottman (eds.), *The Development of Children's Friendships*, Cambridge University Press: Cambridge.

Rawlins, W., and Holl, M. (1988), 'Adolescents' interaction with parents and friends: Dialectics of temporal perspective and evaluation', *Journal of Social and Personal Relationships* (5), 27–46.

Reis, H. T. (1986), 'Gender effects in social participation: Intimacy, loneliness and the conduct of social interaction', in R. Gilmour and S. W. Duck (eds.), *The Emerging Field of Personal Relationships*, Lawrence Erlbaum Associates: Hillsdale, NJ.

Reis, H.T., Nezlek, J. and Wheeler, L. (1980), 'Physical attractiveness and social interaction', *Journal of Personality and Social Psychology*, (38), 604–17.

Reisman, J. (1981), 'Adult friendships', in S. W. Duck and R. Gilmour (eds.), *Personal Relationships 2: Developing Personal Relationships*, Academic Press: London.

Rodin, M. (1982), 'Nonengagement, failure to engage and disengagement', in S. W. Duck (ed.), *Personal Relationships 4: Dissolving Personal Relationships*, Academic Press: London.

Rook, K. (1988), 'Toward a more differentiated view of loneliness', in S. W. Duck (ed.) with D. F. Hay, S. E. Hobfoll, W. Ickes and B. Montgomery, *Handbook of Personal Relationships*, Wiley: Chichester.

Rosenblatt, P. C. (1983), *Bitter, Bitter Tears: Nineteenth century diarists and twentieth century grief theories*, UMN Press: Minneapolis.

Rubin, K. H., Mills, R. S. L., and Rose-Krasnor, L. (1989), 'Maternal beliefs and children's competence', in B. H. Schneider, G. Attili, J. Nadel, and R. Weissberg (eds.), *Social Competence in Developmental Perspective*, Kluwer: Amsterdam.

Rubin, Z. (1974), 'From liking to loving: Patterns of attraction in dating relationships', in T. L. Huston (ed.), *Foundations of Interpersonal Attraction*, Academic Press: New York.

Schachter, S. (1959), *The Psychology of Affiliation*, Stanford University Press: Stanford, CA.

Schneider, B. H., Attili, G., Nadel, J., and Weissberg, R. (eds.), (1989) *Social Competence in Developmental Perspective*, Kluwer: Amsterdam.

Shaver, P. R., Furman, W., and Buhrmester, D. (1985), 'Aspects of a life transition: Network changes, social skills and loneliness', in S. W. Duck and D. Perlman (eds.), *Understanding Personal Relationships*, SAGE: London.

Sherif, M. (1936), *The Psychology of Social Norms*, Harper and Row: New York.

Sigall, H., and Ostrove, N. (1975), 'Beautiful but dangerous: Effects of offender attractiveness and nature of crime on juridic judgement', *Journal of Personality and Social Psychology* (31), 410–24.

Smith. P. K. (1989), 'The role of rough-and-tumble play in the development of social competence: Theoretical perspectives and empirical evidence', in B. H. Schneider, G. Attili, J. Nadel, and R. Weissberg (eds.) *Social Competence in Developmental Perspective*, Kluwer: Amsterdam.

Snyder, M., Tanke, E. D., and Berscheid, E. (1977), 'Social perception and interpersonal behaviour: On the self-fulfilling nature of social stereotypes', *Journal of Personality and Social Psychology* (35), 656–66.

Solano, C. H., and Koester, N. H. (1989), 'Loneliness and communication problems: Subjective anxiety or objective skills?', *Personality and Social Psychology Bulletin* (15), 126–33.

Spitzberg, B., and Canary, D. (1985), 'Loneliness and relationally competent communication', *Journal of Social and Personal Relationships* (2), 387–402.

Sprecher, S. (1987), 'The effects of self-disclosure given and received on affection for an intimate partner and stability of the relationship', *Journal of Social and Personal Relationships* (4), 115–27.

Stroebe, W. (1977), 'Self esteem and interpersonal attraction', in S. W. Duck (ed.), *Theory and Practice in Interpersonal Attraction*, Academic Press: London.

Takens, R. J. (1982), 'Psychotherapist–client relationships and effectiveness of therapy', Paper to International Conference on Personal Relationships, Madison, WI, July.

Thibaut, J. W., and Kelley, H. H. (1959), *The Social Psychology of Groups*, Wiley: New York.

Tolhuizen, J. H. (1989), 'Communication strategies for intensifying dating relationships: Identification, use and structure', *Journal of Social and Personal Relationships* (6), 413–34.

Trower, P. (1981), 'Social skill disorder', in S. W. Duck and R. Gilmour (eds.), *Personal Relationships 3: Personal Relationships in Disorder*, Academic Press: London and New York.

Trower, P., Bryant, B., and Argyle, M. (1978), *Social Skills and Mental Health*, Methuen: London.

Van Lear, C. A., Jr., and Trujillo, N. (1986), 'On becoming acquainted: A longitudinal study of social judgement processes', *Journal of Social and Personal Relationships* (3), 375–92.

Walster, E., Walster, G. W., and Berscheid, E. (1978), *Equity Theory and Research*, Allyn and Bacon: Boston.

Weber, A., Harvey, J. H., and Stanley, M. A. (1987), 'The nature and motivations of accounts for failed relationships', in R. Burnett, P. McGhee and D. D. Clarke (eds.), *Accounting for Relationships*, Methuen: London.

Weiss, R. S. (1974), 'The provisions of social relationships', in Z. Rubin (ed.), *'Doing unto Others'*, Prentice-Hall: Englewood Cliffs, NJ.

Wheeler, L., Reis, H. T., and Nezlek, J. (1983), Loneliness, social interaction, and sex roles', *Journal of Personality and Social Psychology* (35), 742–54.

Wiseman, J. P. (1986), 'Friendship: Bonds and binds in a voluntary relationship', *Journal of Social and Personal Relationships* (3), 191–211.

Wittenberg, M. T., and Reis, H. T. (1986), 'Loneliness, social skills, and social perception', *Personality and Social Psychology Bulletin* (12), 121–30.

Wright, P. H. (1984), 'Self referent motivation and the intrinsic quality of friendship', *Journal of Social and Personal Relationships* (1), 114–30.

Yaffe, M. (1981), 'Disordered sexual relationships', in S. W. Duck and R. Gilmour (eds.), *Personal Relationships 3: Personal Relationships in Disorder*, Academic Press: London and New York.

Author Index

Subject Index